D1610028

Masterless Men

Masterless Men

The vagrancy problem in England
1560–1640

A. L. Beier

Methuen

London and New York

First published in 1985 by
Methuen & Co. Ltd
11 New Fetter Lane, London EC4P 4EE

Published in the USA by
Methuen & Co.
in association with Methuen, Inc.
29 West 35th Street, New York NY 10001

© 1985 A. L. Beier

Photoset by Rowland Phototypesetting Ltd
Bury St Edmunds Suffolk
Printed in Great Britain

British Library Cataloguing in Publication Data
Beier, A. L.
    Masterless men: the vagrancy problem in
    England 1560–1640.
    1. Tramps – Great Britain – History
    I. Title
    364.1'48'0942   HV4545. A3

    ISBN 0-416-39010-2

Library of Congress Cataloging in Publication Data
Beier, A. L.
    Masterless men.

    Includes index.
    1. Tramps – England – History.
2. England – Social conditions.
3. England – Economic conditions.
4. Vagrancy – England – History.   I. Title
HV4546.A3B45   1985   362.5'0942   85-7257
ISBN 0-416-39010-2

To Lucinda

Contents

Contents ix

Acknowledgements

John Donne's observation that 'no man is an island' is certainly true when it comes to writing a book. I have been fortunate to come into contact with a number of remarkable teachers – Geoffrey Elton, Henry Hill, Maurice Lacoste, Alexander Kroff, George Mosse, Robert Reynolds, Lawrence Stone and William Appleman Williams – who helped to equip me for the *métier* of historian, but who also provided a great deal of intellectual stimulation. This book has taken over ten years to research and to write. It has required journeys to the four corners of the country, making me in one friend's words 'the vagrant's vagrant'. But without the support of a number of institutions the task would have certainly taken twice as long, if it could have been undertaken at all. I am particularly indebted to the Social Science Research Council (UK) for an initial grant to conduct research on 'The Vagrant Poor in Tudor and Early Stuart England', and then a year's study-leave to examine the materials collected and to begin writing. My own university granted me a year and two terms of sabbatical leave, as well as a year's unpaid leave, and Lacey Baldwin Smith and his colleagues at Northwestern University were kind enough to welcome me during the latter period. Finally, the Wolfson Foundation assisted with a grant for typing and other expenses in the later stages of the project.

I must also record my gratitude to the archivists of a number of repositories, who have answered a stream of requests for information and photocopies over the years: Caernarfonshire, Chester, the Corporation of London, Doncaster (particularly R. D. Steward), Essex, Greater London, Hertfordshire, Kent, Leicestershire, Lincolnshire, Nottinghamshire, Shropshire, Somerset, Staffordshire (principally F. B. Stitt), Suffolk (Bury St Edmunds and Ipswich branches), East Sussex, Warwickshire, Westminster (especially Margaret Swarbrick), Wiltshire, the National Library of Wales and the Public Record Office. I am further indebted to Lieutenant-Colonel Alan Faith, Clerk to the Governors of Bridewell Hospital, for making available the Bridewell Hospital Court Books, and to the Gov-

xii Acknowledgements

ernors for permission to quote from them. I have also profited from the reactions of a number of groups who have heard various essays in the book: at Arizona State University, Bowdoin College, the University of Chicago, University of Illinois (Urbana), Northwestern University and Princeton University; at the Newberry Library and the Liverpool College of Higher Education; and not least the students in my special subject on Tudor social history. Others have read all or part of the book and given me the benefit of their wisdom, although they are responsible for none of its failings. Peter Clark and Alexander Grant deserve special votes of thanks for going through the entire typescript and helping to transform it into something more readable. Others who kindly read chapters are Roger Finlay, E. R. B. Gibson, De Lloyd Guth, Ivan Roots, Anthony Salerno, Jane Shuter, Paul Slack, Nicholas Webb and Austin Woolrych. For their permission to cite their unpublished theses I am obliged to Julian Hill, Martin Ingram, Joan Kent, Jane Shuter and Nicholas Webb. To the publishers of *Past and Present*, the *Journal of Interdisciplinary History* and *The Problem of the Poor in Tudor and Early Stuart England* I am grateful for permission to reproduce small amounts of material previously published by them. My greatest debts, however, are to those persons who have provided counsel and encouragement at decisive junctures: to Louis Amborn, an understanding probation officer; to Peter Clark, Roger Finlay and Sandy Grant; but above all others to my wife Lucinda, whose partnership is intellectual as well as personal, and to whom the book is dedicated.

Bailrigg
August 1984

Abbreviations

AgHR	*Agricultural History Review.*
AHEW	J. Thirsk (ed.), *The Agrarian History of England and Wales, 1500–1640* (Cambridge, 1967), vol. IV.
APC	*Acts of the Privy Council of England*, ed. J. R. Dasent.
BCB	Bridewell Hospital Court Books, 1559–1660, Guildhall Library.
BIHR	*Bulletin of the Institute of Historical Research.*
BJF	*The Book of John Fisher, 1580–1588*, ed. T. Kemp (Warwick, n. d.).
BL	British Library.
Carus-Wilson	E. M. Carus-Wilson (ed.), *Essays in Economic History* (1954–62) vols I–III.
CLRO	Corporation of London Records Office.
Crisis and Order	P. Clark and P. Slack (eds), *Crisis and Order in English Towns, 1500–1700* (1972).
CRO	County Record Office.
CSPD	*Calendar of State Papers Domestic.*
Cunnington, *Devizes*	B. H. Cunnington, *Some Annals of the Borough of Devizes, 1555–1791* (Devizes, 1925).
Cunnington, *Wilts.*	B. H. Cunnington, *Records of the County of Wilts* (Devizes, 1932).
DAD	Doncaster Archives Department.
DBC	Dorchester Borough Court.
DCA	Doncaster Chamberlains' Accounts.
EcHR	*Economic History Review.*
EHD	C. H. Williams (ed.), *English Historical Documents, 1485–1558* vol. V (1967).
GLRO	Greater London Record Office.

Halliwell	J. O. Halliwell (ed.), *A Minute Account of the Social Condition of the People of Anglesey in the Reign of James I* (1860).
Harrison, *Description*	W. Harrison, *The Description of England* (1577), ed. G. Edelen (Ithaca, 1968).
Herts. Co. Recds	*Hertfordshire County Records*, ed. W. J. Hardy and W. Le Hardy (Hertford, 1905–39), vols I–VI.
Journ.	Journals, Court of Common Council, CLRO.
Judges	A. V. Judges (ed.), *The Elizabethan Underworld* (1930).
KCAO	Kent County Archives Office, Maidstone.
LBR	M. Bateson (ed.), *Records of the Borough of Leicester* (Cambridge, 1899–1905), vols I–III.
Leonard	E. M. Leonard, *The Early History of English Poor Relief* (Cambridge, 1900).
Middlesex Co. Recds	*Middlesex County Records*, ed. J. C. Jeaffreson and W. Le Hardy (1886–92, 1935–7), vols I–VIII.
More, *Complete Works*	*The Complete Works of St. Thomas More*, ed. J. H. Hexter and E. L. Surtz (1965), vol. IV.
NCM	Minutes of the Norwich Court of Mayoralty, Norfolk Record Office.
NCM	*Minutes of the Norwich Court of Mayoralty, 1630–1631*, ed. W. L. Sachse (Norfolk Record Society, XV, 1942); *Minutes of the Norwich Court of Mayoralty, 1632–1635*, ed. W. L. Sachse (Norfolk Record Society, XXXVI, 1967).
NLW	National Library of Wales.
NRQS	*[North Riding] Quarter Sessions Records*, ed. J. C. Atkinson (1884–92), vols I–IX.
OED	*Oxford English Dictionary*.
P&P	*Past and Present*.
PRO	Public Record Office.
Remembrancia	Remembrancia Books, CLRO.
Repert.	Repertories of the Court of Aldermen, CLRO.
Ribton-Turner	C. J. Ribton-Turner, *A History of Vagrants and Vagrancy* (1887).
RR	J. M. Guilding (ed.), *Reading Records: Diary of a Corporation* (1892–6), vols I–IV.
SBR	Shrewsbury Borough Records.
SE	*Books of Examinations and Depositions,*

	1570–1594, transc. G. H. Hamilton (Southampton Record Society, 1914); *The Book of Examinations and Depositions, 1622–1644*, ed. R. C. Anderson (Southampton Record Society, 1929–36), vols I–IV.
Slack, 'Vagrants and vagrancy'	P. A. Slack, 'Vagrants and vagrancy in England, 1598–1664', *EcHR*, 2nd series, XXVII (1974).
SRP	P. L. Hughes and J. F. Larkin (ed.), *Stuart Royal Proclamations* (Oxford, 1973), vol. I.
Statutes	*Statutes of the Realm* (1817; 1963 edn), vols I–V.
TED	E. Power and R. H. Tawney (eds), *Tudor Economic Documents* (1924), vols I–III.
TRHS	*Transactions of the Royal Historical Society*.
TRP	P. L. Hughes and J. F. Larkin (eds), *Tudor Royal Proclamations* (1964–9), vols I–III.
VCH	*Victoria County History*.
WCL	Westminster City Libraries, Archives Department.
Webbs, *Old Poor Law*	S. and B. Webb, *English Poor Law History. Part 1: The Old Poor Law* (1927).
WRQS	*West Riding Sessions Records*, ed. J. Lister (Yorkshire Archaeological Society, 1888–1915), vols I–II.
WYRO	West Yorkshire Record Office.
YCR	*York Civic Records*, ed. Angelo Raine (Yorkshire Archaeological Society, 1939–53), vols I–VIII.

Through tatter'd clothes small vices do appear;
Robes and furr'd gowns hide all. Plate sin with gold,
And the strong lance of justice hurtless breaks,
Arm it in rags, a pigmy's straw does pierce it.

King Lear (1605–6), IV.vi

Note

All quotations from original sources have been modernized. Old style dating has been altered to begin the year on 1 January. Throughout the text 'Bridewell' upper-case refers to London's Bridewell Hospital, whereas lower-case 'bridewell' refers to the institutions generally.

Introduction

This book is about the Tudor and early Stuart vagrancy laws, and particularly about the people arrested under that legislation. Hitherto disregarded in administrative histories of the poor laws or romanticized as an 'Elizabethan underworld', vagrants remain shadowy figures. Elizabethan estimates of their numbers varied wildly from 10,000 to 200,000, and it is just as difficult for the historian, for reasons explained in Chapter 2, precisely to gauge the extent of vagabondage. Despite this fact, it is still possible to conclude that vagrancy was one of the most pressing social problems of the age. It provoked a spate of Acts of Parliament, which encompassed the totality of the country's unemployed and landless population, which was large and growing. Vagrants could face felony charges under many statutes. The crime was taken so seriously because to the dominant classes vagabonds appeared to threaten the established order. They were 'masterless' in a period when the able-bodied poor were supposed to have masters. They also broke with official conventions of family, economic, religious and political life, some even venturing down the dangerous paths of organized crime and rebellion.

To be understood properly vagrants must be seen in their historical context. The first part of the book therefore examines how contemporaries defined vagrancy, the economic and demographic background to the problem, and the impact of migration and urbanization. The second section shows how vagrants deviated from official norms in their relationships, itinerant life-styles and trades. The final part discusses their begging activities, how far they formed a criminal underworld, and the state's responses to vagrancy, including the development of such radical innovations as transportation, impressment and prison-like institutions. The dates in the title are intended as general guides rather than precise bench-marks. The bulk of the evidence comes from the years 1560 to 1640, a period that probably represents the peak of state activity against vagabonds between 1400 and 1700. But the latter dates are more

important for such aspects of the question as the evolution of ideas about poverty and work.

Source materials for the study of Tudor and Stuart vagabondage are rich. Governments poured out proclamations and statutes against vagrants; preachers pilloried them in the pulpits; hack-writers churned out popular pamphlets about them. Thomas More took the problem as the starting point for his analysis of the country's social ills in *Utopia* (1516), and Elizabeth I's leading minister, William Cecil, drew up a memorandum defining vagabondage. Local magistrates sent him and other ministers their remedies for the problem, took lengthy depositions from suspects, and made returns of arrests to the Privy Council. At parish level churchwardens relieved thousands with doles, while constables punished thousands more who tarried too long.

Historians of vagrancy have chiefly consulted literary sources, and when they have examined official ones, it was only those from the top levels of administration. This book, while it does not pretend to be definitive, draws upon local records throughout England and Wales, in addition to the central collections and published literature. The main criterion for inclusion of material has been how far it could answer numerous questions about the vagrant poor. Records of county quarter sessions, of the various borough courts, of houses of correction, especially London's Bridewell, and of arrests at parish level, have all been utilized.

The mainstay of the documentation consists of the examinations of 1604 vagrants arrested in the towns of Chester, Leicester, Reading and Warwick, and in the counties of Somerset and Wiltshire, from 1571 to 1642. The criterion for inclusion of examinations was that suspects were vagrants according to the statutory definitions of the crime. The value of these records is great, but they do have one or two limitations. First, they were sometimes taken from persons suspected of crimes more serious than the misdemeanour offence of vagrancy. This bias is actually an advantage in making it possible to uncover real-life members of the Elizabethan underworld, but it also means that the more dangerous rogues might be over-represented in the sample. As a corrective, I have examined the records of 5046 vagrants punished as misdemeanants – 447 in Essex (1564–1644), 718 in 17 counties (1569–72), 1821 in London (1516–1625), 1060 in Norwich (1564–1635), and 1000 in Wiltshire (1603 –38). I have additionally drawn upon the evidence of nearly 25,000 arrests in 32 counties from 1631 to 1639, which contains personal details of some 5000 persons punished as misdemeanants. But this last body of material has not been used as extensively as the other sources just described, because it covers a relatively short period, does not contain the wealth of evidence found in examinations, and has been the subject of a valuable

study by Dr Paul Slack in 1974.[1] A second reservation about examinations is that they only show suspected offences. Since it is impossible to follow most suspects through the legal process, because of lack of evidence, we have no way of determining their guilt or innocence. It would be wrong, therefore, to take an examination as definitive evidence of an accused's crimes.[2]

Nevertheless, examinations remain valuable sources, because they give fuller evidence than other records. They provide information about vagrants' personal background, including family life, work-histories, sex-lives, haunts and confederates. If issues of guilt and innocence are left aside, this evidence can be assumed with some confidence to be accurate, for magistrates were rigorous in taking depositions. They compared the stories of suspects travelling together, and if there were discrepancies examined them again. Employers and landlords living several miles away were contacted to check accounts, and liars were caught.

Most historians of vagabondage have failed to do the subject justice. Constitutional and administrative histories have treated vagrants as one side of the poor laws' division of the English poor into 'able-bodied' and 'impotent'. This is a narrow approach that shows how government worked, but ignores the context in which the laws were passed, as well as the vagrants themselves.[3] Another school has portrayed vagabonds as a criminal underworld, based upon the 'literature of roguery' that flourished in the period and purported to describe this low-life world. Although more colourful than administrative history, this perspective distorts reality by exclusive reliance upon literary sources; it makes little attempt to distinguish fact from fiction and neglects official records almost entirely, while the context of the legislation and vagrants themselves are once again ignored.[4] Thirdly, some historians have linked the vagrancy problem with demographic changes, above all population growth and migration. It is true that migration was one step down the road to vagrancy, but whether by the time of their arrests most vagabonds were migrants is doubtful, at least in the sense of travelling from one place to settle in another. Furthermore, vagrancy legislation was not confined to the period of rising population between 1530 and 1650. Parliament first enacted the laws in the second half of the fourteenth century, which is a well-known period of population decline.[5]

It is the argument of this book that the vagrancy laws were intended to deal with a new social problem, that is, a large landless element with no firm roots and few prospects. When uprooted, they became 'masterless men', and dangers to the social order. In Professor Walzer's words the masterless man was 'alien from the feudal world, vagabond and criminal',[6] yet he had no stake either in the emerging bourgeois world of discipline. In response, governments legislated that every able-bodied

person lacking independent means must have a master; otherwise they were legally vagabonds. This definition of vagrancy, and of the other crimes discussed in this book, is derived from the legislation and jurisprudence of the period.[7] Where quantitative data are introduced, the figures represent numbers of offenders; repeated offenders are counted but once.

Vagrancy is perhaps the classic crime of status, the social crime *par excellence*. Offenders were arrested not because of their actions, but because of their position in society. Their status was a criminal one, because it was at odds with the established order.[8] Who determines that someone's status is a crime? The argument that crime is not solely 'a quality of the act the person commits, but rather a consequence of the application by others of rules and sanctions to an "offender"',[9] has much to commend it in this instance. There were indeed two sides to the crime of vagrancy: the masterless, to be sure, but also the masters who made and enforced the laws. By investigating the two sides of the relationship, what was perhaps the most intractable social problem of the period becomes comprehensible, and new light is thrown upon the values and preoccupations of an entire age.

Part One
The origins of vagrancy

Chapter 1

The new poverty

To comprehend a period remote from our own, Sir Herbert Butterfield advised, we should discard our preconceptions and discover how people thought and felt at the time.[1] In this chapter, Tudor and early Stuart vagrancy will be examined through the attitudes and policies of the period. The first point to make is that modern stereotypes of the problem must at once be set aside. The Elizabethan vagabond bears little resemblance to the down-and-outs, often middle-aged alcoholics, of the early 1960s in Britain;[2] nor was he at all like the drop-outs involved in counter-cultures later in that decade. If masterless men have modern counterparts, they are the unemployed of the Great Depression of the 1930s, or the jobless millions of today's inner cities.

Sixteenth- and early seventeenth-century vagrancy involved more than being poor and rootless. It was the product of profound social dislocations – a huge and growing poverty problem, disastrous economic and demographic shifts and massive migration – and had important political consequences. In the Middle Ages it involved the breaking of manorial ties, and so was a form of rebellion. It continued to signify rebellion, although for different reasons, under the Tudors and early Stuarts. Governments reacted vigorously to suppress vagrants and in the process brought about major new developments in state control.

Vagrancy legislation dates from the late Middle Ages, but its fullest development came when the problem worsened in the Tudor period. The Acts of Parliament are obvious starting points for a definition of vagrancy and are examined later in this chapter. But if we concentrate upon the laws alone, we risk ignoring their historical context. In fact, the Tudor and early Stuart concept of vagrancy arose from a general re-definition of poverty. The legislation was part of this process, but so was a considerable body of learned and religious opinion. The change was also reflected in literature, for popular writers described an Elizabethan underworld of vagabonds. In the official sphere, we must look beyond statutes to

observe how the laws were enforced by the courts and by the other institutions deployed to check vagrancy.

From these sources it appears that vagrants had five main characteristics. First, they were poor, lacking any regular income apart from wages from casual labour. Secondly, they were able-bodied – 'sturdy', 'valiant' and fit to work. Thirdly, they were unemployed, or in contemporary terms 'masterless' and 'idle'. Fourthly, they were rootless: wandering, vagrant, 'runnagate'. Finally they were lawless, dangerous, and suspected of spreading vice and corruption. The legislation covered other groups as well – the young, certain occupations and ethnic groups – but these were subsidiary to the five main ones. In addition, successive Acts tended to alter in detail the definition of the crime. Clearly vagrancy was a protean concept. Possibly the laws' blanket coverage was intentional, designed to entrap the maximum number of offenders. But it also reflected a conviction in the ruling élites that vagabondage was a hydra-headed monster poised to destroy the state and social order, for of the vagrant's five characteristics the *leitmotiv* that ran through them all was disorder.

THE DE-SANCTIFICATION OF THE POOR

During the High Middle Ages there was a tendency to idealize poverty. St Francis, for instance, taught that beggars were holy, and that the holy should live as beggars. It was an age of great charitable outpourings to the destitute.[3] But after 1300 a more critical attitude challenged the Franciscan one. Already in the thirteenth century some canon lawyers argued against relieving the wilfully idle; in the following century this trickle of criticism developed into a small stream.[4] The sin of sloth was redefined to include physical as well as spiritual vices. The next step was to make idleness a crime, a position that Langland approached when he included Robert the Robber, a vagabond and thief, in his description of Sloth. By 1400 many humanists believed that some types of poverty, far from leading to holiness, caused social disorders and should therefore be suppressed.[5]

The new critiques of poverty sprang from changing ideas and social conditions. The Franciscan ideal was discredited by the great wealth that the order amassed. In addition, in lay society the poverty ideal lost its potency and was replaced by a new set of values, that of Renaissance humanists, which celebrated the value of worldly activity and success. Religious feeling was evolving also. Although good works, including acts of charity, continued to be popular, many of the learned now questioned their spiritual value. They mocked friars and pilgrims as impious frauds.

They rejected beggars and adopted St Paul's dictum that a good Christian worked to pay his way.[6]

One reason for the new attitude was that the poor themselves were changing. By 1250 those in need were no longer only the aged, the infirm and those on pilgrimage. Vast numbers of destitute industrial workers and a veritable 'culture of poverty' had appeared on the urban scene. In the countryside there were hordes of miserable peasants caught between rising population levels and falling incomes. The situation was exacerbated in the fourteenth century. The decline of population opened up prospects of land and high wages after the Black Death. But if peasants formerly tied to a manorial system now had the freedom to move and better themselves, the possibilities of failure also increased.[7] Moreover, late medieval wars and uprisings produced large numbers of rootless brigands and ex-soldiers, which emphasized the point that poverty was dangerous as well as undesirable. The authorities reacted accordingly. In Florence they limited relief to widows and orphans, and in France and England beggars came under suspicion as threats to public order. The administration of hospitals, those centres of medieval charity, became more restrictive: from the fifteenth century they ceased taking all-comers and mainly succoured the local poor.[8]

After 1500 the small stream of critical opinion concerning poverty developed into a flood. Admittedly more evidence survives for the sixteenth century, but that is not the main reason. Nor was it the appearance of a 'Protestant ethic' with a new critique of poverty. The main cause was simply growing poverty and with it vagabondage, as will be shown in the following chapter. Governments of all persuasions took action on the poverty issue and specifically against vagrants. What was involved in the sixteenth century was a more vigorous attack on the problem as it worsened, rather than a fundamental reorientation in thinking.[9]

In Tudor England unemployment was defined as a dangerous crime. To Edmund Dudley, writing in 1509, it was 'the very mother of all vice . . . and the lineal grandame of poverty and misery, and the deadly enemy of this tree of commonwealth'. Sir Thomas Smith reported in 1565 how the unemployed poor were liable to prosecution: if anyone 'not having rent or living sufficient to maintain himself, do live so idly, he is inquired of, and sometime sent to the gaol, sometime otherwise punished as a sturdy vagabond: so much our policy does abhor idleness'. Treating people out of work as criminals might shock modern opinion, but Smith was merely reporting the current state of the law and opinion.[10]

Beggars were also pilloried. Traditionally they were sought out as objects of charity, but now Protestant and Catholic authorities alike decided the 'sturdy' ones were nuisances. They deceived alms-givers,

took relief that the genuine poor needed, and so were no better than thieves. Henry VIII personally amended a provision in the *Bishop's Book* (1537) regarding charity to exclude persons living 'by the graft of begging slothfully', adding that they should be compelled to work.[11] Learned opinion remained hostile in the Elizabethan and early Stuart periods, despite some recognition that beggary was caused by unemployment. In 1583 Philip Stubbes attacked mendicants as 'drone bees, that live upon the spoil of the poor bees' and recommended they be imprisoned and, if still incorrigible, hanged. Even as late as the 1640s reformers such as Samuel Hartlib and Peter Chamberlen, respectively, described the beggar as an 'idle counterfeit' and 'lazy'. Hartlib proposed despatching the difficult ones to work in fishing fleets and to the colonies; or, like Stubbes, to 'hang them at last'.[12]

The implication of all this is that vagrants were no ordinary criminals; they were actually menaces to society. They posed this threat because they were corrupt and social outcasts. 'We know not according to what law or by what conventions they live', observed Juan-Luis Vives in 1526. A century later John Gore said they were 'children of Belial, without God, without magistrate, without minister'.[13] They were physically corrupt, spreading disease and infecting the community. At church festivals the healthy had to rub shoulders with ulcerous and cancerous beggars whose illnesses, Vives stated, 'assail the nostrils, the mouth, and are almost communicated to the hands and the body of those passing by'. In Elizabethan London, it was reported, diseased mendicants cluttered the streets.[14] Another common theme was that vagabonds were responsible for a multitude of crimes. By suppressing them, Vives suggested, 'fewer thefts, acts of violence, robberies, murders, capital offences will be committed'; even pandering and sorcery would disappear. Richard Morison wrote similarly in 1536 that those 'continuing in idleness, fall to stealing, robbing, murder, and many other mischiefs'.[15] Finally, vagrants threatened government and the social order. They 'sow sedition among the people', warned Morison; Henry Smith preached in 1593 that they were 'of the opinion of the Anabaptists, that every man's goods must be common'. Learned opinion altered little in the early Stuart period. Next to civil war, Hobbes observed in *Leviathan* (1651), the greatest danger to England was 'that dissolute condition of masterless men'. Lacking 'subjection to laws, and a coercive power to tie their hands', they would destroy society.[16]

The rhetorical flourishes of humanists and preachers do not always lend themselves to analysis. Certainly it is impossible to capture the meaning that terms like beggar and rogue had for them and their audiences. Today's equivalents might be anarchist, terrorist, or (in some western societies) communist. Nevertheless, certain messages can be

decoded from the stream of vituperation. Clearly, if a person were poor and able to work, unemployment was a crime. Secondly, begging made a person suspect if he were able to labour. Generally these offences posed serious challenges to the moral and physical well-being of society. Thus humanist and neo-Pauline thinking turned upside down the Franciscan conception of poverty and created instead a concept of vagrancy. It remains to be seen, however, whether that concept existed outside the world of dons and divines.

A VAGRANT UNDERWORLD

The learned attack upon vagrants had a popular literary variant that added credibility to the threat. The literature of roguery, as Professor Chandler called it, described a netherworld of vagabonds poised to overthrow society.[17] The unmasking of roguery had a long tradition in medieval literature, but a new feature of the post-1500 version was its description of an anti-society of vagrants. This world was first revealed in a translation of Sebastian Brandt's *The Ship of Fools* (1508), which was followed by a spate of English publications from 1530 to 1630.[18]

Another striking feature of the literature was its claim to verisimilitude. Writer after writer reported having first-hand experience of the vagrant underworld, and that his account of it was the 'true' one. The leading character in the first major tract, *The Highway to the Spital-House* (c.1535–6), was a hospital porter who claimed to know beggars' frauds. Subsequent writers backed up their boasts by anatomizing the world of vagrants. John Awdeley's tract in 1561 listed nineteen different types, besides three kinds of 'cozeners and shifters' and twenty-five 'orders of knaves'. Thomas Harman went further in 1566 and listed the names of 200 purported members of the underworld.[19]

The writers' pretensions to accuracy have impressed modern historians, one of whom compared Harman to a 'trained sociologist'.[20] In practice it is difficult to separate fact from fiction in the literature. Generally the present study finds that legal records present a different picture from the literary one.[21] Nevertheless, the literature of roguery remains a valuable source. In many essentials it reinforced the views of the learned and religious. For example, it paralleled learned opinion in portraying vagabonds as despicable and immoral. The chief vagrant in Harman's view was a 'wily fox'; the female rogue was a 'cow . . . that goes to bull every moon, with what bull she cares not'. The tracts also confirmed that vagabonds were criminals, listing theft and fraud among their misdeeds.[22] Finally, they showed vagrants endangering respectable society and the state. 'These cony-catchers . . . putrify with their infections this flourishing estate of England', Robert Greene warned in 1591.[23]

8   Masterless Men

The literature of roguery went beyond the learned tradition, however, to describe a highly organized vagrant underworld. In 1552 Gilbert Walker said vagabonds were a 'corporation'; to Awdeley they were a 'fraternity', a 'company' with orders; to Harman a 'fleeting fellowship' in which 'rufflers' and 'upright men' were top dogs. At an annual beggars' convention in Gloucestershire a Lord of the Fair was supposed to be elected; a Chief Commander and officers for regiments were also reported. A new recruit, Thomas Dekker wrote, had to 'learn the orders of our house'; to recognize that 'there are degrees of superiority and inferiority in our society'. Even women and children had their assigned places in the vagrant pecking order.[24]

This anti-society was specialized, too. Some vagrants went in for horse theft, others pretended to be shipwrecked, and still others feigned epilepsy. They had a special underworld vocabulary – canting, or Pedlar's French. The *Highway to the Spital-House* provided a sample, and Harman listed over 100 words and phrases. 'Cony-catching', the confidence tricks they played upon the unwary, had infinite variations, but a typical situation had an 'honest gentleman' fleecing a trusting newcomer to London.[25] In such 'real-life' incidents the nightmares of the learned seemed to come true. Finally, vagabonds were suggested to be in league with Satan. Like witches they were thought to harm people with devilish practices and were compared to Robin Goodfellow, the mythical imp. Dekker's *Lantern and Candlelight* (1608) was set in Hell, whose inhabitants were devil-worshippers.[26]

The literary portrayal of vagrancy should be taken seriously, for it was popular and was believed. The pamphlets were great publishing successes. Harman's was reissued in two pirated editions within a year, and William Harrison lifted large sections of it for his 'Description of England', which appeared in Holinshed's *Chronicles* (1577 and many later editions).[27] Between 1590 and 1620 the literature boomed, and writers freely plagiarized and invented to satisfy the demand. Gentlemen's libraries included Spanish picaresque stories as well as the home-grown variety. As far as the pamphlets' credibility goes, one Fellow of an Oxford college accepted some statements in *O Per Se O* (1612) as literal truths.[28] The rogue literature therefore more than confirmed the learned theory of vagrancy; it elaborated and propagated it.

THE MAGISTERIAL POSITION

The learned and the literary views invariably painted the vagrant in broad strokes. The official approach, while similar in its conception of the problem, applied the finishing touches. The menace of vagrancy is no less ubiquitous in government sources, but it is more precisely defined. In

almost any poor law of the period the presumption will be found that the vagabond was poor, able to work, unemployed, itinerant and disorderly; the same holds true for records of arrests. Nevertheless, even in the legal records the vagrant appears as more than the sum of his parts. To officials, as to other commentators, he ultimately represented a challenge to the *status quo* in state and society.

The legal concept of vagabondage originated in the distinction between the able-bodied and the 'impotent' poor. The division dates from the fourteenth century, when Parliament made masterlessness an offence, but its fullest development came under the Tudors and early Stuarts. Most of the thirteen poor laws passed between 1495 and 1610 had as a first premise the discrimination between those able and unable to work. More sophisticated analyses were occasionally developed, as when London officials distinguished nine types of pauper in Edward VI's reign.[29] But where vagrants were concerned the main criteria for guilt remained quite consistent. An Act of 1531, for instance, encapsulated the three characteristics of poverty, fitness for labour, and unemployment by defining the vagabond as

any man or woman being whole and mighty in body and able to labour, having no land, master, nor using any lawful merchandise, craft or mystery whereby he might get his living.

This prescription lasted until a new statute altered it slightly in 1597.[30]

Vagrancy charges might also arise under labour legislation. The Statute of Artificers of 1563 provided that if the able-bodied poor refused to work in husbandry, or left work before their terms finished, they could be arrested and imprisoned. When leaving masters they had to carry testimonial letters; otherwise they faced prosecution as vagabonds.[31] The obligation to labour was enforced regardless of changes of regime. From the reign of Elizabeth I to the Protectorate persons were prosecuted who lived 'vagrantly and not master-fast', refused to work or to accept official wages, worked as casual labourers, and failed to serve the full statutory year.[32] But the reason for regulating the unemployed was not a shortage of labour, as in the later Middle Ages. Rather it was the rising numbers of able-bodied poor that troubled officials. Here the fourth and fifth characteristics of vagrants – rootlessness and disorderliness – entered the equation. Governments generally distrusted economic and social alterations and intervened to control them, although not always successfully. With vagrants they were afraid what might happen if they were left to their own devices. The masterless man represented mutability, when those in power longed for stability. He stood for poverty, which seemed to threaten their social and political dominance. Fundamentally, in pre-

scribing that the vagrant be employed, governments were preoccupied with a problem of disorder.

Official pronouncements leave no doubt about the concern with stability. Proclamations and statutes portrayed vagrancy as the opening of Pandora's box. In Edward IV's reign vagabonds were blamed for sowing sedition; in Henry VII's for murders, robberies and the decay of husbandry; and in James I's for burglaries 'and other horrible crimes and offences'.[33] Even allowing for some exaggeration in these statements, a huge range of groups besides the unemployed were prosecuted.

The young were a special worry and were singled out in numerous statutes. The chief purpose of an Act establishing houses of correction in 1576 was that 'youth may be accustomed and brought up in labour and work'. More often the laws specified punishment and/or compulsory service. Until 1597 those aged from 5 to 14 were usually to be placed in service, although a statute of 1572 ordered them stocked and whipped. Those over 14 were to be gaoled, whipped, and burnt through the ear; after 1597 children under the age of 7 were exempted from prosecution.[34] Such draconian measures reflected a youth problem of huge proportions, as will be seen in later chapters.

Beggars were another troublesome group, as might be expected from the learned view of them. State action again began in the fourteenth century as part of an attempt to make the able-bodied work. Tudor governments intensified the campaign, because they linked mendicancy with disorder. Most poor laws prohibited or restricted begging. An Act of 1536 cited the 'inconveniences and infections' caused by unregulated hand-outs. Whipping was the most common penalty, but others included stocking, forced labour, branding, and incarceration.[35] Local officials enforced the legislation, appointing beadles to police beggars, making censuses to determine which could work, and sending away 'foreign' ones.[36] Suppression was incomplete, however, as will be shown in Chapter 7.

The vagrancy legislation also covered a vast array of occupations: pedlars and tinkers, soldiers and mariners, many entertainers, students, unlicensed healers and even fortune-tellers. What these varied groups had in common was that they were considered potentially 'more hurtful than necessary to the commonwealth', as an Act of Edward VI's reign stated of pedlars and tinkers. Wizards and unlicensed healers were specifically accused of fraud, while entertainers, military men and tinkers were thought to cause disruption, as will be seen in a subsequent chapter.[37]

Gypsies and the Irish were also treated as vagrants. The first were covered by a distinct body of legislation, but were essentially viewed as vagabonds. The Irish were included in an Act of 1572 that ordered them

back to Ireland. Both groups were accused of sedition and treason, but by the seventeenth century the Irish were considered the more dangerous. As well as being aliens, they came to England in waves of immigration caused by war and famine. To make matters worse, the native Irish were associated with popery and rebellion. The peculiar mores and family structures of these outsiders are considered below in Chapter 4.

The laws were employed, finally, against disorders that were not even in the statute books under vagrancy. A Somerset Don Juan's 'idleness' in 1609 involved luring young women to alehouses and seducing them. Disorderly and drunken behaviour landed others in trouble. For example, a man was arrested in 1574 after quarrelling with his female companion in a Cheshire alehouse. Vagrancy charges even crop up in disputes between neighbours. Elizabeth Owen was whipped in Westminster in 1611 for slandering neighbours. As with witchcraft, such cases probably reflect community tensions more than anything else.[38]

Migrants were also policed under the legislation. When poor relief became law in the reign of Elizabeth I, officials began 'warning out' immigrants under threat of vagrancy charges. This was to stop them from burdening the poor rates. By law the poor were entitled to succour in their birthplaces *or* their last places of residence. Because anyone moving to another parish might be eligible for relief in two places it was natural, if inhumane, to query settlement rights and treat claimants as vagrants. The effect was to turn honest immigrants into vagrants by denying them residence rights.[39] Finally, some offences against property were treated as vagabondage. Along with vagrants, petty thieves were sometimes despatched to houses of correction. Occasionally even vandals were so handled: a Witham cutler was sent to an Essex bridewell in James I's reign for his 'idle and vagrant life' after destroying a gentleman's fish pond.[40]

Thus the omnibus statutory definitions of vagrancy were not purely theoretical. Admittedly not every offender showed all the marks of the vagrant; nor were all five characteristics necessary for prosecutions to take place. Small numbers of offenders did not fit the stereotypes: the few who accumulated substantial bank-rolls; some sedentary persons like Elizabeth Owen; cripples who were occasionally charged; and groups like pedlars who worked but whose trades were suspect. And of course not all the poor were vagrants. As was seen above, the fit and the disabled were considered differently. Nor were all migrants *ipso facto* vagrants. Migration was common among all classes of society in this period.[41] Finally, not all itinerant criminals were prosecuted as vagrants. We shall observe in Chapter 8 how the transient population contained an element, albeit a small one, which perpetrated more serious crimes. An even smaller minority openly attacked the *status quo* in politics and religion. This was

the Elizabethan underworld as far as it existed, but vagrancy was usually the least of their sins.

CONCLUSIONS

Vagrancy legislation therefore reflected a new kind of poverty after 1300, that of 'masterless men'; persons no longer having manorial ties, but who were now subject to the buffetings of the market economy. In response, the stereotype of the sturdy beggar developed, which diverged sharply from the Franciscan idealization of poverty in the High Middle Ages. The stereotyping was the work of a wide range of learned authorities and was ultimately enshrined in the law. In the process vagabondage was defined as a social and political danger much like witchcraft. If witch-belief provided spiritual explanations for evil, the vagrant supplied common or garden ones. Destitute, rootless and masterless, he seemed part of a conspiracy to destroy society.

It would be tempting, considering contemporary fears about vagrants, to conclude that governments lived under veritable siege from them. Certainly it is still commonly believed that English governments of this period were weak, because they had no standing armies and no paid police forces.[42] Judging by the example of vagrancy, however, this is a misleading view. The English state, as Chapter 9 shows, developed a number of institutions to control vagrants that were novel and greatly extended state authority.

One of the new institutions was examination procedure which, as well as supplying the basic documentation for this study, provides a concluding illustration of the political context of vagrancy. It first appeared in a vagrancy statute of 1383; thereafter it was extended to other offences. By the mid-sixteenth century a magistrate's examination was common prior to a suspect's appearance in court. The procedure sprang principally from the extension of state authority. Thus twenty of the thirty or so statutes that prescribed it before 1555 contained new social and economic controls.[43] It was specifically deployed to deal with new and exceptional crimes, especially those thought to threaten the state and social order, such as treason, witchcraft and vagabondage. These offences also involved a new concept of collective crime: of a good society *versus* a wicked one; of Christians against covens of witches; of rightful rulers against treasonous plotters; of law-abiding citizens against anti-societies of rogues. Examinations were designed to discover the conspiracies through detailed questioning of suspects about their movements, confederates and haunts.[44]

The concern for order is obvious in the procedure's development in England. It was first passed into law after the Peasants' Revolt of 1381 in

an Act chiefly concerning disorder and vagrancy. Its application is first well documented in the aftermath of Ket's Rebellion in cases mainly involving seditious words. Finally, it received its most detailed statutory statements in 1554–5 in the wake of numerous rebellions and conspiracies.[45] As this evidence clearly shows, vagrancy legislation was part of a larger extension of state authority, which was responding to disturbing new social and political changes.

Chapter 2

The growth of vagrancy

To understand contemporary fears about vagrancy, one must realize that the problem grew at an alarming rate between 1560 and 1640. The main reasons were population growth, landlessness, and the penury and insecurity of wage-labour. Already in 1520 England had considerable numbers of poor. Then for over a century they experienced increasing hardship; not only occasionally when famines and epidemics struck, but year after year, decade after decade. Chronic destitution resulted from long-term demographic and economic changes, and it was fertile soil for the growth of vagabondage. Between 1620 and 1650 these developments reached a crisis point, and the condition of the vagrant poor sharply deteriorated.

THE NUMBERS ISSUE

Contemporaries' estimates of vagrant numbers are nearly worthless. Harrison thought the national total in 1577 might be 10,000, but just two decades later a Cornish magistrate put it at 200,000, with 10,000 in his shire alone.[1] The conjectures continued to fly thick and fast in the next century: according to one author, some 'wise counsellors of state' in James I's reign believed that 80,000 vagabonds were roaming the country; under the later Stuarts the guesses ranged from 30,000 to 100,000.[2] Even local estimates fluctuated wildly, one source putting the number in London in Edward VI's reign at just 200, while another claimed 30,000 haunted the place in 1602. London vagrancy did rise dramatically in the period, but both these figures are nonsense.[3]

None of the foregoing guesses can be trusted, because they give no indication of their evidence, if they were based on any. They simply confirm that contemporaries saw vagabondage as a 'dark figure': an immense and growing crime that was essentially indeterminate. The only figures to take at all seriously are those of Edward Hext, a Somerset JP

who in 1596 reckoned that English vagrants numbered 300 to 400 per county, plus 30 to 40 gypsies. Projected to England and Wales, these figures would mean 16,000 to 20,000 vagabonds. Hext was an active justice who himself arrested offenders, but even his statistics are suspect. They were based on his Somerset experience, which might be untypical, and are from a crisis period when war and famine no doubt caused a short-term increase in the problem. Even if Hext's totals were accurate, we have nothing reliable to which to compare them.[4]

In fact, we are unlikely ever to possess accurate statistics for the total numbers of vagabonds, since there were no national censuses and no registers of the unemployed. Records of arrests show that 24,867 persons were convicted for vagrancy between 1631 and 1639, or an average of 4447 a year. Constables' accounts of the same period suggest that convicted vagabonds made up just 6 per cent of itinerant paupers travelling long distances. Yet it would be misleading to take these figures as indicating the true numbers or, more importantly, as a measure of people's perceptions and experience of vagrants. Possibly 29 per cent might have been 'recidivists', as Chapter 8 shows, who were recorded more than once. Allowance must also be made for lost and incomplete records (how much is uncertain), an imponderable which makes all calculations extremely dubious. For their part, constables' accounts are deceptive in their categories of transients. In reality, there was considerable overlap between groups of transient poor: 'non-vagrants' such as Irish beggars, gypsies, ex-soldiers, and disabled persons were actually apprehended as vagabonds, as later chapters show. There are still further reasons why a global statistic for vagrants is likely to be misleading. First, it ignores the fact that many more people would have experienced vagrancy for brief periods of their lives because of upheavals linked to life-cycles and employment prospects. As is shown below, adolescents, often servants and apprentices, were especially vulnerable, but that did not mean they became vagabonds for life. Secondly, it would be simplistic to think that people are only considered threats to the social order if their numbers are great. If anything, the numbers pursued in witch-hunts past and present suggest that small conspiracies are feared more. Vagabonds were thought to form just such a conspiratorial underworld, as the previous chapter showed. Thirdly, it must be remembered that, while vagabonds might be few in number, they had 'high visibility', because they were on the move, usually strangers in the places they passed, and were often begging and thus frequently in 'face to face' relationships with the public. These conditions of their existence undoubtedly made them appear to be more numerous than they were. Finally, their numbers increased dramatically at certain junctures: in the countryside in summer; after military campaigns; and during economic crises. The 1620s and 1630s saw sharp rises

ranging from two- to ten-fold, depending upon the parish. For all these reasons it seems that vagrancy will remain a 'dark figure' to which it is impossible to attach a tidy sum total.[5]

It is possible, nevertheless, to chart a deterioration in the vagrancy problem, based upon records of arrests. Admittedly these might reflect official enthusiasm or laxity in enforcing the laws, so we are fortunate to have evidence from national searches in 1569–72 and 1631–9, when local officials were kept on their toes and regularly reported arrests to Whitehall. Only a fraction of the documentation probably survives, but it is sufficient to indicate the changing levels of vagrancy. In the first campaign 742 arrests were reported, and in the second, 24,867. This does not signify that vagabondage increased 34-fold over the period. Far fewer shires' returns survive from the first round-ups (18 compared with 32), and they cover a much shorter period (8 months as against 96). Adjusting for these factors would bring the Elizabethan total to just over 15,000, which means that the total of 25,000 under Charles I represents an increase in vagrancy of around 65 per cent. This rise slightly exceeded the rate of population growth, which was just under 60 per cent between 1571 and 1636.[6] That vagabondage was growing at roughly the same rate as the population, despite government efforts to eradicate the problem, helps explain why it was taken so seriously.

But there was worse to come. Between 1620 and 1650 vagrancy was exacerbated by deteriorating demographic and economic conditions. This period was the grand finale of a disastrous century marked by rising population, rents and food prices, and declining real wages. It also saw a massive depression in the cloth industry and blockages in traditional channels of upward social mobility. The result for the poor was a deepening crisis; it is no coincidence that parish poor relief was first widely enforced, and that large-scale emigration overseas began then.[7] Among vagrants the picture was equally grim. As later chapters show, they were arrested in larger and larger groups as families and children swelled their ranks. They also moved longer distances at faster rates in order to scrape a living. Between 1560 and 1640, therefore, vagrancy worsened both quantitatively and qualitatively.

POVERTY: DIMENSIONS AND STRUCTURES

One precondition of vagrancy was a large pauper population, which possibly doubled in size in the period. Analyses of taxation, census and military records of the 1520s show the destitute making up 13 per cent of the population of Babergh hundred (Suffolk) and 20 per cent in Coventry.[8] In later decades the problem seems to worsen: Elizabethan and early Stuart surveys of the poor, of which a dozen or so survive from

around the country, show them normally accounting for 20 to 30 per cent of the community.[9] Matters did not improve in the later seventeenth century. Exemptions for poverty in Hearth Tax records show from 29 to 44 per cent living in need in two Midlands counties in 1670, while Gregory King's national estimates for 1688 imply that 51 per cent were economic burdens on the country.[10] None of these figures should be treated as statistical certainties. Some originate from just one or two places; others represent averages of data for large areas or over long periods. The incidence of destitution obviously varied from place to place, and could change abruptly when epidemics and harvest failures struck. Furthermore, the criteria for defining people's needs might be affected by circumstances such as which government body was involved and what its aims were. Nevertheless, these estimates are the best available, and they are more likely to understate than to exaggerate the problem's true extent, because they often omitted migrants, vagrants, persons receiving in-door relief, and those on the edge of poverty. They also confirm what is suggested by the demographic and economic data; that is, that England had substantial and growing numbers of poor.

Raw figures of poverty levels indicate the problem's rough proportions, but they do not explain vagrancy. Poverty has many faces, and some are more likely than others to bear that of the vagabond. By the standards of industrialized societies virtually everyone living in Elizabethan times might be considered poor: backward technology, and rudimentary levels of sanitation and medical care, made death and discomfort omnipresent. The economy was underdeveloped; regular work and incomes were the exceptions. Productivity was low, and unemployment was high, affecting about a third of the population according to contemporaries. Still others were 'underemployed', because most work was seasonal and dependent on the harvest. Those adults who were employed bore tremendous burdens. This was because of the population's age-structure, which included about twice as many persons as today under the age of 16. Despite widespread child labour, fully productive adults were therefore in short supply, while dependent youngsters were numerous.[11]

Again, these remarks about poverty in pre-industrial societies leave the story unfinished. In reality destitution was more dynamic and varied than the broad distinction between pre- and post-industrial allows. Fundamental to the problem in England was the changing relationship of the bulk of the population to the land. The decisive shift occurred in the later medieval period. In the High Middle Ages the poor were comparatively firmly rooted on the land, even during the thirteenth century when the population grew and destitution increased greatly. There were various responses to the deteriorating conditions, none of which seems to

have led to a significant growth of vagabondage. Many peasants, for example, managed by assarting on wasteland and in forests. But even those tied to manors adapted. At Halesowen the poorest smallholders simply became poorer and poorer, living shorter lives than the better-off, marrying later (if at all), and having smaller families. Another response is seen on Cambridgeshire manors, where destitution was soaked up through temporary concessions of land to the poor.[12] All this changed with the fourteenth-century crisis. At first the lords were unable to resist the pressures for mobility and high wages, and for a few generations after 1380 smallholders and wage-earners prospered at the lords' expense. But the lords were careful not to lose complete control over their lands,[13] and when demographic and economic conditions changed after 1500, the plebeians whistled a different tune. They were no longer part of a manorial economy, but now they faced the chill wind of the marketplace.

Of course, the picture was not all black in the sixteenth and seventeenth centuries. The 'lower sort' in England, unlike their French counterparts, did not starve in great numbers.[14] Some listed as destitute in taxation records were probably young adults who were in service or newly married. Later in life they might leave the ranks of the poor and even prosper; some husbandmen and craftsmen accumulated considerable quantities of household goods. In addition, although smallholdings did not proliferate as they had in the thirteenth century (and continued to do in many parts of France), the English poor still had resources to fall back upon. They retained gardens and crofts where they grew some food; they kept livestock on the commons; and they supplemented their incomes through casual labouring and cottage industries. When times were bad, they no doubt received assistance from relatives, neighbours and friends. Vagrancy was also unlikely to threaten them at all stages of life, for as is demonstrated below it mainly occurred among adolescents after they had left home and entered the labour market. The severity of the conditions giving rise to vagabondage also varied over the period. Although the authorities were concerned about the problem in the early sixteenth century, it was in the later sixteenth and early seventeenth centuries that it reached its most menacing proportions, because of the developments examined in the next section. Then from the mid-seventeenth century vagrancy waned as conditions changed, including (as it is argued in the Conclusions at the end of this book) the widespread enforcement of statutory poor relief. But in the meantime, particularly between 1560 and 1640, the poor no longer had the security of smallholders in a manorial economy and received a severe buffeting in the marketplace. Governments intervened on an unprecedented scale to check the social consequences, and so there is some truth in Tawney's assertion that the poor laws were a social necessity after villeinage ended.[15]

Censuses of the poor leave little doubt about their vulnerability to vagrancy. Eighty to 90 per cent were able-bodied and therefore liable to arrest if they begged, were unemployed, or met any other of the laws' criteria. As regards age, poverty was nearly universal. As might be expected, the very young and very old were affected, but so were people in the prime of life between the ages of 30 and 60, who made up 30 to 40 per cent of the total. The only group seemingly to escape were adolescents and young adults in the age-group 16 to 30, especially males. They were often away in service, apprenticeship, and the armed forces or, if at home, unmarried. But even this group had only brief reprieves, and they were especially prone to vagrancy. Those able-bodied adults at home mainly suffered from unemployment and low wages. They were not automatically granted poor relief, even if they were settled in the community, although their children might receive it. Not surprisingly the settled poor were there one day and gone the next: half of Warwick's paupers disappeared in less than five years in the 1580s through death and migration. Males were particularly volatile, because they left home for the reasons mentioned, but also because they deserted women and probably died younger.[16]

Poverty also varied spatially and temporally. The belief that towns were the worst hit is quite wrong, largely the result of better record-keeping; in fact the countryside was also affected. The Hearth Tax records show many villages with 40 per cent and more of their inhabitants in poverty, and the general average was about the same as in towns. Of course the incidence of social problems varied between regions. Many classic nucleated villages had fewer paupers because smallholders had often been squeezed out and resident squires kept the places closed to in-migration. By contrast the scattered settlements of fen and woodland, often without resident lords, were open to squatters and had higher poverty levels.[17] Towns were also centres of in-migration by the poor, but even there the impact was selective, with most huddling in suburban slums rather than the centre. London's fantastic growth seemingly put it in another league from most towns, but the next chapter shows that its social problems were not unique. Finally, the fortunes of the poor might change overnight: the numbers of Warwick's poor doubled in 1587 after a poor harvest.[18]

POPULATION GROWTH AND DISPOSSESSION, 1500–1650

One reason for the growing destitution was that the country's population nearly doubled from about 2.7 million in 1541 to 5.2 million in 1651. Even allowing that at the latter date England was only one-tenth as populous as today, growth still spelt trouble. Obviously the numbers of the poor

would have increased if they had simply reproduced as fast as the population generally. But things were worse than this because of the special character of the rise, which resulted from high fertility rather than falling mortality levels. In other words the period witnessed a baby-boom such as occurred after the Second World War, but in this instance compounded over 100 years. The upshot was that, despite high rates of infant and child mortality, the problem of great numbers of unproductive youngsters was greatly intensified.[19]

The economy offered little relief to growing poverty, and agrarian changes made matters worse. Agricultural and industrial output rose, but whether it surpassed population growth or made much impact upon unemployment is doubtful. In agriculture some technological innovations were introduced, but production was chiefly increased by extending cultivation. Harvest yields on some carefully managed lands doubled, but even then just kept pace with population and failed to stifle the rise in food prices.[20] Manufacturing was similarly sluggish. The old argument that England experienced an 'industrial revolution' in the period is misleading. Production rose sharply in a few industries, but they were untypical of an economy that remained largely rural and underdeveloped in 1640. The leading industry, cloth manufacture, was 'scarcely affected by cost-reducing innovations' and suffered long bouts of depression between 1550 and 1640. Few towns were able to employ unlimited numbers of migrants. The most notable industrial expansion was in domestic production in pastoral and woodland areas, and in towns (or parts of towns) outside gild control.[21]

The main economic trends offered little comfort to the poor. Rises in food prices averaging about 4 per cent a year might not seem much by the standards of the 1970s and 1980s, but the inflation was sustained for nearly 150 years and had serious consequences. Those who did not produce their own food, which included most of the poor, had to purchase it at inflated prices in the marketplace. Meanwhile, wages were rising half as much as food prices because the supply of labour outran the demand: real wages for *both* agricultural and industrial labour fell by as much as 50 per cent. Even if some élite craftsmen had capital to fall back on, wage-work by itself (as will shortly be seen) was unlikely to provide a living for the bulk of wage-earners, who had also to rely upon smallholdings and charity. Industrial prices were similarly depressed, rising half as much as food, so that apart from the exceptions noted this sector offered little hope. The best economic prospect was unquestionably land, but this was precisely the resource denied to the English poor.[22]

Historians used to think that England ceased to be a land of small-holders in the eighteenth century, but now they see the process beginning in the Middle Ages. Without any question, however, the demo-

graphic and economic shifts of the sixteenth and early seventeenth centuries accelerated this development. The greatest pressures were upon smallholders in open-field villages. One dramatic case was Chippenham, a Cambridgeshire chalkland village where the proportion of landless householders rose from 3.5 per cent in 1279 to 32 per cent in 1544, and on to 63 per cent in 1712, and where middle-sized holdings of 15 to 50 acres were nearly wiped out in the early seventeenth century. If not always so dramatic, the same pattern is well documented for many areas of traditional open-field husbandry. Growing landlessness is also evident at the bottom of the heap among farm labourers, who were initially smallholders who occasionally worked for wages: those without land, apart from small crofts and gardens, rose from 11 per cent in the mid-sixteenth century to 40 per cent in the mid-seventeenth.[23]

The causes of dispossession included population growth and commercialized agrarian relations. The rise in population led to greater competition for holdings, rising rents, and the proliferation of uneconomic smallholdings. By 1600 it barely paid to farm less than 30 acres of arable. Yet even in good times in Elizabeth I's reign few smallholders held more than 4 acres. Under the early Stuarts there was still further fragmentation of holdings and recourse to wage-work to make ends meet. The rising corn prices of the period were unfavourable, because most smallholders kept livestock and bought their corn in the market. Far better placed were the lords and big peasants, who engrossed the smallholder's lands and enclosed the commons he used for grazing.[24]

Enclosure has often been considered a leading cause of vagrancy, and the issue is still debated. Estimates of 300,000 persons displaced under the early Tudors have been reduced to 34,000 for the longer period from 1455 to 1637.[25] But enclosure was just one of many pressures upon smallholders who, as Tawney correctly perceived, were displaced by a complex agrarian revolution. He focused upon customary tenants, by far the largest group. While arguments persist over how much legal security they enjoyed, we do know that a good half of them had no rights of renewal and that two-thirds were subject to increased rents. These were supposed to be 'reasonable', but in fact outstripped the rise in food prices. Tenants unable to pay big fines had to move on, even if they were not formally evicted.[26]

Of course enclosure was a point of leverage upon smallholders. It involved more than simply erecting hedges around one's lands. The whole pattern of agriculture in open-field villages was altered from a communal to an individualistic one. Sometimes entire villages were converted by the agreement of major landholders, including rich peasants; occasionally by just one of them. Whichever the case, the result usually involved the extinction of common rights of grazing, the

smallholder's life-blood. Enclosure did not cease or even decline after 1520. The later Tudor period saw as much as before and the process continued through the next century.[27]

Yet another threat to smallholders was engrossing, which involved the extinction of whole farms and villages for conversion into veritable sheep ranches. The destruction of entire villages largely ceased about 1520, but engrossing was still occasionally stimulated by high wool and low cereal prices. When food prices rose suddenly amidst a wave of engrossing, as in 1549 and 1607, the poor rebelled.[28] Large landholders had other weapons as well. Where tenure was weak, in addition to raising rents, lords of manors returned holdings to the demesne without renewing them and converted copyholds to leaseholds. Where tenants had secure holdings that gave the lord poor returns, he shifted maintenance responsibilities to them, allowed properties to fall into disrepair, imposed new services and revived old ones. All in all, the big fish were well placed to swallow up the small fry.[29]

Although we are unlikely ever to have a final tally, thousands were undoubtedly displaced in England's agrarian upheavals. Many, probably most, started new lives elsewhere – in towns, woodland and fenland regions – and avoided an immediate descent into vagrancy. But migration was often a stop-gap, as will be demonstrated in the next chapter. Furthermore, the significance of the dispossession of the smallholder goes beyond those initially uprooted. Henceforth the social order largely excluded the type of smallholding peasant found in medieval society. By 1600 the English people had had the country's major resource seized from their grasp; at a time, ironically, when their requirements for food and housing were increasing. Where were they to find refuge? Where indeed, wondered preachers and politicians terrified of popular uprisings.

WAGE-LABOUR: A WAY OUT?

Wage-work was one possible escape route from destitution. It consisted basically of two types, the one living in as a servant or apprentice in which payment was chiefly in kind; the other doing day-labour in agriculture or a craft, mainly for cash. Some uncertainty surrounds both positions. Regarding the first we are told that the master/servant relationship was the lynch-pin of a patriarchal society in which 'every relationship could be seen as a love-relationship'.[30] Might the poor have found refuge in patriarchal households? Controversies about day-labour centre upon the standard of living it afforded, especially upon whether the decline in real wages has been exaggerated. In relation to vagrancy it is necessary to determine how much security the poor found in wage-work generally. The short answer, it seems, is a qualified 'not much'. Neither living-in nor

day-labouring was likely to provide a permanent stay against poverty, for uncertainty and insecurity were problems inherent to these positions. In addition, in purely cash terms begging was a genuine alternative by the early seventeenth century.

Living-in, dependent workers were probably the largest element in the labour force. They formed about two-fifths of the population with occupations and status recorded in seventeenth-century villages, mainly working as servants in husbandry; and between a half and two-thirds in towns, most of them apprentices and domestics. They performed various jobs and served terms of varying lengths, but in other respects they had a certain unity. Legally, both service and apprenticeship were forms of servitude. Dependent workers put themselves at the will of masters for shelter, board and clothing. In return, their masters had the right to their labour and the authority to discipline them.[31] These workers were also of roughly similar wealth. Some well-off ones turn up in London, but the majority were property-less, receiving minimum cash wages amounting to pocket money. They also had similar life-experiences, for their positions were supposed to be temporary ones in a 'life-cycle'. They usually entered service in their early to mid 'teens and left in the mid to late twenties.[32]

The system of dependent labour provided temporary relief. The children of the poor were generally placed with the 'better-sort', who were the biggest servant-keepers. To governments the system was a means of keeping the growing numbers of young people under control; the poor laws actually prescribed apprenticeship as a remedy for poverty. But whether the system was viable over the long term appears doubtful, because economic and social changes were undermining it. In any case, dependency was subject to a multitude of upheavals that actually caused vagrancy.

Dependency declined in the period and was increasingly replaced by short-term hirings on a cash basis. The change took centuries, but was well under way in the sixteenth and seventeenth centuries. Between 1520 and 1700 the numbers of living-in workers fell by something like 50 per cent: from perhaps 20 per cent of the total population to just 10 per cent.[33] There were many reasons for the shift away from living-in labour. First, the dissolution of the monasteries put several thousand living-in servants out of work, who probably did not find immediate employment. Secondly, between 1590 and 1620 the aristocracy cut the numbers of their servants from an average of one hundred or so each to three or four dozen – hence the complaints of a 'decline of hospitality'.[34] Thirdly, apprenticeship ceased to be the main avenue for entry into trades and crafts. Interlopers now set up in suburbs and in the countryside outside gild controls. In London apprentices formed about 15 per cent of the popula-

tion in 1600, but a century later the figure was just 4 or 5 per cent. Finally, agricultural labour was increasingly hired on a casual, cash basis, which gave employers greater flexibility and trimmed their costs.[35] As with the land question, therefore, opportunities for the poor in service and apprenticeship were drying up between 1560 and 1640.

Living-in was an unstable as well as declining prospect, and instability led to vagrancy. Dependent workers in fact formed a substantial and possibly growing element in the vagrant population. They made up nearly half of those arrested who had trades listed in Essex from 1564 to 1596; 56 per cent of those taken into Bridewell from 1597 to 1608; and in Norwich a third between 1564 and 1610, rising to two-thirds from 1626 to 1635.[36] Of course we might expect such large turn-outs, since dependent workers were numerous. But this *caveat* fails to explain why persons in theoretically stable positions should have become vagrants.

One reason is that they were exceptionally mobile. Between a half and two-thirds of farm servants switched masters yearly; seventeenth-century diaries show that living-in servants who stayed more than a year were exceptional. They changed locations as well as masters. Of twenty-six servants living in Cogenhoe (Northants) in 1628, only one had been in service there two decades before; of sixty-seven in Clayworth (Notts) in 1688, the number there a dozen years earlier was similarly just one. Nor did apprentices settle once their terms finished: in Norwich the proportion was just one in six; in London, one in three.[37] With all this chopping and changing, many inevitably ended up out of work.

It is impossible to say whether master/dependant relations were generally harmonious. Many masters probably had stable and caring relationships with servants, as Laslett suggests. On the other hand, there is considerable evidence that breakdowns occurred, causing vagrancy. A plethora of conduct books was published in the period advising masters and dependent workers how to maintain concord. But the literature's clear message is that conflict was common. William Gouge's hundred pages on masters and servants are a catalogue of discord.[38] The official record suggests a similar picture. Statutory requirements for servants – a year's contract, a quarter's notice, and 'reasonable and sufficient cause' before leaving – imply that ruptures were a problem. Moreover, apprentices' indentures normally required them not to steal from masters, gamble, fornicate, buy or sell except for the master's profit. These provisions and the master's right to mete out 'reasonable correction' suggest that sweetness and light did not always prevail.[39]

Conflicts arose over basic issues of terms and conditions. Disagreements over food and clothing, important elements in the dependant's wage, led to breaks.[40] This is not surprising considering the master's huge powers. Thomas Platter described England as 'a servant's prison, because

their masters and mistresses are very severe'. Whoever was to blame, disputes occurred. Masters allegedly starved their charges, neglected the training of apprentices, and encouraged them to steal. Dissension led to violence. Correction was supposed to be moderate and reasonable, but some masters went overboard. For their part, menials sometimes gave as good as they got.[41]

Contrary to the regulations, masters dismissed workers before their terms finished. They let them go when they became ill and unable to work, and when they themselves fell on hard times. Another source of vagrancy was flight. Some youngsters found the adjustment to service difficult, and once truancy began it tended to continue. William Scarlett, incarcerated in Bridewell in 1620, had run away six times.[42] It was such youngsters who filled the houses of correction, and from there the slide into vagrancy and other crimes could be quick and certain. Theft also disrupted patriarchal relations. It was almost customary to lift something from masters when quitting their service. Some stole out of genuine need, others because of grudges, and still others for gain.[43]

Another source of upheavals was illicit sexual unions, which resulted in vagrancy, especially for female servants. Sometimes servants took up together, left masters, and ended up on the road.[44] But masters themselves were also involved. Alice Smalley was taken into Bridewell in 1606 after abandoning a bastard child in London; the alleged father was her master, a local girdler. Such blatant violations of the patriarchal ideal appear regularly in court records.[45] Fellow-servants and masters were not the only males involved, for masters' sons raped and seduced female servants.[46] The upshot for females could be disaster: pregnancy, discharge from service (although that was unlawful), punishment as vagrants by officials terrified of supporting a bastard child, and the birth of the child in a lonely place.

Dependency looks increasingly to have offered limited help to the poor. It provided temporary refuge for many teenagers and young adults, but the system was in decline, which must have exacerbated unemployment and vagabondage. When workers did live in, mobility and conflicts with employers meant that menials fell foul of the vagrancy laws. Finally, whether most dependants successfully completed the life-cycle and set up on their own is doubtful. At Ealing in 1599 their mean average age was 25, suggesting that many adults were finding no permanent niches. Furthermore, the majority of servants in husbandry whose settlement examinations survive ended up as destitute day-labourers.[47] On a number of counts, therefore, dependent workers faced a deteriorating situation.

Little is known about independent wage-workers, even though their numbers and importance were probably growing. Everitt's figures sug-

gest that perhaps a third of the population lived from wages, as do Gregory King's.[48] However, imprecise nomenclature in most sources means that only local records are accurate, and they are too scattered and variable to be meaningful. Moreover, the line between working for wages and being self-employed was a fine one. The person who worked purely for cash wages was probably exceptional. It is well known that the farm labourers studied by Everitt were actually smallholders who occasionally worked for wages. Many craftsmen were paid what amounted to a wage by capitalists running 'putting-out' systems. Casual labourers in agriculture often received food and drink in part payment. This almost infinite variety in wage-workers makes generalizations problematical.

Nevertheless, it seems that the wage-worker living out also faced serious difficulties. He experienced a major erosion in living standards and status because of adverse conditions between 1500 and 1650: the growth of population, which put downward pressure on wage levels; the differential between food prices and wages of two to one, which had the same effect; and the squeeze on the land and the sluggishness of industrial production discussed above. Among vagrants, the numbers of labourers and journeymen fell in the period (see Appendix, Table XI), but this is misleading. The status of persons arrested is not always clear, so that someone listed as a shoemaker or weaver might in reality be a journeyman. Occupational mobility also meant that wage-work was dropped for other lines. Furthermore, the evidence of social origins suggests that vagrants were chiefly drawn from the low-paid: servants, apprentices, labourers and the poorer crafts.

As Professor Hill has shown, wage-labour was synonymous with poverty in the sixteenth and seventeenth centuries.[49] The belief was well-founded. Wages were commonly thought to be a supplement to another source of income such as a smallholding. The decline in the purchasing power of wages appears to have been dramatic at nearly 50 per cent. It is true that it has been argued that these figures have no meaning in the case of those building craftsmen who were small businessmen of substance. But how typical they were remains to be seen; certainly there were also poor building craftsmen who did rely mainly upon wages and whose future was less kind.[50] Where farm labour is concerned, we know that it was also under pressure: on top of wages falling by about half in real terms, those holding less than an acre rose fourfold between 1560 and 1640. Similarly, the cottar-miners of the Stannaries and Derbyshire sank into poverty from the 1580s because of the rising cost of living.[51] It is therefore unlikely, despite the possible exception of some builders, that wage-workers prospered in the period. Many no doubt joined the ranks of migrants and vagrants.

Wage-labour was not only badly paid; it was irregular. Daily wage-rates

tell us nothing about how many days people worked. Most employment was seasonal, agricultural work reaching a peak in the summer months and tailing off until the following spring. Even industrial employment fluctuated seasonally: in Prescot in Lancashire, it was reported in 1640, the local poor dug coal in summer and begged in winter.[52] Crafts were also subject to economic crises. Poor harvests, which came on average every four years, caused unemployment among industrial workers, because the demand for their goods depended on agricultural profits. Trade slumps threw thousands out of work, particularly in the cloth industry. Depressions occurred in 1562–4, 1571–3, 1586–7 and almost constantly from 1614.[53] Wage-work, then, offered limited assistance to the poor before the mid-seventeenth century.

Under these circumstances it is not surprising to find that the traditional channels of upward social mobility for the 'lower sort' were closing in the first half of the seventeenth century. London apprentices were increasingly recruited from the sons of the well-off artisans and traders of the Southeast rather than from the offspring of the poorer upland zone.[54] Land and work were at a premium as population growth peaked and the cloth industry slumped between 1620 and 1650. It was the young, above all, who suffered in these conditions. The records of Richard Napier's mentally disturbed patients between 1597 and 1634 show that those in their twenties were most at risk of all age-groups, appearing before him at more than twice the rate warranted by their numbers in the population; economic uncertainty and reverses were leading causes of their anxieties.[55] Further consequences of blocked opportunities for the young are clear at Warminster between 1640 and 1660, where the authorities kept records of householders and young males. They show that the young men were exceptionally mobile in the period, at least a third leaving the town in the 1650s alone. Among emigrants to North America in the seventeenth century, about half were in their twenties, and once again economic difficulties figured prominently in their departures.[56]

With conditions as desperate as this, begging was a real alternative. By the early seventeenth century a licensed beggar might make a better living than most wage-earners; better indeed than many smallholders. Armed with an official licence or a counterfeit, both of which were readily available, a mendicant might gather 6d a day. In villages the authorities regularly doled out 1d to 2d per person, but in the towns, where vagrants mainly congregated, they gave up to 6d and 1s. If 6d were the daily average, then a licensed beggar should have made over £9 a year, which compares very favourably with the £1 6s granted to resident paupers, as well as with servants' wages, which were about £2 p.a. in the 1630s, not including diet. It was also as much as agricultural labourers were earning in the early seventeenth century.[57] If vagrants had official letters issued

under the Great Seal, which were also counterfeited, their takings might have surpassed the labourer's and even smallholders with 30 acres. Finally, unlike labouring, mendicancy was carried on all year round in many towns.

CONCLUSIONS

It is clear that the prospects of the English poor were far from bright in the sixteenth and early seventeenth centuries. They were unlikely to starve and survived through various makeshifts, but in losing the security of landholdings, many found few anchors to moor them. A position in dependency afforded temporary but insecure refuge. Working for wages as a craftsman or farm labourer living out was even more perilous, because that meant being exposed to the pressures of the market. Until population growth tailed off and wages picked up after 1650 it is unlikely that wage-earning on its own was a viable proposition. Even those with smallholdings like the Mendip cottar-miners and the agricultural labourers faced increasing hardship. With the bottom elements of society in a state of upheaval, the poor laws were necessary to control poverty. But not all the poor were succoured: under one-fifth of adults in Norwich in 1570 received relief, just over half the poor in St Mary's Warwick in 1587, and only about one-eighth in St Martin's Salisbury in 1635.[58] For many, therefore, migration and begging were the only alternatives – but then they risked arrest under the vagrancy laws.

Chapter 3

Migrants and vagrants

Elizabethan and early Stuart England experienced exceptionally high levels of migration, particularly by the poor. To what extent did such movement provide an escape from the growing destitution examined in the previous chapter? We shall probably never be able to generalize about the fate of poor migrants as a group, because of patchy evidence. Nevertheless, this chapter attempts to throw some light on the subject through an analysis of the geographical origins of 6100 vagrants and by a detailed study of London, which saw remarkably high immigration levels in the period. In the light of this evidence, migration appears as a slippery slope rather than a safety net for the poor.

THE RISE OF SUBSISTENCE MIGRATION

Strictly speaking, vagabonds were not migrants at all, since they were not usually making 'a permanent or semi-permanent change of residence'. Rather theirs resembled the 'continual movements of nomads and migratory workers', who fall outside modern definitions of migration.[1] Vagrants, as is shown later in Chapter 6, lived in a state of almost perpetual motion: few had much prospect of settled homes, and few had had them in the recent past. Thus to lump them together with migrants would do violence to the facts. It also seriously underrates the precariousness of the vagrant condition. Viewing migration and vagrancy as distinct, although related, processes allows one to consider the relationship between them.

Migration was common among all classes in the sixteenth and early seventeenth centuries, but there is good reason to think that the poor were most dramatically affected. It has been suggested that there were basically two types of migrant: first, 'betterment migrants', recruited chiefly from the 'better-sort', who moved comparatively infrequently and over short distances; secondly, 'subsistence migrants', drawn principally

from the poorer classes, who moved farther and more often.[2] In practice this meant that a craftsman or farm labourer migrated about twice as far, and a servant three times as far, as a gentleman or yeoman tended to do. Certainly from an early date the bottom levels of society were exceptionally mobile. In Northamptonshire in 1524 the rate of migration among persons taxed on wages, who were generally poor, was seven times higher than that among the more affluent assessed on lands and goods. Chopping and changing was frequent, as we have seen, among servants and day-labourers.[3]

The chronology of migration by the poor is difficult to chart, because of the variety of the sources and the differing methods used in their interpretation.[4] But some salient points are clear. The first is that migration was by no means unheard of in the Middle Ages, but we have little idea what proportion of the total population might have migrated.[5] Nor are we in a position to measure the overall distances moved, because manorial, surname and apprenticeship records only show where people embarked and disembarked, so to speak, and ignore intervening stops. Yet judging by the available evidence, fields of migration were quite limited in this period. In the early fourteenth-century Midlands, for example, immigrants most commonly originated within 10 miles in villages and middle-rank towns, and the vast majority came from within 20 miles. In larger towns the field was more extensive, but even in London it did not surpass 40 miles, and most immigrants sprang from the Home Counties.[6]

Migration appears to have increased in the later Middle Ages, particularly after the Black Death. In the countryside the amount of movement rose considerably, although whether distances increased there is unclear.[7] In the case of towns, however, they clearly did. In York those coming from over 20 miles mounted by about half; in London the proportion from outside the Home Counties doubled from 40 to 80 per cent between 1300 and 1500, as the pattern developed of large numbers coming from distant parts, especially the North.[8] The period also saw the appearance of the long-distance subsistence migrant. He is visible in the records of Kentish towns from the 1370s and 1380s, but his numbers did not begin to proliferate until the last quarter of the fifteenth century, when the engrossing of farms, urban unemployment, and renewed population growth began to squeeze the poor.[9]

From about 1500 there is evidence of growing long-distance migration, above all to southern towns from the poor pastoral uplands of the west and north.[10] The later sixteenth and early seventeenth centuries witnessed an acceleration of this tendency. Admittedly some of the long-distance newcomers were well-off and destined for apprenticeships in leading City Companies, but there was a parallel increase in long-haul

moves among the poor, which reached a peak about 1640. Between 1580 and 1640 the mean average distance moved by migrants to Kentish towns was about 60 miles, but among the poorer trades the figure was closer to 100. Thereafter the pattern changed. The mean average nationally fell by about half between 1660 and 1730, and the occupational profile was reversed, with the 'better-sort' moving the longer distances.[11] The late Elizabethan and early Stuart period also saw the appearance of a great host of itinerant paupers, which expanded greatly as time went on and which was permanently uprooted. Thus between the mid-fourteenth and the mid-seventeenth centuries England experienced major shifts in migration patterns: from mainly local to more long-distance moves, the latter rising significantly betwen 1580 and 1640, including a frightening increase in the numbers of transient poor.

The reasons for the rise in long-distance movement were similar to the causes of destitution examined in the previous chapter: the growth of population; agrarian dislocation in open-field villages; problems of unemployment and underemployment; and downward pressures upon wages. In these circumstances migration possibly acted as a safety-valve which relieved the danger of local starvation. But it also reflected the desperate state of the poor, who were having to move greater distances to make a living. Movement increased sharply in periods of crisis, above all in the 1590s and the decades from 1620 to 1650. Harvest failures, wars and trade depressions cut people adrift in great numbers at these junctures. Three Midland parishes averaged fourfold increases in numbers of 'poor travellers' from the 1610s to the 1630s; in the latter decade they each relieved between about 1000 and 2000 licensed beggars of various descriptions, many of whom were moving great distances. Even more disturbing, there was a sharp rise – in the order of 100 per cent – in the proportion of families among this itinerant population.[12] The transient poor thrown up in these upheavals, like vagabonds, hardly deserve the description of migrant at all, since they were usually on the road collecting alms rather than making permanent changes of residence. Perhaps they should be considered the desperate extreme of subsistence movements.

Given the conditions in which pauper migration occurred, it is not surprising that it led to vagrancy charges. The most common migrants were, in all likelihood, the poorest members of society. Because they moved farthest and most frequently, they ran the greatest risk of being permanently uprooted. In crisis periods the line between legal movement and illegal vagrancy was very fine. In fact, as we know, convicted vagrants formed only about 6 per cent of the total population of transient poor in the early seventeenth century, but there was considerable overlap between the two groups. They had similar trends in family structures, as is shown in the next chapter, and they both included gypsies, soldiers and

Irish. An accusation of vagrancy was always likely once a person was down and out, because officials regarded mendicancy and casual work with suspicion. A beggar relieved as a 'poor traveller' in one village might be arrested in the next if he acted suspiciously or was troublesome.

Another reason for migration leading to vagrancy is that the legal mechanisms were lacking to enable smooth changes of residence. Indeed the poor laws erected obstacles to movement by the poor and arguably increased vagabondage. They required three years' residence to establish a legal settlement for most of the sixteenth century; after 1597, and until the settlement law of 1662, the rule was one year. Ironically, the wider enforcement of poor relief in the early seventeenth century probably exacerbated vagrancy, because if the migrant looked like being a burden on the poor-rates, he was ejected. Officials used all the means at their disposal, legal or otherwise, to shift strangers, whom they turned into vagrants. If anything, settlement probably became easier for the poor under the later Stuart legislation, as it is argued in the Conclusions at the end of this book.[13]

Migration also resulted in vagabondage because migrants found problems in their new habitats, which meant they were scant improvement on their old ones. Migrants were especially prone to vagrancy if they originated in centres of high immigration, including towns, woodland and pastoral areas, as the following regional analysis of vagrants' origins attempts to show.

THE GEOGRAPHY OF VAGRANCY

The documentation for vagrants' geographical origins is abundant, if scattered. Records of county quarter sessions, borough courts, houses of correction and national search campaigns provide evidence for most parts of the country. The only major lacuna is Wales, but this is partly filled by evidence from Chester and Shrewsbury, which received many Welsh immigrants, and from Monmouthshire in the 1630s. Most of the records list the vagrant's place of birth or last residence. The authorities sought to determine this information for the purpose of sending offenders 'home', even though they might have left the place years before and had no further connection with it. This procedure, which was based upon statute law,[14] probably aggravated vagrancy by senselessly shifting the poor around and causing settlement disputes between parishes. It was also subject to abuse by vagrants, who lied about their origins and travelled around the country with the seeming blessing of magistrates.

None the less, the information is still valuable. It is likely to be accurate for the majority of vagrants, even though some counterfeits slipped through. Moreover, the evidence shows some clear patterns which allow

migratory movements to be linked with vagrancy. Magistrates did not differentiate consistently between places of birth and last residence, so that it is impossible to document phases of migration from, say, country to town, and town to city. Instead they often vaguely referred to a person as being 'of' a place. Finally, there was probably a tendency to overstate urban origins the further a person was from 'home', because a distant town might be more familiar than a little-known village. But since the law required offenders to be returned to parishes having a legal responsibility for them, it is possible to exaggerate the significance of this distortion.

The Southeast

This area was something of a crossroads for the country's vagrants, and the authorities were aware of its cosmopolitanism. The Recorder of London reported that a round-up netted over 100 vagrants in 1582, but that only twelve were from the metropolis itself; the same year at Maidstone sessions the JP William Lambarde observed of Kentish rogues that 'the most part be of foreign shires'.[15] The Southeast indeed drew contingents from most parts of Britain, and from abroad in London's case. As the figures in Table I (see Appendix) show, the region especially attracted them from the Southeast itself, from the western counties between London and Bristol, and from East Anglia, Lincolnshire and Yorkshire. But Hertfordshire also pulled large numbers from the Midlands. The region drew noticeably, too, upon the Celtic fringe, apart from Scotland: in London from 1604 to 1610 almost one in 8 came from Ireland or Wales; in Essex from 1564 to 1620 the figure was one in 20; and in Colchester from 1630 to 1664, over 1 in 10.[16] Ireland provided almost a fifth of the total vagrants arrested in London in 1630-1, although this was the exceptional result of recent famine there. The capital was the only part of the country noticeably to attract foreign vagrants, although the number was never great: 1 to 2 per cent from France, Spain, the Low Countries and the occasional runaway 'blackamore'.

The South and West

The counties between London and Bristol mainly saw vagrants move in a west-to-east direction, which was also the prevailing current nationally. Despite its proximity, the Midlands never accounted for more than a tenth of those arrested in Berkshire and Wiltshire; nor did East Anglia and the North make up more than a small fraction. Most transients originated in the region itself (almost half in Wiltshire, 1603-20), in the Southeast (two-fifths in Reading, 1623-41), and in Wales and Ireland (over one in 7 in Wiltshire by 1621-30). Thus the region caught a great deal of traffic across southern England. In particular, there was movement along the south coast to Portsmouth and Southampton, to Devon and Cornwall

through Dorset and Wiltshire, and to the western ports of Minehead and Bristol through Berkshire and Wiltshire. Not all roads led inexorably to London, but this was certainly the main direction of the flow. Just how powerful was the capital's pull can be seen at Reading, where over a quarter of the vagrants arrested were born or last lived in London or its near suburbs (40 of 138).[17]

The Southwest (Somerset, Devon, Cornwall)

The west-to-east flow was even more striking in this region. Almost no vagrants apprehended here came from north of Gloucestershire. The vast majority were from the area itself (over half in Somerset's case; just over two-fifths in Devon and Cornwall); from the South and West (in Somerset a fifth, many of them from near-by Bristol (32 of 94); a tenth in Devon and Cornwall); and from the Southeast (about a tenth in all places). Wales and Ireland also sent many vagrants to the region as, for instance, in Devon and Cornwall, where close to a third came thence.[18] The west-to-east movement was obvious in Somerset from 1607 to 1636, where most of the southwesterners came from Devon and Cornwall (135 out of 232), counties which accounted for almost a third of the total arrested. Those from northern parts were mainly from Wales (22) and Bristol (32) and from the east, Dorset (18), and Wiltshire (20). The Irish provided the single largest contingent of vagrants in Devon and Cornwall in the 1630s, although the Cornish ran a close second (77 and 71 respectively).[19]

The Midlands

In so vast an area the flows of vagrants are not surprisingly less obvious. Much as in the Southeast, they converged from all directions. There was a large group from the region itself – roughly a half in most places – with especially large contingents from neighbouring shires: in Staffordshire, over half from the West Midlands between 1606 and 1633; in Nottingham-shire, 1604–39, and Leicestershire, 1584–1640, a third from the East Midlands. Under Elizabeth the Midlands drew roughly a fifth of its vagrants from the North and the same from southern England. But in the seventeenth century the balance changed: in Leicester between 1584 and 1612 the south provided almost 25 per cent, but its share fell below 15 per cent between 1613 and 1640.[20] The main area of origin to advance was the North, which rose from 17 to 30 per cent, with Lincolnshire and Yorkshire providing the largest single groups, but the Northwest and Northeast also showing increases. Thus Derby officials reported in 1631 that most vagrants seized there had drifted down from Yorkshire and more remote northern parts.[21]

Another major current in the Midlands came from Wales. The influx dated from Elizabethan times, when a tenth of those apprehended in

Northamptonshire came from the principality. Similarly in Worcester in 1584 it was said of the poor who descended upon the city that 'the most part [came] forth of Wales'.[22] In Shrewsbury, too, a large part of the poor population came from the shires of Brecknock, Merioneth and Montgomery: in 1641 a survey of inmates showed over half from Wales (95 of 160), Montgomery leading the pack with 35 and Merioneth accounting for 14, while the West Midlands provided 51.[23] Once again, the flow was from west to east.

Wales

The evidence is too sparse to allow generalizations about the whole principality, but in Monmouthshire in the 1630s the biggest stream of vagrants came from Herefordshire and the Welsh counties to the north and west (77 of 106 cases). When those from Monmouthshire itself are included, Herefordshire and Wales made up almost the whole (100 of 106). The mountainous shire of Brecknock, with a total of 38, was especially prolific in sending vagrants southwards, so that the pattern here is similar to the Midland one.[24]

The North

Once again the documentation is sparse, with none at all for the North-east and Lincolnshire. But there is a good deal for Lancashire and Westmorland in the 1630s and for Yorkshire in the 1640s and 1650s. Cheshire makes up for the sporadic information elsewhere by a fairly continuous run from 1570 to 1630. A striking feature of vagrants' origins in the North was their localism. In Yorkshire from 1638 to 1660 over half came from Yorkshire or Lincolnshire. While these admittedly were the country's largest counties in area, so that it was necessary to travel further than elsewhere to leave their borders, similar proportions in Lancashire and Westmorland originated in the region (352 of 668 persons).[25] Cheshire was more cosmopolitan, with only a quarter to two-fifths originating in the Northwest. It was one of the few shires in the west to attract vagrants from the east, with between 1 in 5 and 1 in 7 coming from the West Midlands, depending upon the period, and those from Lincolnshire and Yorkshire making up about 1 in 10. This cosmopolitanism is explained by Chester's position as a leading centre in the Northwest for trade, ecclesiastical, military and political life, and for traffic to Ireland. It was the only place in the North to attract vagrants from southern England (roughly 1 in 10); by comparison, Yorkshire drew only about 1 in 20 from regions south of the Midlands.

Why the North failed to attract many southerners is not difficult to explain. Despite the importance of the old centres of Chester and York, and the rising stars of Manchester and Newcastle upon Tyne, the region

remained poor and remote. Its scattered settlements, poverty and great distances between market towns made it an unfavourable prospect for the vagrant poor. What was more, the climate was probably wetter, making travel uncomfortable. While the northern hills may not have terrified everyone as much as they did Defoe a century later, this combination of circumstances must have discouraged vagabonds.[26]

The North therefore attracted vagrants mainly from other remote areas. Cheshire pulled them from Wales and the Northwest itself, especially south Lancashire (the Fylde), North Wales (Denbighshire, Caernarfonshire and Montgomeryshire), but also from Staffordshire and Shropshire to the south and east. Yorkshire drew over a quarter from the Northeast (County Durham, above all), the Northwest and Scotland. Although these influxes were by no means just from one or two sources, they were more often from west to east or north to south than *vice versa*.[27] This drift southwards and eastwards can be observed in miniature in Yorkshire, where of 26 vagrants arrested who came from the North Riding, only 5 were caught in that riding, while the other 21 were seized in the East or West Ridings. The North Riding itself mainly drew vagrants from Scotland, Durham and the Lake Counties (21 of 30 cases).

East Anglia

Here the evidence comes from Norwich and Suffolk, where again a large share of vagrants were native to the region: roughly half in both places, but rising to three-quarters in Norwich in the exceptional 1630s.[28] Recruitment was not entirely parochial, for the North sent groups of a tenth to a fifth depending upon place and time, with a trickle from the Midlands ranging from 2 to 8 per cent. Perhaps most surprising is the substantial number from the south, running at between 15 and 30 per cent apart from the 1630s. East Anglia is one of the few instances in which movement occurred from south to north on any scale, and indeed on a level greater than in the opposite direction. The explanation might lie in the remoteness of Norfolk and Suffolk from the main north-south routes, so that vagrants travelling south from the North and the Midlands missed out these places. But that does not explain why the region attracted them from the south. As at Reading, the answer perhaps lies in sheer proximity. But the wealth of the region would also attract southern vagrants: to Norwich, the nation's second city and an expanding centre; to Suffolk, one of its richest shires; and finally to the harvest work available in this major region of cereal production.[29]

General trends

The evidence demonstrates that vagrants moved in distinct directions after pulling up stakes, above all towards the southern and eastern parts

of Britain from the more northern and western ones; the major exceptions were East Anglia and, to a lesser extent, Cheshire. There were, in addition, clear corridors through which they rambled. London and the Southeast were a major junction of the avenues running north to south and west to east, although the flow was never one way and various routes might be taken. In the Midlands and the North, as in the Southeast, the west-to-east, north-to-south currents intersected, and the same movement was obvious in Welsh influxes into Cheshire and Shropshire, although they also shifted southwards into Welsh shires like Monmouth. In the rest of the North traffic was more localized, but even there the directions were broadly similar to the south and the Midlands.

Movement generally was out of upland areas of the north and west into lowland ones to the south and east: from Wales into Cheshire and the Midlands; from the Northeast into Yorkshire; from the North Riding into the East and West Ridings; and from Brecknockshire, Herefordshire, and Carmarthenshire into Monmouthshire. Further evidence of the pattern is found in Lancashire, where the lowland parts north of the Ribble attracted transients principally from the upland regions of Lakeland, the West Riding and east Lancashire; and in Staffordshire, where they came from the highland parts of Dovedale and the Peak district – from places with such likely names as Butterton in the Morelands and Draycote in the Moors, as well as from the towns of Ashbourne ('in the Peak') and Buxton.[30] The same tendency is found, finally, in Somerset and Yorkshire. The former county is neatly divided between a highland area to the west and 'village England' to the east. Among Somerset vagrants apprehended in Wiltshire between 1598 and 1638 a majority sprang from the upland regions of the shire and their edges, even though in terms of proximity one would have expected the eastern lowland region near Wiltshire to have been in the lead. The example of Yorkshire is still more decisive, where nearly three-quarters of the county's vagrants arrested in neighbouring shires came from the Pennines and their borders.[31]

Another place from which vagrants commonly came was the woodland. Those arrested in Wiltshire came from the New Forest in Hampshire, Bruton and Selwood forests in Somerset and the Forest of Dean. Nearly a fifth of Somerset vagrants seized in Wiltshire between 1598 and 1638 came from Bruton or Selwood (33 of 171 cases), while in Somerset itself the place that sent more than any other was a forest town, Frome Selwood.[32] Other woodland communities that produced exceptional numbers of transients included Rockingham and King's Cliffe in Northamptonshire.[33]

EXPLANATIONS

Contemporary observers thought that forest and pastoral regions produced vagrants because their denizens were generally wicked. In 1589
Puttenham described those who lived in forests as 'vagrant and dispersed
like the wild beasts, lawless and naked'. The barrister John Cooke
referred to forest communities in 1648 as 'dens, and nurseries of li-
centious people, where there are many close alehouses that are receivers of rogues, and thieves'. Officials similarly saw the inhabitants
of these places as 'drones devoted to thievery, among whom are bred the
very spawn of vagabonds and rogues'.[34]

One specific reason for official hostility to forest communities was
fiscal, when early Stuart projectors met resistance to their attempts at
enclosure schemes. Another was that the inhabitants, as well as destroying timber and game, lived free of resident squires and parsons,
which it was said led to 'idleness, beggary and atheism, and consequently
disobedience to God and the King'.[35] Thieves occasionally used forests as
hide-outs, but that has little to do with why these regions produced
vagrants. In fact, they were centres of high rates of in-migration and
population growth in the sixteenth and seventeenth centuries.

Immigrants from open-field areas poured into woodland and pastoral
ones. Although originally characterized by scattered settlements, some
upland communities became larger than lowland ones. The woodlanders
were poor as well as numerous. In leaving open-field villages they put
behind them the threats of enclosure, rising rents and engrossing. But
their escape from poverty was temporary, because their new settlements
soon filled up with poor. Warwickshire and Northamptonshire forest and
pastoral regions had significantly higher numbers exempt from the
Hearth Tax because of poverty than mixed-farming areas.[36] The poor
were thick on the ground in these sorts of places long before the Resto-
ration. In east Somerset concern was expressed about unemployment
and food supplies for the poor as early as the 1580s; the wood/pasture
region of Norfolk was reported in 1631 to contain 'many poor, and none
of them all ordinarily having any corn but from the market'.[37]

These places were poor because of their economies. The dominant
agricultural pursuit was grazing, which was expanded in the period by
assarts and disparking. As a result, husbandry was dangerously tipped
towards pasture, and the inhabitants came to rely on outside corn
supplies. The growing population, together with partible inheritance
customs, produced land shortage. Then these regions turned to industries to make their living, classically the cloth industry, although a
multitude of others also developed.[38]

The combination of pastoralism and industry was dangerous. It meant
that forest communities were caught between the Scylla of famine and the

Charybdis of trade slumps. When harvests failed, their corn supplies dried up; when trade faltered, they were out of work. Since trade often collapsed because of a bad harvest – owing to greater elasticity of demand for industrial goods – these communities were terribly vulnerable. In 1586 the clothworkers of east Somerset were 'not set on work, whereby in this time of dearth of corn and victual they lack their common and necessary food'; similar conditions produced a 'tumultuous assembly of poor' there in 1622.[39] Thus the extraordinary growth of forest and pastoral communities combined with economic fragility to produce poverty and, ultimately, vagrancy.

Of course not all vagrants came from pastoral and forest areas. Many sprang from towns located in, or on the edges, of such places: in Somerset 58 of the 88 urban vagrants came from such centres (including Bath, Dulverton, Frome Selwood, Minehead, Taunton and Wells); in Yorkshire the vast majority of urban vagrants originated in places neighbouring on the uplands (37 of 46 cases). But there were also little clusters of lowland vagrants. Chester and the Bolton area of Lancashire drew them from lowland Lancashire, especially the coastal Fylde. In Bolton in 1637 more transients came from west of a line from Salford to Lancaster, which is largely lowland, than from the uplands to the east. Another clutch of lowlanders came from the northern rim of Norfolk – from Wells, Cromer, Holt and North Walsham – but why these places produced numerous vagrants remains to be discovered.[40]

At the end of the day, however, the vagrant poor were pre-eminently urban in origin. Although the proportion varied – in Cheshire, 1571–1600, and Norwich, 1630–5, as low as a third; in Reading, 1623–41, two-thirds; and in London, about nine-tenths throughout the period – the overall mean average was three-fifths (see Appendix, Table II).[41] Urbanization in part accounts for this high figure, for the urban population quadrupled from 1500 to 1700 while the country's as a whole only doubled, so that by 1700 nearly 1 in 5 persons lived in urban centres.[42] Yet the share of vagrants coming from towns was more than twice the proportion of town-dwellers in the global population, which suggests that persons of urban background were especially prone to vagabondage.[43]

The reason is that, as in woodland cum pasture regions, the growth of towns often outstripped their ability to provide for migrants, and the upshot was vagrancy. Not all centres measured up to the general fourfold rise in urban population, of which London alone accounted for about half, but many expanded, especially after 1570. Some grew by births outrunning deaths, but immigration was necessary for the growth of most towns. London, for example, must have been attracting an average of over 7000 migrants each year from 1605 to 1660, and this figure takes no account of persons who came and left again, which might raise the total

by 50 per cent. Roughly 400 migrants a year fuelled the growth of Norwich in the late seventeenth century.[44] But such influxes posed a social challenge to towns, even quite small ones. A connection between poverty and towns is evident from an analysis of the Warwickshire Hearth Tax: in 1670, places with over 200 households had on average 16 per cent more paupers than villages with under 20 households; those that grew more than 100 per cent from 1563 to 1670, which were invariably towns, had 10 to 15 per cent more poor than places that increased by less than 50 per cent. It was especially the towns experiencing expansion in manufacturing in north Warwickshire which attracted poor migrants.[45] It is sometimes possible to pinpoint migrants among the urban poor. In Norwich in 1570 1 in 8 had come to the city in the previous decade, while in Warwick in 1587 the proportion was 1 in 10. As in woodland areas, food supplies were a major challenge to the authorities. When enclosures uprooted the poor in the countryside, Cooke observed, they were 'driven into market-towns and corporations, which are so populous, that every unseasonable year for corn threatens a present dearth'.[46] Unemployment, health care and housing presented further problems. Dispossessed and rootless, many of the migrant poor ended up living from casual labour, doles and crime.

'LONDON CANNOT RELIEVE ENGLAND'

Why urban centres failed to assimilate migrants, so that they became vagrants, can be explained for the case of London. The capital was admittedly exceptional in size and rate of growth, but no town will be entirely typical. In fact, provincial towns experienced similar problems to the capital's, however different in scale, as is demonstrated in the next section.

London's growth in this period was dramatic. The overall metropolitan population was about 120,000 in 1550, and rose to 200,000 in 1600, and no less than 375,000 in 1650.[47] This rapid expansion caused serious social problems, which grew even more quickly than the population. There was a threefold increase in City householders needing poor relief, c.1550 –c.1600, although its population had risen by just a quarter. (The City grew much less rapidly than its suburbs.) Vagrancy arrests increased still faster, rising twelvefold from 1560 to 1625, a period in which the metropolitan population only quadrupled.[48] Observers were struck by this growing destitution amidst the splendour of the Elizabethan capital. They sought explanations for the phenomenon, and more than one blamed in-migration by the poor and masterless. A Christ's hospital official listed among those descending upon London in Elizabeth I's reign:

all soldiers wanting wars to employ them, all wounded soldiers . . .
servingmen whose lords and masters are dead . . . masterless men
whose masters have cast them off . . . idle people, as lusty rogues and
common beggars.

The idle came, he said, 'hearing of the great liberality of London'.
Similarly, John Stow noted in 1598 how London relieved its paupers, but
'also the poor that from each quarter of the realm do flock unto it'.[49]

These statements contain some, but not the whole, truth. It was shown
above that the capital attracted vagrants from all points of the compass.
But a striking development of the period was that more and more of them
originated in the metropolitan area itself, defined here as the City, its
suburbs and Middlesex. Until 1580 those born or last resident in this
catchment area formed 20 to 30 per cent of the total, and those from the
Southeast as a whole about 40 per cent. After 1600, however, the
proportions rose to 50 per cent from the first area and 60 per cent from
the second, which were increases of 100 and 50 per cent respectively.
From the standpoint of distance, those originating within 10 miles
of London Bridge more than doubled, so that by 1600 about half of
the total were in this category.[50] Of course, although the majority of
vagrants reported birthplaces or residences in the metropolis, many were
probably migrants. Thirty per cent claimed to be born in London,
but an overall total of 52 per cent said they came from there, and
the difference must be explained by in-migration. In addition, the rising
numbers of vagrants of local origin might be caused by London's growing
share of the country's population, which roughly doubled in the Elizabethan period.[51] But juggling these figures still fails to explain why a
majority of vagrants came from London itself by the early seventeenth
century. This development suggests that, whether they were born there
or not, living in London was the critical element in the problem and that,
contrary to contemporaries' statements, vagrants did not actually arrive
in the metropolis as vagrants, but became down and out because of
conditions there.

Of course, not all the migrant poor drifted into vagrancy in the capital.
Kinship links provided stability for some: nearly two-fifths of female
migrants had relatives in London; over a fifth actually lived with their kin.
Ethnic connections drew together Huguenot, Irish and Jewish newcomers in the seventeenth century, and people from the same shires and
towns formed clubs from the 1630s to dine and drink together.[52] Apprenticeship and service gave a stable home environment for many, as well as
some practical training, while the gilds provided fellowship and economic protection to the freeman during his working life and some security
in old age. Civic and parish office-holding, which it is argued was

widespread, bolstered feelings of solidarity and ensured that City parishes were well organized in social matters, including poor relief. These are also signs of an incipient youth culture, which drew groups of apprentices together for religious and social occasions. This development might have been expected, given the high levels of immigration, made up in all likelihood mainly by the young. Finally, the highly developed civic pageantry probably helped to create a sense of belonging.[53]

It is questionable, however, whether these institutions were able to cope with the flood of migrants. Kinship and ethnic links only involved minorities, and we have seen that service and apprenticeship were temporary, fragile relationships. The freedom and office-holding were widespread, and poor relief well administered in the intramural City parishes, but the same was not true outside the walls. Whether royal entrances and Lord Mayors' shows had much impact in these lawless parts seems doubtful. Youth culture, as will shortly be demonstrated, was a double-edged sword, which might cause instability as well as solidarity. To contain the rising tide of social problems, new institutions were developed. From the 1550s Bridewell hospital was used to punish vagrants and other offenders, and from the 1590s provost-marshals were appointed with wide powers of arrest. It is impossible, once again, to determine the exact proportion of migrants who fell foul of the vagrancy laws, but the numbers being sent to Bridewell during the 1620s suggest it was substantial. The mean average was about 1500 a year, most of whom were probably migrants, which was a significant share of the average annual immigration of 7000.[54]

Migrants to London became vagrants because the city was unable to provide them with secure housing and employment. Newcomers crowded into extramural parishes and slum conditions resulted. These parishes were growing much faster than intramural ones, but not until about 1620 did they actually surpass them in total population: in 1640 the ratio was still only 3 to 2. Yet between 1574 and 1642 vagrants of extramural origin outnumbered intramural ones by a margin of 3 to 1, which confirms that parishes outside the walls were exceptionally burdened with social problems.[55] Mortality rates were exceptionally high there, too, even by London standards. Destitution generally was also extremely severe. From the 1570s the Court of Aldermen ordered wealthy parishes within the walls to assist poverty-stricken ones outside. Even Westminster experienced these problems. The records of St Margaret's parish and the Court of Burgesses show people living, having children, and dying in the streets there, literally on the doorsteps of the Court and Parliament.[56]

Furthermore, extramural parishes were plagued with poor housing. Landlords divided houses for multiple occupation, crammed people into

cellars and threw up hovels in alleys. The space left by the dissolution of the monasteries was largely filled by 1570; in 1580 the housing problem reached crisis proportions and the government intervened. But it was too late, and soon the outskirts of London were notorious for crime and poverty. A decade later Southwark was described as providing 'nurseries and seminary places of the begging poor that swarm within the City', and the Privy Council wrote to Middlesex JPs in 1598 about 'base people and . . . lewd persons that do keep evil rule, and harbour thieves, rogues and vagabonds' in Shoreditch, St Giles without Cripplegate, and Clerkenwell. In the same year Stow described slums springing up in Southwark and the eastern fringes.[57]

Housing unquestionably improved in some parts of seventeenthcentury London, but whether social conditions in these extramural parts saw much amelioration is questionable. In 1608 Dekker wrote of 'the infection of the suburbs'. They were 'caves where monsters are bred up to devour the cities themselves', where all kinds of criminal were found:

> Would the Devil hire a villain to spill blood? There he shall find him. One to blaspheme? There he hath choice. A pander that would court a matron at her prayers? He's there. A cheater that would turn his own father a beggar? He's there, too. A harlot that would murder her new-born infant? She lies in, there.

John Graunt noted in 1662 that in the large out-parishes 'many of the poorer parishioners through neglect do perish, and many vicious persons get liberty to live as they please, for want of some heedful eye to overlook them'. Children went in gangs there, throwing stones at windows and coaches, and whipping horses so that their riders were thrown. According to Dr George's findings, many of these places were still centres of poverty and crime two centuries later.[58]

The outskirts were important in the lives of migrants and vagrants. Because officialdom was weak, they might gain footholds in alehouses and lodging-houses. Table I (in the Appendix) shows that long-distance migrants were conspicuous among vagrants arrested in Elizabethan Westminster, where only about 1 in 20 was from the London area and 2 in 10 from the Southeast. In intramural parishes the comparable figures were 1 in 3 and 4 in 10.[59] From the periphery they crept into the centre to seek work, to beg and pilfer. There was something like a state of war between the City authorities and the suburban vagrant. The latter came into the centre where a bevy of officials caught him, sent him to Bridewell hospital for chastisement, and then back outside the walls. Lacking any tight controls over these areas, however, they could not solve the problem, for what was to prevent the vagabond from returning again and again? Governments surveyed suburban housing in order to halt sub-

dividing and jerry-building; Southwark hired a man to harass lodgers under James I; and in 1637 an official survey was made of houses in which the poor were housed.[60] But whether these measures dampened in-migration is most doubtful.

It is hard, at a distance of centuries, to imagine the effects of large-scale vagrancy upon everyday life. Contemporary observers were appalled, and the Bridewell Court Books suggest that their reaction was justified. These records show that boys and apprentices filled the streets, mobbing passers-by, begging, selling ballads, brooms and pamphlets, and shining shoes. They show them stealing from shops and stalls, purses and pockets, even lead from roofs. By the end of Elizabeth's reign London was experiencing large-scale juvenile delinquency, and officials feared these vagrant youths as potential rioters.[61]

The reason for the plethora of idle youngsters was that the metropolitan economy was incapable of providing them all with regular work. As well as living in slum conditions, the migrant was likely to be underemployed, when not unemployed. Ironically, London's economy was expanding during the period. Its rise to a monopoly position in English cloth exports, its growth as a centre for conspicuous consumption, and its booming agricultural trade must have generated considerable demand for labour. In the manufacturing sector there was expansion in leather goods, brewing, soap-making, ship-building and the docks, silk-throwing and framework knitting, and a proliferation of many new trades.[62] But the common preoccupation with growth involves a danger of ignoring the scale and mode of production. For example, the numbers employed in privately-owned ship-building might have 'multiplied several times over' from 1540 to 1640, but the operations of London ship-builders remained small, none employing over 100 men in peacetime. The docks, too, continued to be small-scale operations up to 1660.[63] Units of production usually involved no more than a master and a few apprentices and journeymen, as in the traditional gild system. Living-in apprentices and servants were the mainstay of the labour force, accounting for half the work-force listed in parish burial registers before 1600.[64]

But employment was erratic in this system. Relations between masters and workers were particularly fragile. When plague struck or trade collapsed, masters discharged servants and apprentices. The latter were a volatile group, many quitting before their terms were up, and the majority leaving the capital when theirs finished. Servants and apprentices were indeed most prone to vagrancy of all London's socio-economic groups, accounting for almost three-quarters of the Londoners whose occupations were listed in Bridewell records from 1597 to 1608, thus surpassing even their substantial share of the labour force.[65] After 1600 living-in labour, as we have noticed, declined and was replaced by casual

hirings, particularly outside the walls, which were even more erratic. Cloth was still the most important trade, and when exports slumped thousands were thrown out of work. The constraints on production were arguably exacerbated by the capital's peculiar demographic features. High mortality rates meant even shorter working lives than elsewhere, and high in-migration flooded the labour market with young and inexperienced workers.[66]

It is also probable that the supply of migrant labour surpassed the demand. Some vagrants indeed reported visiting London and finding no situations. Richard Rose of Whiteparish in Wiltshire failed to find work in 1631 and was caught 'rambling up and down the city' and incarcerated in Bridewell.[67] London's vagrancy problem was so massive, especially on the outskirts, that it spilled over into the rest of the country. In Essex between 1564 and 1644 a sixth to a fourth of the vagabonds arrested had come from the metropolis, while in Reading from 1623 to 1641 the proportion was over a quarter. When it is possible to discover their parishes of origin, they came overwhelmingly from the peripheral ones: 29 of 31 in Reading, and 26 of 32 in Salisbury.[68]

Why, if conditions were so dreadful in London, did migrants continue to congregate there? One reason was that wages were significantly higher – perhaps a half to two-thirds greater than elsewhere in southern England – and in a period of declining real wages that must have been a consider-able spur.[69] Another reason was that nationally the harsh demographic and economic conditions that caused long-distance migration continued to apply up to the mid-seventeenth century. Finally, provincial officials despatched their poor to the capital to get rid of them. York officials ordered two boys, probably orphans, to be sent to London in 1577; and, in 1581, another to be 'sent to London by a carrier' unless he found work locally. A poor law of 1597 actually empowered parish officers to levy rates to 'apprentice' children in this way, and the law was enforced. The Somerset parish of Edington directed two children of a vagrant widow to be 'placed' in London in James I's reign, and Westmorland regularly sent children to Leeds, Halifax and London in the 1630s.[70]

The dangers of migration to London were great for unsuspecting country youths. Their home parishes appear to have made minimal arrangements for placing them with an employer, so that payments to the children were really just bribes to take them away. Once in the carrier's cart, the problems began. A Shropshire carrier was hauled into Bridewell in 1575 for fathering a child on a migrant girl *en route* to London; other youths were simply dumped in the streets and at alehouses. In 1579 the Court of Common Council ordered that carriers abandoning youngsters should be imprisoned and then forced to take them home. A Christ's hospital official proposed in 1587 that the City stop carriers bringing

children under the age of 18 to the capital 'unless [they] be well provided for, [so] that they be not left to loiter up and down the city for want of masters, as a number do at this day'. But abandoned children still turned up. A Buckinghamshire girl was nearly starved to death after being brought up and left by a carrier in 1601.[71] Officials might send for the miscreants and make them take youngsters away, but with hundreds of carts entering London it is obvious that inspecting every passenger, not to mention children who came alone, on foot or on horseback, was a sisyphean task.

Some migrants to London never left again because they died there. The metropolis was a dirty and unhealthy place, even for those with positions; for those out of work and homeless, it was positively lethal. London's burial records abound with references to vagrants dying in the streets and near-by fields. The parish of St Botolph's without Aldgate, for example, listed the following burials from 1593 to 1598:

> Edward Ellis a vagrant who died in the street.
> A young man not known who died in a hay-loft.
> A cripple that died in the street before John Awsten's door.
> A poor woman, being vagrant, whose name was not known, she died in the street under the seat before Mr. Christian Shipman's house called the Crown . . . in the High Street.
> A maid, a vagrant, unknown, who died in the street near the Postern [Gate].
> Margaret, a deaf woman, who died in the street.
> A young man in a white canvas doublet . . . being vagrant and died in the street near Sparrow's corner being in the precinct near the Tower.
> A young man vagrant having no abiding place . . . who died in the street before the door of Joseph Hayes, a brazier dwelling at the sign of Robin Hood in the High Street . . . . He was about 18 years old. I could not learn his name.

These entries admittedly come from famine years, but even in good times one could find dead vagrants on one's doorstep in Elizabethan London. Nor was the problem confined to extramural parishes; the corpses even turned up in main thoroughfares like Leadenhall.[72]

Despite the capital's perils, the poor still thronged to it. In Leicester between 1584 and 1640 and in Somerset from 1607 to 1636 the most common destination mentioned by vagrants was London.[73] In spite of the risks, London might still have been a better bet than staying at home in upland regions and many towns. But in addition, London's glamour was an established myth. 'I hope to see London once ere I die', sighed Davy, Justice Shallow's servant, in 1597. The same year an itinerant procuress told a Sittingbourne woman to take her best clothes, leave her husband

and move to London, because 'here in the country it was very hard and miserable living, but a woman having good apparel might live with great pleasure in London'. Similarly, a Dorchester lad took off on a spree in 1631 after someone told him 'he might live very well' in the capital. In the mid-Elizabethan years it was accepted that 'London draws unto it great concourse of people of all sorts'. But many were poor, and so the writer appended the *caveat* that 'London cannot relieve England'.[74]

PROVINCIAL TOWNS

London was different from other towns because of its exceptional growth, but its vagrancy problem was not unparalleled. The differences were in degree rather than in kind. Elizabethan Warwick's population of 2500 was a small fraction of the capital's, but it grew by nearly half between 1544 and 1586, which strained the town's economy, forcing officials to intervene to deal with poverty. Moreover, the main judicial business in Warwick was vagrancy.[75] This town's experience was repeated in others up and down the country. The severity of urban poverty was still obvious in Hertfordshire in 1635, when officials reported that 'in the country villages the poor people and their children are provided for. But in the market towns, masters are wanting, all men of ability having apprentices already settled with them'.[76]

The forms that destitution took in provincial towns were similar to London's. Like the capital, they had poor migrants packed into suburban slums that bred vagrancy and other crimes. In Warwick it was the West Street ward that had most poor in 1582. Exeter's poorest suburbs had significantly higher mortality rates than the rest of the city when epidemics struck: St Sidwell's on the north end attracted the migrant poor and produced vagrants to exceptional degrees. Similarly, in Dorchester, Salisbury and Shrewsbury the poor huddled at the town's end.[77] No wonder, then, that so many London vagabonds had originated in other towns.

CONCLUSIONS

Although generalizations about the migrant poor as a group are out of the question, the hazards they met after pulling up stakes were evidently considerable. If diseases did not kill them, then unemployment and crime might well cut them adrift in the unsteady conditions of Elizabethan and early Stuart times. Whatever towns offered to the imaginations of the poor, their promise was often illusory, and the same was true of forest and pastoral villages. Even those who emigrated to the Americas in the seventeenth century found that conditions there were no Garden of Eden, as a later chapter will show.

Of course, those who stayed at home were probably no better off than their footloose cousins. They faced deteriorating living conditions in the early seventeenth century and were themselves cast upon the highways in rising numbers as a result of dislocation caused by famines, wars and economic crises after 1590. Fundamentally, there was no way out for the English poor. If the alternative was starvation or, ultimately, a life on poor relief, it is perhaps not surprising that many chose migration and some chose crime. They did not have the historian's advantage of hindsight and could not know that the odds were against them in this terrible lottery.

The fate of the migrant poor was not, however, only a matter of concern to themselves and to historians of a later age. England's ruling élites, as was shown in the first chapter, were terrified of vagrants, linking them with a vast range of evils which they thought posed a grave threat to the *status quo*. The chapters that follow attempt to capture the meaning of that threat, based not on the rhetoric of their enemies, as has usually been done, but through an analysis of the lives of vagabonds themselves – their family structures, their peregrinations and haunts, their occupations, and finally their crimes. In this way we will achieve a better understanding of the danger to established society presented by vagabonds; and, in the final chapter, of the often ferocious policies directed against them.

Part Two
The structure of vagrancy

Chapter 4

A promiscuous generation

Vagrants were a menace to the social order because they broke with the accepted norms of family life. If the ideal was the patriarchal household, they had no part in it, and for that reason they were considered pariahs. In John Downame's opinion in 1616 they were 'a promiscuous generation, who are all of kin, and yet know no kindred, no house or home, no law but their sensual lust'. Another observer reported in 1653 that they were 'married under hedges, [their] children born in barns and under hedges [and] there baptized', and a year later Richard Younge claimed they 'have not particular wives, neither do they range themselves into families, but consort together as beasts'.[1] There was some truth to these strictures, although from the 1620s English, Irish and gypsy vagrants were increasingly arrested in families. Vagabonds also formed a variety of liaisons *en route*, but these were often impermanent and illegal.

FRAGMENTED FAMILIES

If the normal household of the period contained a married couple, children and servants, then vagrants were a radical departure from it.[2] Ignoring local variations, couples and their children made up only a third of the vagrant population. The remainder were men and women who were single, at least while they were on the road, and children and adolescents without parents (Appendix, Table III). Of course, that does not mean that two-thirds of vagrants had no living kin. Children and spouses were not examined by justices in some cases,[3] even though they accompanied vagabonds who were; some had abandoned their families; and others travelled with siblings. Nevertheless, complete families were far less evident on the road than in settled communities. The main reason is undoubtedly poverty. If a person had some landed property, as in traditional peasant societies, it was possible to marry, have a family and keep it together. But for those who had none, which we know was the

condition of many Englishmen in the period, the chances of settling down were limited.

Family structure among vagrants is a story of fragments, of individuals cut adrift from kin and masters. The majority were single males, who were especially numerous in the greater cities, as Table III shows. In London between 1516 and 1642 the proportion was 70 per cent; in Norwich from 1564 to 1635 it was 55 per cent; and in Chester, Essex, Leicester, and Wiltshire between 1564 and 1644, over 50 per cent. The predominance of single males is in part caused by their being the most common migrants. In particular, their great numbers in large urban centres is explained by high levels of in-migration by male servants and apprentices. Resident paupers, conversely, showed a decided imbalance in favour of females, which was probably because they lived longer than men, but also again because of greater male migration.[4] Finally, males may have been arrested more than females because the authorities considered them greater threats, and because women itinerants were charged with prostitution rather than vagrancy. Whatever the cause, family fragmentation was a national problem by 1610, when a vagrancy statute stipulated that persons who deserted their families were to be punished as incorrigible rogues and felons.[5]

The disintegration of families took many forms, but a classic one was desertion by the male partner. One in every 12 female adult beggars in Warwick in 1587 had been abandoned (7 of 84 cases), and considering that some women took to the roads to search for men, that figure is probably on the low side.[6] Men departed for many reasons – poverty and debt, family disputes, impressment and adultery. Once made, the break could be lasting. A Yorkshire vagrant told Somerset officials in 1624 that he had not set eyes on his wife and six children for eight or nine years. Even a brief absence could plunge families into desperate poverty. After John Sheppard left his wife and six small children in Bedfordshire in about 1633 they sank into penury, the woman finally dying. Some 'single males' were clearly nothing of the sort.[7]

Vagrant women were basically of three sorts: those looking for husbands who had deserted them, prostitutes, and unmarried pregnant girls. Some spent months tracking down husbands, relying upon rumours and chance meetings, while risking punishment as vagabonds. Alice Knight of Romsey went to Southampton in 1577 to search for her husband, an errant shipwright, but he was not there and she was locked in a cage for vagrancy. A Lincolnshire woman seized in Warwick in 1582 had tracked her husband all over the Midlands until she cornered him in a fair in the town, but he escaped after promising to meet her in an alehouse, purloining her cloak into the bargain! There are few instances, by contrast, of women leaving their menfolk and children.[8]

Prostitutes were not always cut adrift from families. Some were pushed into the life by penurious parents – for example, Agnes Harcote, aged 14, who was sold 'with the consent of her own mother' at 6d a time in London in 1560. In country areas some married women committed adultery for a few pennies. But in the larger cities prostitution usually involved professionals cut off from family life, living in bawdy-houses where clients visited them. The most notorious concentration in London was on the Bankside, but there were houses all over the metropolis and plenty of women who plied the trade outdoors. A Southwark boy hauled into Bridewell in 1578 had allegedly committed fornication in the open street with a harlot named Kate, while in 1627 Margery Dubber was seized 'in the night putting her hand into a man's codpiece'. One did not have to go very far to find a prostitute in Elizabethan London, and they were regularly sent to Bridewell as 'nightwalkers'.[9]

The pregnant girl without means or a husband must have been a common sight in Tudor and early Stuart times. Illegitimate births are thought to have peaked in the late sixteenth and early seventeenth centuries. The rise was caused by poverty, which made marriages impossible, the failings of the marriage laws, discussed later, and strict regulation by parishes.[10] The chance of pregnancy outside marriage was always great, because birth-control devices were primitive if not non-existent. With marriage delayed normally until the mid or late twenties, people had to find outlets for their sexual drives outside the marriage bed. Men had intercourse with prostitutes, but also with ordinary single women. The result was unwanted pregnancies and social problems that included vagrancy.

Some unmarried girls took to the roads by choice to hide a pregnancy; others because they were 'encouraged' by parents; and still others because they were expelled by masters or the parish. Thus the girl and her parents might avoid the stigma of bastardy and dump the baby far away, and her home parish and the father could shed the responsibility for supporting her and the child.[11] Elizabethan and early Stuart parishes engaged in long, expensive and cruel disputes in which mother and baby were shunted back and forth. The result was a great traffic of girls, their infants and the fugitive fathers. Somerset girls went as far as Wales to have their bastards,[12] and to London they came from all parts of the country. That was because of the anonymity of the metropolis, where they might live in obscurity during the pregnancy and then leave the child after it was born.[13] As Table III shows, there was a rise in female vagrants from under a fifth, 1560–1, to almost two-fifths, 1624–5, in Bridewell, and extramural parishes were especially pestered. Over a third of Elizabethan Westminster's vagrants were women, whereas in the provinces the proportion was rarely more than a fifth. In St Saviour's, Southwark,

single women made up over half the lodgers noted in 1619 and 1622, and two-thirds of them had children with them or were pregnant. They gathered in these suburbs because officialdom was comparatively weak there, but also for the opportunities for prostitution near the Court and on the Bankside. The problem of prostitutes and their bastards assumed major proportions in 1615, when City officials issued an order 'for the finding out of Queans that leave their children in the streets . . . whereof some by reason of the cold and lack of sustenance have died'.[14]

After being turned out, pregnant women had their children in odd places. In Westminster they were reported 'travailing of child in the street'. Elizabeth Holland, a Somerset girl, bore her stepfather's child on a church porch in Wales in 1618; and Clare Crowe, a widow consorting with a tinker in 1634, gave birth on the road at the town's end of Luton.[15] Once a child was born, the single mother's problems mounted, assuming that she herself survived. The high infant mortality rates, together with infanticide and abandonment, probably carried away many babies. But women still turned up carrying them on their backs and suckling them in the streets and highways. When economic conditions deteriorated under the early Stuarts, more and more transient women appeared with children. Katherine Constable and Mary Washington, punished in Kent in 1636, had eleven children with them and not a husband in sight. Single women with infants were frequently so hard-pressed that they had to abandon them. One had the audacity to deposit hers on the Lord Mayor's doorstep in 1603.[16] But women usually bore the brunt of bastardy charges, and vagrancy was one result of the problem.

The dissolution of families was also hard on the young, and there is little doubt that vagrancy was mainly a young person's crime. This was in part because the young formed a huge share of the population, 40 to 50 per cent of whom were under the age of 21.[17] But vagrancy was also caused by bastardy and abandonment, high mortality (which meant many orphans), and conflicts between parents and children, and masters and servants. Evidence of vagrants' ages is sparse, but it suggests that youth predominated. A list of those incarcerated in Bridewell in 1602 showed 97 per cent under age 21 and 54 per cent below 16; in Norwich between 1595 and 1609 the comparable figures were 72 per cent and 52 per cent respectively. In Crompton near Oldham, an upland parish where mining had attracted migrants from south Lancashire and Yorkshire in 1597, 75 per cent of the 'goers abroad' were under age 21 and 50 per cent under 16. Vagabonds in smaller towns and rural parishes were generally older, with only about half under 21 and a third under 16 (Appendix, Table IV). Age-distributions no doubt varied, so that high immigration to London, Norwich and Crompton resulted in youthful populations. It is impossible to state categorically how vagrants' ages changed in the period

because of the patchiness of the data. Averaging the evidence indicates that the proportion below age 16 declined from 43 to 29 per cent, and below age 21 from 67 to 47 per cent in the years 1623–39 as compared to 1570–1622. The greatest rises were between ages 21 and 60, apart from Colchester, where over sixties were especially diligently noted. These figures must be hedged with reservations, because the documentation for the later period is mainly from rural areas, where the age-structure was probably biased towards the elderly. The exception is London in 1630–1, where Bridewell officials noted children consistently; these, assuming they were all under age 16, formed 42 per cent of the total compared with 54 per cent in 1602.[18] Certainly a rise in vagrants' average ages after 1620 is to be expected, considering the harsh economic conditions of the 1620s and 1630s which uprooted whole families, as has been shown; but it would be wrong to press this evidence very hard.

Fortunately, we need not rely solely upon statistics. Literary evidence confirms that youth was a group with special problems. Richard Morison complained in 1536 about the 'young and lusty, [who] neither have, nor yet will learn any honest occupation . . . but continuing in idleness, fall to stealing, robbing, murder, and many other mischiefs'. Another observer wrote what amounts to an analysis of juvenile delinquency in Elizabeth I's reign. He argued that a chief cause of vagabondage was 'the bringing up of youths without virtuous exercises'. Until age 12 or 13 they were allowed to play in the streets, 'which breeds in young age great idleness, a disease hard to be cured'. For the next five years they were given odd jobs, gathering firewood and acorns, gleaning wheat and turning spits at church-ales. By the time they entered service in their late 'teens they were 'idle, slothful, and unkempt', so that they were in and out of service. Then from age 21 'fall they to whoredom and set up with a bag and a wallet . . . or else forthwith go to plain thievery'.[19]

The youth problem was probably at its worst in London, but it was not confined to the capital. From the northern borders in 1541 it was reported that the young were forced through lack of work to thieve in Scotland and England; in Elizabethan Exeter John Hooker found 'troops and clusters of children, boys and elder persons [who] lie loitering and floistering in every corner of the city'.[20] The continued rise in population caused social problems requiring official intervention. Three Norfolk hundreds reported in 1638 'many young people which live out of service by reason of the multitude of them'. It was not unheard of to meet children wandering alone. Edward German, aged about 10 and discovered roaming in Leicestershire in the winter of 1586, was 'almost devoured with lice'. Two boys aged 5 and 6, who turned up scavenging in Stafford in 1614, said they had come from school in Shrewsbury over 30 miles distant.[21]

Efforts to train and employ the poor not surprisingly focused on the

young. The theory was that if they had a 'virtuous bringing-up' and practical training, they would secure positions and avoid vagrancy. From Juan-Luis Vives's Bruges scheme of 1526 to Samuel Hartlib's London one of 1646, the employment of children was widely discussed, and governments took action on the problem. London's Christ's hospital was established to care for them. One of the aims of the vagrancy Act of 1576 providing for houses of correction was the employment of youth, and bridewells in London and elsewhere were supposed to put young offenders to work. The theory made sense because otherwise, as commentators realized, they would 'stuff prisons and garnish gallows trees'. But work-creation schemes mostly failed and the authorities had to resort to more drastic measures, which included sending youngsters away to cities, as seen in the previous chapter, but also to the New World and to fight in the Thirty Years War.[22]

The youth of vagrants was not simply the result of their great numbers causing unemployment. It also shows that groups who today would be expected to be among the most protected were in fact at risk. Children became vagrants because of parental neglect, especially if they were illegitimate. A girl found lying in the streets of Elizabethan Westminster turned out to be the bastard daughter of a local man. In 1600 Norwich officials had to write to a putative father 'to keep his bastard at the town of Cringleford and not suffer him to run roguing about'.[23] Vagabonds also included orphans who were born to the itinerant life, while others had had settled homes but their parents had died, many probably in epidemics. Still others begged and wandered because they were unrelieved by local officials, and after rows with their masters.[24] Conflicts with parents also landed the young in trouble. London parents sent their rebellious offspring to Bridewell to be disciplined. William Knightly was brought in as a rogue in 1575 because he 'will not tarry with his mother and father'. Similarly, Agnes Chalkley was arrested in 1603 and punished for abusing her mother.[25] Neither nuclear families nor patriarchal households were sufficiently stable to keep the young off the streets and highways of early modern England.

Most vagabonds were single persons, but the proportion of females and families rose from the late sixteenth century in most places (Appendix, Table III). Only in Cheshire were there changes in the opposite direction, and even there the proportion of children rose, while Norwich experienced fluctuations that are difficult to explain. Nevertheless, both Norwich and London, which traditionally attracted large numbers of single males, witnessed a levelling off in the proportion of males and increases in females by about a tenth after 1600. The rises in females and families are explained by the economic and political crises in early seventeenth-century England. These events, as has been shown earlier,

caused a dramatic increase in the transient population and the doubling of the proportion of families in their ranks in just two decades. Since vagrants formed part of this rootless host, it is not surprising that families increased in their ranks as well.

The question of large gangs

Their enemies were correct in thinking that vagrants had alternatives to settled family life, but the image of them often wandering the countryside in troops of forty to fifty is mistaken. Elizabethans did not usually underestimate the proportions of the vagrancy problem, but they were aware that large contingents were rare, with the partial exceptions of gypsies and the Irish. English rogues, Hext wrote, travelled two or three to a bunch. Gypsies, although they sometimes belonged to groups numbering dozens of members, broke up into clusters of four to six, Dekker noted.[26] Vagrants occasionally gathered in force at fairs and markets and in isolated outbuildings, but on the road they seldom travelled in groups of more than three: up to 1620 the great majority (between 51 and 88 per cent depending on time and place) were arrested in ones and twos. Admittedly examinations sometimes ignore dependants, thus exaggerating the smallness of groups, but when dependants were regularly noted in Wiltshire constables' presentments and Essex house of correction calendars, the majority were still in ones and twos (Appendix, Table V). A gathering of more than five vagabonds was a rarity. It might be argued that a lone constable was unlikely to tackle the large gangs, so that few were recorded, but this is not convincing, because some big troops were apprehended. Thirteen gypsies were seized in Great Chesterford in Essex in 1566, and groups of thirteen and seventeen vagrants were arrested in Wiltshire in Charles I's reign.[27] Large companies existed; there were just not very many of them.

Vagrant bands did increase in size in the first half of the seventeenth century, especially after 1620. In Essex groups of three or more rose from 12 to 39 per cent of the total; in Leicester the increase was from 16 to 33 per cent; and in Wiltshire it was from about 28 to 50 per cent (Appendix, Table V). The mean average size of vagrant groups remained small in the 1620s and 1630s, a matter of three or four persons, but it was rising. The explanation is not that many troops of a dozen or more were appearing, but that those numbering three to seven members were on the upswing. Even small clutches of vagrants worried officials, because they were a departure from the norm among such offenders. A comparison of vagrants and other offenders in the Chelmsford house of correction from

1597 to 1644 suggests why vagrants were considered dangerous. Among the others, who included runaway servants, mothers of bastards, adulterers and scolds, only 3 to 4 per cent were in groups of three or more, and between 1597 and 1620 almost 85 per cent were alone. That figure then fell between 1621 and 1644, but still stuck at 66 per cent. By contrast, solo vagrants made up only 53 per cent and 33 per cent in the same periods (Appendix, Table V). That vagrancy was more likely to involve two or more persons than many other crimes helps to explain official trepidation. It was one thing to arrest a solitary troublemaker; rather more daunting, one imagines, to seize a suspect with one or two companions.

Among the large troops of vagrants were some strange collections. One group arrested in Essex in 1590, which numbered six adults and over twenty youths, had journeyed from the bishopric of Durham, apparently collecting children whom they were licensed to place in service. A second such company turned up in Leicester in the 1620s, this time from Ireland. It included a couple and eleven children for whom they were to find apprenticeships and, similarly licensed, had visited Liverpool and London.[28] If genuine, these examples shed some interesting light on the unemployment problems of the upland areas, noted earlier, in the early seventeenth century. Another curious assembly resulted from a round-up of gypsies in Yorkshire in 1596 in which 196 men, women and children were seized, of whom 106 were tried and condemned to death at York sessions. Nine were actually executed but the remainder were spared. One of the troop was licensed to conduct them to their places of origin and was allowed seven months for the job, but they only got as far as Lancashire before the licence was confiscated. Although they were probably all gypsies, it appears that they were collected together by officials and did not normally travel as a group.[29]

Gypsies

Gypsies did, however, form a genuine alternative society, as many do today. They remain a shadowy group in the Elizabethan period, despite literary studies, which have mainly focused upon their dress, origins and crimes without investigating their family structures and relationships with society at large. Tudor governments passed a number of statutes specifically aimed at them. An Act of 1530 stipulated that they should forfeit their goods and be banished from the country within fifteen days, if they had been convicted of theft; the rest were to depart within sixteen days. The Act was enforced, for in 1543 twenty-four gypsies were issued with papers to quit the country. Another statute of 1554 contained similar provisions for banishment and felony charges for any who remained. Still another of 1562 continued the felony charge, but ordered that those born in the country were to be placed in service.[30]

Gypsies were distinct from English vagrants in travelling in large troops. Groups numbering 20, 40, 49, 80 and 140 were reported by Tudor magistrates. The Somerset justice Hext noted in 1596 that they numbered 30 to 40 per shire, although he said that because they 'went visibly in one company' they were less dangerous than English rogues. In *Lantern and Candlelight* Dekker also claimed that gypsies were 'commonly an army about four score strong'; in 1610 'Martin Markall' reported a group at Devil's Arse-A-Peak in Derbyshire that 'go always never under 100 men or women'; and two years later the author of *The Art of Juggling* said the same.[31] Court and parish records of the seventeenth century, however, suggest smaller groups. At quarter sessions they usually numbered five or six persons, and at one assize in 1577, nineteen were committed, although it is unclear whether they were arrested together.[32] But most court records probably underestimate the size of gypsy groups, because children under 14 were exempt from trial. A more accurate impression is gained from the accounts of parish officials who gave them doles, which show a mean average of 15.7 members in the seventeenth century.[33] The discrepancy between the large troops reported by some sources and the parish records has a number of explanations. Some authors clearly exaggerated the size of gypsy gangs for rhetorical purposes, and some groups were official creations like that in Yorkshire in 1596. Other reports like the one of 140 from Staffordshire in 1539 were pure rumour, while some others were probably temporary encampments and gatherings such as those supposed regularly to be held at Devil's Arse-A-Peak and near Blackheath. It is also possible that gypsy units became smaller in the period because of official harassment. The author of *The Art of Juggling* remarked that, because of the statutes passed against them, 'they divide their bands and companies, into diverse parts of the realm'.[34] But whatever the explanation, the conclusion is inescapable that gypsies travelled in much larger groups than other vagabonds.

Like English vagrants, they were supposed to have recognized leaders. 'Martin Markall' wrote that the first Romany leader in England was Captain Giles Hather, and that his concubine Kit Callot was Queen of the Gypsies. Jonson's *Masque of the Gypsies* of 1621 began with one leading a horse carrying five children, described as 'the five princes of Egypt'.[35] Some of the references to royalty may have been poking fun, but both officials and gypsies treated some of them as chiefs. 'Two leaders of the gypsies' were committed to Canterbury gaol in 1546, and George Portingale, who led a contingent of seventeen of them to Wigan in 1602, was called 'Captain of Egyptians'. Some seventeenth-century Romanies claimed to be kings and queens: Margaret Finch, a Kentish one who lived to age 109, was the first queen of the Lambeth encampment; a Warwickshire group was reported to have chosen a man named Hern as their king

in 1673; and in 1687 in Camberwell Robert Hern and Elizabeth Bozwell, 'king and queen of the gypsies', were married.[36]

There is good reason to accept these claims as genuine, for gypsies still recognize royalty. But the problem is to determine how one achieved the status and how far a monarch's authority extended. In the present century gypsy royalty is based upon wealth and lineage, with the latter the crucial element. Some families claim authority extending over the whole of the country.[37] But the significance of kings and queens in the sixteenth and seventeenth centuries is less obvious. Gypsies may have paid them obeisance at annual meetings and in regular encampments, but their groups of three or four nuclear families were little affected by royalty in their day-to-day existences on the road. When arrested, their leaders parleyed with officials or were made examples of, but royalty rarely entered into the matter.[38] The main consequence of recognizing their own royalty was to differentiate gypsies from English mores and government. Modern studies show that 'the title gypsy chief, even when bestowed by gypsies upon a gypsy, does not amount to much'. Sometimes the titles are used to boost fortune-telling businesses at the seaside; Scottish tinkers even used to hold funerals for dead kings and queens to drum up custom among non-travellers.[39]

The most pervasive relationships among gypsies were kinship-based. Those brought to trial had the same surnames in two-thirds of cases, and at least half were probably members of the same nuclear family, which was the basic unit of gypsy troops. Hence the common portrayal of a couple travelling with their children strapped on a horse. Gypsy groups of the seventeenth century usually included three or four nuclear families, thus providing a classic example of 'chain migration'. The etchings of Jacques Callot portray these large, peripatetic units on the continent in the 1630s.[40] Even when surnames were different, it is probable the groups of families were related in the manner of the *vitsa* of the American Rom, which include the families of siblings and possibly first cousins. Of course, some gypsy groups may also have been formed for self-protection or for economic purposes.[41]

Gypsies were also different from English vagrants in having a language of their own, Romany. A group apprehended in Normanby in 1650 'did sometime speak in languages which none who were [near]by could understand'. Romany was 'spun out of three other tongues, viz. Latin, English and Dutch', and was invented 'to the end their cozenings, knaveries, and villainies might not so easily be perceived', according to one Jacobean writer. Modern scholars have demonstrated that Romany is the product of many languages: the gypsy hegira from India through Europe can be charted linguistically from the vocabulary picked up along the way. But Romany was also the result of isolation from the culture of

the society in which they had come to rest. This segregation, together with gypsy links with vagrants and crime, is seen in borrowings between Romany and canting vocabulary.[42]

The usual gypsy employment was thought to be fortune-telling by palm-reading. The statute of 1530 stated that they pretended 'that they by palmistry could tell men and women's fortunes, and so many times by craft and subtlety have deceived the people of their money'. 'Martin Markall' wrote that when they came to country towns 'they pitifully cozen the poor country girls, both of money, silver and the best linen, only in hope to hear their good fortunes told'.[43] Officials arrested them for such offences. Thirteen 'women and children, all in one company, miserable poor people, and of the quality of runnagate gypsies' were gaoled in Norfolk in Charles I's reign for reading palms. Gypsies were also accused of introducing sleight-of-hand tricks to England. But besides these illicit lines of work they were horse-dealers, blacksmiths, tinkers and scrap-dealers. The index of the original series of the *Journal of the Gypsy Lore Society* lists 135 trades that they practised.[44]

Gypsies looked different from the rest of the population. The fifteenth-century *bourgeois* of Paris reported that children 'had their ears pierced and wore a silver ring in each ear, or two rings in each'. The men were 'very dark, with curly hair', and the women 'the ugliest you ever saw and the darkest, all with scarred faces and hair as black as a horse's tail', with 'no dresses but an old coarse piece of blanket tied on the shoulders with a bit of cloth or string'. Their apparel was 'odd and fantastic' and designed to attract crowds, Dekker stated. The men wore 'scarves of calico or any other base stuff, hanging their bodies like morris-dancers with bells and other toys'; the women, 'rags and patched filthy mantles uppermost' but with fancy undergarments.[45]

Although different in many respects from English vagrants, gypsies were seen and treated similarly. A separate body of legislation covered them, but it described them in terms usually reserved for vagabonds. In the 1530 statute they were portrayed as 'using no craft nor feat of merchandise' and going 'from shire to shire and place to place in great company and used great subtle and crafty means to deceive the people'. The 1554 Act stated that a gypsy would not be punished if he would 'leave that naughty, idle and ungodly life and company'. And a search order for London in 1569 included 'all vagabonds, sturdy beggars commonly called rogues, *or Egyptians*', while a Derbyshire order of 1629 lumped gypsies together with

> suspect persons, rogues, both sturdy beggars and begging vagrants, some whereof pretend to be petty chapmen, hucksters and higglers, and others tinkers, and others palmsters, fortune-tellers.[46]

Gypsies and English vagrants merged in the official view for four reasons. First, they both led itinerant and masterless lives. For instance, Portingale, who was arrested in Wigan in 1602, cropped up again in Wiltshire in 1608 and in Essex in 1611.[47] Secondly, some vagrants may have taken on the speech and apparel of gypsies. The statute of 1562 referred to persons who dressed up as gypsies and imitated their speech and manner. Some English tramps might have joined gypsy troops but it is doubtful that many did, considering the traditionally closed nature of their clans and the severe penalties involved.[48] A third reason for the merging of the two groups is that, although foreign immigrants in the previous century, by Elizabethan times most gypsies were born in England, a fact recognized when the Act of 1562 abolished banishment for the native-born. But if they were considered natives, then governments had to develop some means of dealing with them. In the event the answer, as with vagrants, was compulsory service, thus blurring the distinction once again.[49] Finally, gypsies were suspected of similar offences to vagrants, including larceny and cheating. They were also considered threats to the government. Thomas Cromwell wrote in 1537 to the President of the Council for the Marches of Wales that they committed 'felonies and treasons unpublished', and the Privy Council stated in 1592 that they were 'seditious people', 'disordered and tumultuous'. In fact the Earl of Huntingdon ordered armed forces to Leicestershire in 1613 to break up a troop of them. Gypsies remained alien in many respects from English vagrants, but that did not prevent them from being banished and imprisoned; in one instance, for those who associated with them, from being sentenced to hang.[50]

The Irish

Irish vagrants travelled in large troops, too, but unlike Romanies they were also apprehended in ones and twos. Families were common, including siblings with children. For example, Robert Leigh, his wife, their two children, his sister and her child, were punished as vagrants near Honiton in 1633. But other factors besides kinship drew the Irish together. In a group of seventeen seized in Wiltshire in 1629 the three families had different surnames, and these companies were probably drawn together by common origins or embarkation points. Two families apprehended together in the county in 1637 came from the same area of County Cork.[51] The Irish also moved in large bands because of their extended family structures at home. Sixteenth-century Hibernians were noted for their casual attitudes towards incest, bastardy, divorce and adoption, which must have resulted in strange family configurations. Even today Irish travelling-folk share with their forebears the extended family pattern and a flexible attitude towards relationships.[52] Moreover,

Irish vagrants went in large companies because they tended to arrive *en masse*, especially in the western counties, while further east they broke up into smaller units. They literally arrived by the boat-load in times of famine, war and rebellion. The Cornish gentleman Richard Carew observed during the troubles of 1602 that Ireland 'sends over yearly, yea and daily, whole ship-loads of these crooked slips'.[53]

An incident near Bristol in 1630 provides a graphic illustration of the arrival of a boat-load of migrant Irish. The ship, the *Peter* of Dungarvan, deposited between 40 and 80 of them near Portishead Point in the month of May (the estimates varied according to the witness, the captain giving the lower one). The passengers were literally dropped, as observers' statements make clear:

> they saw many of the women and children carried upon men's backs from the said boat through the water to the shore, and that the first man that came ashore (by wading in the water) brought with him a long rope and tied the end thereof unto a rock whereby it might be a stay unto the passengers coming through the water (breast high) from the boat to the land.

The captain, Maurice Keysons, *alias* Curry, had led them to believe 'that when they came into England they should have all things plenty, and when they came to men's houses they should have meat, drink, and money'. A tailor from County Clare reported that he, 'being but a poor man, sold all that he had to bring him over into England, hoping that by begging he and his wife and children should be relieved'. The captain had persuaded them to leave all the food they had on the ship, 'for that they should have victuals enough in the country at every man's door'. He had carried on a regular trade in migrants for two years, charging 4s per head for the passage, by his admission making about £15 per crossing, which suggests the number on this voyage was closer to 80 than the 40 he claimed. He had also dropped Irish beggars in Devon, Cornwall and Wales, had four more voyages planned when he was caught, and for a return cargo usually sailed to Swansea where he loaded his 8-ton bark with coal. His defence of the business was proto-nationalist: 'as long as there were English in Ireland, he would bring Irishmen into England, for if Englishmen would depart from Ireland, then the Irish had no need to come into England'.[54]

Another reason Irish vagrants were arrested in large companies is that entire communities and families were periodically uprooted there. They came over in waves: when English settlement began and rebellions occurred in 1569 and 1579–83; in the early 1600s when the English forces embarked on a policy of 'planned genocide by starvation'; and from 1628 (significantly, the year Keysons began his sailings) to 1660, when the

country suffered famine (1628–9), civil wars (1641–3) and conquest (1649–52).[55] These events affected different groups, but the common result was to throw victims on to the roads, which for many led to England.

The Irish were thought to be barbarous enough on their own soil, but even more obnoxious when they came to England with their dubious morals, dirty habits and popery.[56] Governments employed two procedures to handle them. First they bought them off with official doles; secondly, they punished them as vagrants and returned them to their own land. The policies were sometimes pursued concurrently, with an official paying one Irishman to go away and whipping the next for no obvious reason. A vagrancy statute of 1572 ordered Irish vagabonds and beggars to be sent home after punishment, yet Irish itinerants were given relief before and after the Act: in 1585 London officials paid £10 to get rid of some.[57] From 1628 the same policies were pursued on a larger scale, as the problem dramatically worsened. In just one day that year Bridewell officials despatched thirteen Irish vagrants to sea. That apparently was the tip of the iceberg, for in April the following year the Privy Council and the Lord Mayor corresponded about 'loose and vagrant persons' in the metropolis, who included 'very many Irish'. The provinces, too, reported swarms of Irish beggars, especially in the western shires. But even the Home Counties and East Anglia made complaints, and finally in 1634 the government issued a proclamation that all the Irish should be punished.[58] Despite penal measures, parishes continued to relieve them, especially once rebellion broke out in 1641 and thousands of Protestant settlers returned as refugees. It would be a remote place indeed that did not witness the passage of some Irish beggars in the 1640s. In the parish of St Mary le Strand, Westminster, between 1621 and 1637 just one or two received doles each year. But in 1637–8 the total rose to 8, in 1638–9 to 16 and in 1648–9 to 80. London saw a massive influx in 1630–1; in Wiltshire the Irish share of the transient population rose from 0.3 per cent in 1603–20 to pass 10 per cent in 1621–38; and similar, although smaller, rises occurred in Chester and Leicester (see Appendix, Table I for the last three places).[59]

Although they aroused fear and loathing, gypsies and the Irish were few in number compared with English vagrants. Harman stated in 1567 that over 100 Irish beggars had come over during the past two years, but that was not many, even if the statement referred solely to the Home Counties. Hext estimated in 1596 that gypsies numbered 30 to 40 per shire, but even taking the top figure it does not amount to much more than 2000 for England and Wales.[60] Rather than sheer numbers, it was the fact that the gypsies and the Irish were alien groups that caused resentment. Of the two, the Irish were probably seen as the greater threat. They

travelled in large companies and descended upon the country in waves, sharply augmenting the vagrancy problem, while the gypsy population was much more stable. But in addition the native Irish were associated with popery and rebellion, which disturbed England's rulers and in some measure the populace. If there is a parallel in the Great Rebellion to the 'Great Fear' of 1789 in France, it is the Irish scare of 1641, when rebellion there sent shock waves through England.[61] The great influx of Irish refugees during the previous decade had no doubt prepared the ground for that panic.

Dangerous liaisons

Vagabonds formed new relationships *en route*, which disturbed the authorities. Men and women formed illicit ones and were sometimes married under dubious authority. Others were already married and committed adultery and bigamy. Family-type relationships were also recreated by the adoption and theft of children. Younge and the other commentators were correct that vagrants were promiscuous, although whether they were more so than the rest of the population is uncertain. Certainly the latter were no angels, judging by the numbers of immorality cases in church and civil courts. Such charges were partly the result of repressive official attitudes in sexual matters, but the offences were undoubtedly there to be prosecuted. The church courts traditionally handled these crimes, but the secular arm was also increasingly active in this area, with Parliament legislating against sodomy, swearing, drunkenness and bigamy, while justices and constables inquired into disorders ranging from bawdry to buggery.[62] Since accusations were most likely to be made by neighbours, vagrants were probably prosecuted rather less than the settled population.

Whether bigamy led to an itinerant life or *vice versa*, the two went hand in hand, because the bigamist often journeyed between different partners. After bigamy was made a felony punishable by death in 1604, few confessed offenders appear among vagrants. Before then, however, some were clearly untroubled about having more than one legal partner. A Salisbury man seized in Exeter in 1564 had both his wives with him, while a vagrant cook admitted to Bridewell officials in 1604 that he had married four women, three of whom were still living.[63] Unmarried or dubiously joined couples were common among vagabonds. When officials questioned couples closely they found about a third to be uncertainly wed: 11 of 35 in Wiltshire examinations, 1603–38; 18 of 56 in Leicester ones, 1584–1640. Since others probably lied and got away with it, at least half were probably unmarried by the strict rules of the church. Magistrates sometimes went to great lengths to determine whether couples were legally married. This was possibly to discover whether their evi-

dence could be used against one another, for if they were properly married it could not.[64] The usual procedure was to examine each partner separately and then to compare their stories. They were asked where they were born and where they lived before marrying; where and when they were married, including the name of the church, the day and year, and the names of the minister, witnesses, and the man who gave the bride away; where they had spent their wedding night and had lived since the wedding; details of their children, including names, ages, birthplaces and burial places; and whether they had had banns properly published and could produce a marriage certificate. Such rigorous interrogation inevitably meant that liars were caught. A few were simply inept, like an Essex pair who disagreed in Dorchester in 1632 about where the event took place, who the parson was, who gave the bride away, whether she was a widow or not at the time, where the wedding dinner was held, and the names of two of their five children. By comparison, William and Elizabeth Searchwell of Tower Hill had rehearsed their stories well, but still fell foul of the Dorchester magistrates in 1634 when they listed five children and got the name of one wrong.[65]

When detected, they pleaded mitigating circumstances. Women protested that they had taken up with men after promises of marriage, which were in fact legal contracts of marriage.[66] Marriage law was a complicated tangle, involving five separate stages: the first two included written and verbal contracts, the third the proclamation of banns, the fourth the actual church wedding and the fifth, the sexual union. Each stage seems to have been considered a *degree* of marriage. A woman who had had two bastards by a Scot told Bridewell officials in 1606 that they were 'handfast', that is betrothed, which was only the second of the five steps, but a legally valid contract just the same and a common form of marriage in remote parts of the realm. The messy state of the law inevitably produced back-sliding and confusion. A case in point is an itinerant surgeon who stated of the woman accompanying him in Leicester in 1608 that 'he is married to her, and he is not married to her, for they are betrothed the one to the other and therefore they are man and wife before God'.[67]

Vagrant couples also reported marriages in 'lawless churches' by renegade ministers and in peculiar jurisdictions. These vicars did a roaring trade in dubious marriages, not only among vagabonds. Up to 1754 London had over 100 chapels in which one could be married without banns being read: St James's, Duke's Place, alone celebrated 40,000 matches between 1664 and 1691 that were strictly illegal. In some country parishes a third to two-thirds of marriages were by licence (without banns) or irregular in some other sense.[68] Vagrants were unlikely to conform even to these illicit procedures, since the government ordered vicars not to marry them early in Elizabeth's reign. And considering that

large numbers of the settled population did not bother to get married in church, it is not surprising that vagabond couples were often dubiously joined.[69]

Not all the relationships of vagrant couples were casual and short-term. Some reported spending five years and more together, stated their willingness to take the vows legally, and protested that they would not forsake one another.[70] In any case, the authorities' treatment of young lovers was always likely to encourage them to cut loose and live in sin. Officials actually broke up love-making sessions and split up partners permanently. In London in 1641 William Leicester and Elizabeth Ouncestead were 'taken in a suspicious manner of incontinence and locked up in a chamber and the bed warm'. Although they denied any misdeed and the matron at Bridewell inspected the girl and found she 'never knew man', he was packed off to the East Indies. Later that year London officers caught an apprentice and his girlfriend in bed after breaking the door down.[71] No wonder some couples absconded to escape official controls. Such illicit unions, while having a semblance of normal family life, reinforced official disapprobation of vagrants and arguably exacerbated the bastardy problem.

Vagrants were not averse to stealing children and accepting unwanted ones, which also had the effect of recreating, in some small measure, nuclear family patterns. Gypsies allegedly made off with the young, but other cases appeared to involve English vagrants. A Warwickshire woman, accused of having taken a child near Chelmsford in 1575, claimed that its parents had given it to her at a fair in Norfolk.[72] Vagabonds probably mainly stole the offspring of the poor. Two women vagrants were sent to Bridewell in 1621 for 'stealing away a little child, formerly the mother thereof lying in, in Bermondsey Street in the cage'. Under James I child-theft reached the level of a regular trade in the metropolis. It was probably stimulated by the official transportation of children overseas, a subject which is examined in the final chapter. Two women were incarcerated in Bridewell in 1624 'suspected to have combined together to buy and sell children.'[73]

Bastard children, for obvious reasons, were especially likely to be passed to vagrants. At Nottinghamshire sessions in the early seventeenth century JPs normally required the child's father not to give it to a passing vagrant. But that is exactly what happened in Staffordshire in 1616, when a man who made a neighbour's maid-servant pregnant took the baby and 'bound it upon the back of a rogue'.[74] The fate of the child stolen by or given to a vagrant was unkind. The woman accused of taking the one in Essex had hurt it after only a week, and allegedly offered a shilling to a boy to drown it. The rogue who took the Staffordshire baby 'neither had wife nor means to give it nourishment, whereby the child in short time

miscarried and died'. Susan Hobbes, a vagrant entrusted with an infant whose parents had allegedly died in Newgate, had two teenage daughters of her own and another 10-year-old girl with her in Reading in 1627. The baby was apparently too much for her – too small to walk, 'untoward' and 'a strong child', who bit and scratched – so she reportedly killed it by breaking its skull.[75]

A baby or child was a useful ploy to gain the goodwill and pennies of the public. The child of a Norwich woman was handed over to another for begging in 1565, while a woman taken into Bridewell in 1624 was described as 'a common child-bearer, to beg with'.[76] Youngsters were also put to work stealing. Two girls were encouraged to thieve as well as beg in Elizabethan Chester by the woman with whom they lodged, while an Irishman persuaded a boy to drive stolen sheep to market in Somerset in 1623. Children were also handy for burglaries, because they could crawl through small apertures.[77]

CONCLUSIONS

To sum up, gypsies and the Irish travelled in large companies, and to some extent family-type units were formed among English vagabonds by taking new partners and stealing or adopting children. But it was exceptional to find vagrants in very large troops, and even when couples and their children increased in number in the early Stuart period they rarely accounted for more than a third of the total. Above all, vagrancy was a crime of the young male. Even such family relationships as existed on the road were often casual and unstable. Persons departed, sometimes never to return, or only to meet many years later. A Hertfordshire family arrested in Salisbury in 1624 had two children and an apprentice with them, but when re-arrested eleven months later they had only one child left.[78] Disease, the gallows and gaol fever must have cut short many lives. Vagrants were therefore mainly thrown together by coincidence and circumstances. Their relationships were evanescent ones, and this made them dangerous in the eyes of those who ruled.

Chapter 5

On the road

The vagabond, William Harrison wrote in 1577, 'will abide nowhere but runneth up and down from place to place . . . to and fro over all the realm'.[1] Considerable periods of vagrants' lives were spent in motion, but the nature of that mobility deserves closer examination than commentators such as Harrison gave it. In particular, it is worthwhile studying the extent and pace of their movements, the places they frequented, when and how they moved about, and where they received food and shelter, for the results of this analysis show that the ramblings of vagabonds, far from being aimless, had definite patterns, and that mobility increased in the crisis years of the early seventeenth century. They also suggest further reasons why vagrants were at odds with the social order. On the one hand, a peripatetic existence augmented their isolation, because they were uprooted from settled communities and mainly received hospitality on a cash basis in alehouses. On the other, their mobility also increased their everyday contacts – and conflicts – with the established order, because it took them to centres of population and to public gatherings. That made them highly visible and aggravated the official tendency to view them as bogymen.

The documentation for vagrants' movements is good, if variable. The procedure of sending them 'home', whereby officials recorded birthplaces or last residences, produces evidence of limited value, because it fails to indicate where and how long they had meandered since embarking on their travels. A vagabond might be arrested only 50 miles from his birthplace, but could have tramped hundreds of miles over several years since his original departure. Justices' examinations, however, normally give evidence of mobility in the past. The records vary in the thoroughness with which they were compiled, but they normally provide details of past movements and yield figures indicating the minimum levels. The distances travelled by vagrants have been measured as the crow flies, which of course generally underestimates the length of the journeys. But

even though the documentation tends to understate the level of mobility, it leaves no doubt that vagrants were uprooted and mobile.

THE ROAD GOES ON

Tramping the roads was a permanent condition for most vagrants. They reported having 'small dwelling' and 'no abiding place'. One told Montgomeryshire justices in 1568 that he 'dwells nowhere, nor has no abiding but there as he may have work'; another, seized in Leicester in 1594, said that he 'has no dwelling, but is a traveller abroad for his living'. When pressed by magistrates, they might produce places of birth or previous residence, but in reality few had regular abodes. In Warwick in the 1580s just fifty of 130 vagrants could claim a home, and few had had households of their own. Many had been cut loose for years, some for periods exceeding a decade. A woman apprehended in Cheshire in 1574 stated that 'she has used the art of begging from her cradle', while Anne Morris told Chester officials in 1629 that she had left her home sixteen years earlier, since when she had 'had no place of abiding'.[2]

Commentators thought the vagrant ranged from one end of the country to another: the Somerset justice Hext put the typical distance at 200 to 300 miles. Although that was an exaggeration, they could cover considerable mileages. In Charles I's reign a Nottinghamshire man boasted he could walk 30 miles on a winter's day, despite being lame, and such a distance was not impossible considering the journeys reported by others. Some itinerants roamed widely in their travels. A couple arrested in Staffordshire in the same period said that they had 'heretofore lived in most of the shires of England and beyond seas'. The odyssey of Thomas and Isabell Wylde, a pedlar couple, took them from one end of the country to the other in 1582. In mid-March they set off from Settle to travel to London. By the time of their arrest, a fortnight later in Warwick, they had passed through six counties and covered about 260 miles. They had travelled about 15 miles a day, partly on foot, in spite of carrying wares and transacting business along the way.[3]

It would be misleading, however, to think that vagabonds covered great distances in short periods of time. The opposite is closer to the truth. In Warwick in the 1580s, seventy-four travelled on average 2.25 miles per day or about 68 miles per month.[4] That does not mean that a typical day's march was 2 or 3 miles. Rather, movement was a matter of stop and go, halting for a few days to work, beg or steal, then making 10 or 12 miles. When long distances were covered, they were done in slow stages, a matter of weeks and months rather than days. But evidence from Reading suggests that vagrants were moving faster and further by the 1620s and 1630s. The seventy-four reporting detailed movements had rambled on

average 2.85 miles per day and 85 miles a month, an increase of a quarter over Elizabethan Warwick.[5] The spurs behind increased movement were economic crises and, after 1630, greater official harassment.

Although displaced, most vagrants were arrested within several days' travel of their places of origin. Averaging the totals shows that 53.3 per cent were apprehended within 50 miles of birthplace or last residence (Appendix, Table VI). Three groups can be distinguished according to their distances from 'home' when arrested. First, there was the short-distance vagrant who was roughly 20 miles from his origins and often much less, the treatment of whom varied. In the countryside he was often tolerated. Thus a constable's report from an Elizabethan village observed of beggars that 'we see very few come [unless] it be such [who] dwell so near that they may go home again the same day'. Similarly a Wiltshire constable stated in 1626 that two poor women begged at his door, 'which he punished not, for that they were old and neighbours', and Norfolk justices reported to the sheriff in 1631 that 'if any do beg, they are but near dwellers'.[6] Large towns such as London and Norwich also had high proportions of vagrants from near by, but were not so tolerant. As we saw earlier, they faced great problems of disorder, because of the large influxes of migrants who readily drifted into vagabondage.

The second type of vagabond was regional in his movements. Rather than remaining within the confines of his town or shire he strayed 45 miles from home – the median in the early seventeenth century – and thus a few days' travel. At minimum, then, he would reach the border of an average-size county and might well wander beyond. Edward Smith, seized in Warwick in 1581, had only travelled 20 miles from the town in any one direction but had crossed the county's boundaries twice, while a West Midland seamstress, who travelled from market to market to buy and sell, 'to get a penny to help to maintain her', had visited Bishop's Castle, Ludlow, Wellington and Oswestry before her arrest in Shrewsbury in 1600.[7]

The third type moved long distances, at least 80 to 100 miles. He not only left his immediate locality and region; he was likely to be arrested in another part of the country altogether. Those apprehended more than 100 miles away formed between a fifth and a third of the total, depending on the time and locality (Appendix, Table VI). The very long-distance person, found over 200 miles from his origins, accounted for about a twentieth. Long-distance vagrants were selective in the regions they favoured. Southern England was popular, those originating over 100 miles away rarely falling below a fifth of the total, and usually standing between a quarter and a third. In the Midlands and the North, in contrast, the proportion never rose above a sixth; in Lancashire and Westmorland in the 1630s it was only 1 in 20; and in Yorkshire from 1638 to 1660, 1 in 11.

About the same time London and Suffolk each drew a fifth from beyond 100 miles; Kent, Surrey and Sussex, just over a third; and Devon and Cornwall, nearly half. In some cases these were special circumstances. The high figure for Devon and Cornwall is explained by influxes of Irish; the comparatively low figure for Reading of 1 in 7, by frequent arrests of persons from London. But in general southern England drew the vagrant poor from greater distances than the rest of the country.

Vagrants were apprehended in places increasingly distant from 'home' in the early seventeenth century. In Chester and Leicester those coming from over 100 miles rose by 10 per cent; Cheshire, Essex and Wiltshire also saw increases in the 51–100 mile range, and declines in the 0–50 bracket; and those coming from over 200 miles away rose by 14 per cent in Wiltshire constables' records from 1621 to 1638 (Appendix, Table VI). In Cheshire the rise was largely made up of persons from Wales, while in Wiltshire the Irish were the key group. In that instance famine conditions in Ireland were responsible, but the share of English vagrants from beyond 50 miles also increased in the period.

In sum, vagabonds had severed their ties with settled communities, but their peregrinations were not random or boundless. They tended to be arrested in regions from which they had sprung, and in cities a majority might well come from within 10 or 20 miles. Although they ran up considerable mileage, it was covered over long periods and punctuated by stays in one place. That was one reason they fell foul of the authorities. If they had simply passed through without stopping, they would have escaped the stocks and whip more often. But vagrants were moving greater distances by the early seventeenth century, which no doubt reinforced the stereotype of footlooseness.

OBJECTIVES

Vagrants gave various reasons for being on the road (Appendix, Table VII). There was some variation between different places, which is explained in part by magistrates' lines of questioning: in Wiltshire they paid special attention to destinations, while in Essex examinees often confessed crimes. Roughly two-thirds of vagrants' stated purposes are accounted for by visits to specific destinations, to kin, seeking work, and other subsistence activities. Apart from crimes, which are examined in a later chapter, the remainder of their objectives were a miscellany that included settling gambling debts; pursuing various persons; bringing money to persons in gaol; having shoes mended; seeking relief for fire losses, shipwrecks and injuries; getting medical attention; and simply having a good time. A statistical table cannot really do justice to the variety of missions, and the lack of stereotyping in these statements

suggests that they contain some, if not the whole, truth. In addition, a quarter of vagabonds claimed to be working, and another tenth reported looking for work. While some statements were probably false, sufficient evidence exists of work-histories for the subject to receive separate treatment in the following chapter.

Vagrants reported travelling to specific places in a fifth of cases. In Cheshire a common one was Ireland; London was a frequent target in Leicester and Somerset; and in Wiltshire the most usual were Bath, Bristol, London and Salisbury. In other cases they simply reported that they were returning home. Errands involving kin were important, accounting for a fifth of cases, but these appointments were often vague and may have provided an excuse to be footloose. However, some did link up with kin beyond the immediate family and at some distance. A Somerset man travelled over 20 miles to Gloucestershire in 1622 to see a cousin, and another man from the county journeyed into Berkshire about the same time to work in husbandry with a kinsman. Vagrants also came to London on the strength of kinship links.[8] Another kin-related mission was the placing of children in service: a Derbyshire woman accused of theft in Leicester in 1596 claimed to be returning from placing a child in service in Southwark. People also travelled to visit relatives in gaol: Joan Wood visited her son in Leicester gaol in 1598, bringing him food, drink and 2d in cash. Finally, love entered into vagrants' motives. A South-ampton man left the city in 1577, 'partly for lack of work and partly because he had offered himself unto Sybel Pearce', a Christchurch woman who had run off with a local miller.[9] While the evidence of vagrants' aims should be treated cautiously, its variety and the emphasis upon practical survival have a ring of truth.

HAUNTS AND HABITATS

Masterless men overwhelmingly frequented towns, as the vagrancy Act of 1547 noted. In examinations most (58.9 per cent) of the places they reported visiting had markets (Appendix, Table VIII). There were variations from place to place – for example, in Cheshire only about two-fifths of places visited had markets, which is explained by the comparative scarcity of market towns in the North and Wales. But generally towns were frequented more than was warranted by their share of the total population, and the proportion increased in the seventeenth century.[10] There were two main reasons for resorting to towns. One is that, because vagrants were chiefly urban in origin, it was natural for them to flock there; a second, that even though many towns experienced difficult times in the period, they still had facilities that attracted vagabonds: alehouses for refreshment and lodgings; places to squat during the winter, such as

barns and brick-kilns; and a variety of public gatherings at which they could engage in subsistence activities.

Market days and fairs acted like magnets in drawing vagrants to towns. Copland noted in Henry VIII's reign that beggars 'walk to each market and fair, and to all places where folk do repair', and 'keeping market' was frequently mentioned. A whetstone seller reported to Chester magistrates that he travelled from market to market to make his living, while two women seized in Devizes in 1631 regularly sold pedlary in eleven market towns in four counties. In London vagrants were described as a 'haunter of the markets to pilfer' and a 'common frequenter of the markets'; some actually slept rough in them.[11]

Almost a thousand fairs were held each year in England and Wales. Most towns and many villages held at least one, and they were popular resorts of vagrants. Warwick's on 1 May, Bartholomew's Day, and St Simon's and Jude's; Shrewsbury's and Chester's on Midsummer day; Reading's on St James's Day; and Leicester's in early December: they all attracted mobs of them.[12] In 1571, forty-seven vagabonds were arrested in Cambridge, 'the number whereof were so great . . . by reason of the confluence to and from Stourbridge fair'. If Dekker is believed, there was even an annual beggar's fair, which was held on the Holy Rood days in Tewkesbury, where 'you shall see more rogues than ever were whipped at a cart's arse through London, and more beggars than ever came dropping out of Ireland'. Norfolk JPs reported that 'dangerous rogues' frequented fairs there in the 1630s and ordered strict watches kept.[13]

For many vagrants fairs provided opportunities to cadge a living. Even though fairs and the traditional open markets faced growing competition from private marketing, they remained the centres of economic life. The fair was a place to buy and sell, but also to settle debts and to seek work. Various traders used them, especially livestock dealers: one arrested at Bartholomew fair in Warwick in 1583 had visited ten other Midland gatherings in the past few months. Pedlars also made their livings at such meetings. Chapmen seized in Warwick in the 1580s named fairs at Lichfield, Pershore, Redditch and Tamworth that they had attended; an Oxfordshire woman apprehended at Corsham fair in 1631 had recently visited three fairs and five markets in Oxfordshire and Northamptonshire.[14] The hiring of labourers took place in autumn fairs, where the men 'stood in rows in the market-place, with ribbons in their caps to indicate their craft'. These meetings were probably the last resort for those who failed to find work through other channels. The authorities sometimes frowned upon hiring-fairs; for example, in Buckinghamshire in 1631, where apprentices were said to 'take a lawless liberty to place themselves' at Thame fair.[15]

Such assemblies undeniably attracted ne'er-do-wells, especially

thieves. Harman claimed that upright men rendezvoused with their doxies at fairs and markets, 'where they meet to pilfer and steal from stalls, shops, or booths'. In *Bartholomew Fair* (1614) the fair's entertainments were a cover for pickpockets. These gatherings presented golden opportunities to the crook: victims with large sums of money; plenty of distractions for unwary bumpkins; shops and stalls full of goods; and crowds in which to mingle and disappear. Fairs also attracted professional gamblers. Officials were often primed for trouble on these occasions. In London a double watch was ordered during Bartholomew fair in 1621, while the authorities in Chester, Leicester and Shrewsbury regularly made large numbers of arrests.[16] Fairs and market days were social occasions, too; fixed points in the calendar when vagrants met friends and relations, at which 'good cheer' abounded. At such events groups assembled numbering five or six members, who were related to or knew one another. They also came for entertainment. A Shropshire man attended Midsummer fair in Chester in 1577 because 'he heard of the plays here', and a wandering woman reported 'there were minstrels playing, and there they made good cheer' during a Nuneaton fair in 1582.[17]

Vagabonds flocked to all kinds of holiday gathering. In London special watches had to be ordered in Easter week and at Midsummer in 1610. In the countryside parish feasts – called revels or watches in the Southwest; wakes, garries and helpales in the Midlands and North – attracted throngs of them. At these fetes 'food and drink were abundant, courtship and every kind of social intercourse flourished, and the hardship of life was obliterated'. But officials took a dim view of them. In 1612 West Riding justices ordered feasts to be suppressed, because they attracted 'vagrants, persons and men of lewd disposition'. Wakes were similarly suspended in Staffordshire in the reign of Charles I, because it was feared 'no small evil may ensue by drawing together of rogues, vagabonds, and other idle persons', and because of plague. However, the campaign failed, vagrants continuing to name feasts they had attended.[18]

Vagabonds made their way to all manner of public event, making the statement 'you have the poor always with you' literally true of Elizabethan England. They attended plays, bear-baitings and horse-races; stationed themselves where the nobility passed in coaches; flocked to sermons and Sunday services; and swarmed to aristocratic funerals to receive a meal and a dole. At the obsequies of the fourth Earl of Northumberland in the late fifteenth century 13,000 were said to have been relieved. Although hand-outs on this scale declined in the sixteenth century, 3000 to 4000 beggars might still appear at an aristocratic burial in the 1580s, and they continued to throng to upper-class funerals into the 1620s.[19]

Vagrants also journeyed to take cures at Bath, Buxton and Holywell.

The vagrancy statute of 1597 stated that such great numbers gathered in these towns that they were overwhelmed by the cost of maintaining them. The traffic in cripples was certainly considerable. St Margaret's, Westminister, regularly sent them to Bath for cures, and the records of southern shires show them on their way there from most of southern England.[20]

They turned up, too, at official functions, including quarter sessions, the assizes, the Council in the Marches and elections.[21] They even plagued the monarch's Court. In 1526 the Knight-Marshal was ordered to see to the punishment of 'vagabonds and mighty beggars, also of un-thrifts and common women', who congregated there. But the press around royalty did not cease. James I wrote to the Virginia Company in 1619 about vagrant youths who bothered him at Newmarket, suggesting that they be transported to the colony. Charles I was just as sensitive about the problem. Three 'lewd women that follow the Court' were despatched to Bridewell in 1630; the Privy Council wrote in 1634 to the Lord Mayor about the swarms in the capital, 'even near his Majesty's Court'; and at Middlesex sessions in 1641 constables were ordered to punish vagrants in Hyde Park and other places near the King's palace.[22] Not even the mightiest of the land entirely escaped the attentions of the wretched. Vagrants were seemingly omnipresent.

SEASONAL SHIFTS

Vagrancy was thought to wax and wane according to the season. In summer vagabonds flocked to the countryside; in winter they frequented towns. Beggars, Copland stated, 'all summer keep ditches and busks . . . but in the winter they draw to the town'. The runaway apprentice-turned-rogue, an author noted in 1625, spent his time 'fatting himself with the lazy bread of summer, tumbling (during that season) in a hay-cock with his dell; and in winter, lying snug in a brick-kiln with his doxy'.[23] The summer months saw most movement, and required official vigilance. Sir Thomas Smith wrote that 'in the warm time the people for the most part be more unruly . . . even in the most calm time of peace'. Justices had therefore to meet at the beginning of summer to suppress vagabonds. When the Privy Council ordered special searches between 1569 and 1572, they were scheduled from April to October, especially late summer.[24]

Judging by their dates of arrest, vagrants followed the observed season-al patterns in many places (Appendix, Table IX). In rural areas movement picked up in March and April after a winter lull, remaining at a high level to September, while the months after October saw a lower rate. The pattern is evident in Cheshire before 1601; in Essex, Somerset and Wiltshire; and to some extent in Norwich from 1564 to 1635, Leicester

from 1584 to 1640, Salisbury from 1599 to 1638, and Doncaster, 1627–8.[25] The seasonality of movement is hardly surprising, considering travelling conditions in pre-industrial England. Winter journeys were possible, but shorter days and wet and cold weather must have made them unpleasant. There were probably many vagrants like the one who stayed all day in a barn near Warwick in January 1581, 'because it did snow', and another who broke his journey in county Durham in December 1653, 'disliking the weather'.[26] Another variable was the harvest, which drew vagrants to the countryside to work in summer, as is shown in the next chapter. The dissipation of the previous year's bounty in spring and summer also stimulated subsistence moves. Langland remarked in *Piers Plowman* that 'beggars, at Midsummer (when corn begins to grow scarce), sup without bread', and the comment was still valid in the early seventeenth century. Finally, deficient crops set exceptional numbers moving to towns. After the poor harvest of 1622 London officials reported a 'multitude of wandering and idle beggars and vagrants resorting hither' because of 'the hardness of the time'.[27]

People regularly moved in the spring and summer to find employment and to beg. A Lancashire vagrant stated before Chester magistrates in 1612 that he was on his way to Oxfordshire, 'where he had usually yearly about this time of year heretofore gone to work in husbandry'. Likewise, a Berwick widow told Maldon officials in 1630 that every spring she came south to gather peas and make hay in the London area. Anglesey vagrants went begging every summer: women known as *gwragedd cawsa* for cheese, wool, hemp and flax; others called milk-wives for milk, butter and cheese; and their menfolk for grain and seed at harvest time.[28] Another factor affecting seasonal movements was the timing of fairs, of which over 70 per cent were in the six-month period from May to October, a mean average of almost 120 per month. In the rest of the year fewer than fifty a month took place and in January, only nine. In the south of the country, where the growing season was more advanced, they reached their peak number in May; in the north, where the harvest came later, in August. A close relationship is discernible between summer fairs and increased vagrancy arrests: in May in Leicester, Reading and Salisbury; in June in Chester and Colchester; in July in Reading; and in August in Warwick (see Appendix, Table IX).[29]

On the other hand, many towns were troubled with vagrants in winter as well as summer – for example, Chester (1601–30), Colchester, Leicester, London, Reading, Salisbury and Warwick (Appendix, Table IX). The shorter winter days actually meant increased vagabondage in London, the Lord Mayor warned aldermen in 1604: 'towards winter (the evening growing dark) many loose, lewd and vagrant persons have been found to wander about the streets and to lurk in corners . . . under colour of

begging'. Towns offered shelter from an inclement countryside. They also attracted itinerants if they held winter fairs: thus there were high numbers of arrests in October in Chester, Colchester, Leicester and Warwick; in December and January in Salisbury; in February in Norwich and Reading; and in March in Colchester and Salisbury.[30]

Official action affected seasonal movements, too, because in some places poor relief was only provided during the winter, making wandering and begging necessary for the rest of the year. London officials informed a beggar named Margaret Morris in 1553 that 'she shall be relieved in the winter season in the house of the poor in Southwark', but in the remainder of the year she was to 'give herself to honest labour'. In seventeenth-century Shropshire full pensions for the aged poor were similarly limited to the winter months, and from April to October they had to find other means of support.[31]

GETTING AROUND

A good deal is known about the transport of goods in Tudor and Stuart times, but far less about passengers.[32] Most vagrants travelled on foot, but they also used horses, wagons, carts and boats. The case of an unemployed Norfolk weaver journeying to London in 1621 shows the diverse facilities available even to down and outs. He rode to the capital by wagon and, finding no work there, embarked in a tide boat that took him from Wapping to Grays Thurrock. Then he tramped across Essex, but, tiring, mounted a horse, with which he was later apprehended near Billericay. Some vagrants owned their own horses, especially if they were petty chapmen; others borrowed or hired them in their businesses; still others, like the Norfolk weaver, allegedly rustled them. Vagrancy and horse-theft were natural bedfellows: if someone were on his uppers and tired of walking, there was a strong temptation to take a horse from a field and never turn back. Finally, some vagabonds hitched rides: a Lichfield woman accepted one from a stranger between Hawarden and Chester in 1609.[33]

For long distances the most common means of travel were carriers, whose long wagons became popular from the mid-sixteenth century. They carried twenty to thirty passengers, both rich and poor, as well as goods, were drawn by six or more horses, and made 10 to 15 miles a day. By the early seventeenth century most provincial towns had regular carrier services to London.[34] Vagabonds also journeyed by water, especially in the capital. The Aldermen of Billingsgate were ordered in 1569 to appoint men to attend the landings of the Gravesend barges, which allegedly brought rogues and masterless men to the City. But the action was apparently ineffective. Two further orders were issued in 1572, and

the Bridewell Court Books show vagrants still arriving by water thirty years later.[35] If the poor wanted to travel, there were plenty of means at hand and little the authorities could do to stop them.

One means that governments devised for controlling the vagrant poor was the passport, an institution to be examined in the final chapter. In practice such a document was the key to almost unhindered mobility, because it gave them the right to travel and to receive relief from officials along the way. But from the authorities' viewpoint the system was imperfect. Vagrants used it to ramble around the country begging and did not return to their native parishes as required by law. Moreover, a lively trade in counterfeit papers developed, as is shown in Chapter 7. Keeping vagrants to the most direct route home required co-operation between constables, which did not always happen. The Privy Council wrote to the Lord Mayor in 1569 about vagabonds with passports who 'craftily [d]o spent their time in passing idly [and] do stray far out of their right ways', but evasion continued. A vagrant seized in Lincolnshire in 1631 lied to magistrates about his origins and was sent to two further places before coming clean. In the following year a Wiltshire magistrate observed that vagabonds were having passports made by justices stating distant destinations, which enabled them to 'travel from the remotest parts of the realm to the remotest from thence'. Such abuses, which Hartlib considered to be a major failing of the poor laws, were unlikely to endear vagrants to those who ruled.[36]

HOSPITALITY

As well as keeping large numbers of servants and retainers, hospifality traditionally included the provision of food and lodgings for travellers and visitors. It was notably dispensed by the Church, gentry and aristocracy, but the sixteenth century changed that. In the Reformation many institutions that had provided succour were dissolved. For their part, the landed upper-classes were hard-pressed by inflation, addicted to new types of conspicuous consumption, and made economies in hospitality.[37] Yet good Christians continued to be expected to take in itinerants. Becon urged in 1564 that tithes be used to 'succour and comfort the poor . . . the hungry, the naked, the harbourless, the wayfaring man'. 'Hospitality hath respect unto all men, but chiefly to strangers', preached Archbishop Sandys in Elizabeth I's reign. In *Christian Hospitalitie* (1632) Caleb Dalechamp was more discriminating, and specified 'the entertaining of *honest* guests and travellers'.[38]

In practice, vagrants received limited assistance from the traditional founts of hospitality. When they named places in examinations where they lodged and had refreshment, alehouses and inns were the most

common, forming 41 per cent of the total, followed by the houses of persons below gentry rank with 33 per cent (Appendix, Table X). Some of the latter group no doubt included members of the public relieving needy vagabonds, but others were letting rooms for cash and some were probably running unlicensed alehouses. These considerations, together with the likelihood that some 'masters' were also alehouse- or inn-keepers, mean that the majority of instances of hospitality very likely involved cash rather than charity. Certainly the old-style entertainment of all-comers by the Church and landed élites, if it was ever more than a myth, was a dying practice. Only very rarely were more than 10 per cent of vagabonds succoured by these former dispensers of largesse, even if they did still flock to their jamboree funerals. In fact, a higher proportion of vagrants slept rough than had relief at the gates of great houses in the early seventeenth century. It is also noticeable that comparatively little assistance flowed from kin; again, less than 10 per cent of cases, confirming that vagrants were quite thoroughly cut off from their roots.

Many more vagabonds were received in inns and alehouses, principally the latter, since inns were mainly élite establishments. Alehouses were a different matter: often just one or two rooms; limited to providing food, drink and lodgings; cheaper and catering for the popular market. They were also more numerous, by perhaps five or six to one in a total of some 20,000 hostelries in 1577.[39] Almost every village had one, and most towns had several. To the vagrant they were places of refuge in an ever-changing landscape: as well as a roof over his head and food and drink, they provided somewhere to meet relatives and companions, to pawn and sell stolen goods, and to plan crimes. Just how significant tippling houses were to masterless men is suggested by one vagrant's stopping-places during a western trek in 1612:

> First night, the Saracen's Head in Farringdon;
> Second night, the Star in Abingdon;
> Third night, an unnamed alehouse in Wallingford;
> Fourth night, the Hand in Reading;
> Fifth night, the Shoemaker's Last in Newbury;
> Sixth night, the Black Boys in Andover;
> Seventh night, the Chequers in Winchester;
> Eighth night, an unnamed alehouse in Amesbury;
> Ninth night, a barn five miles from Amesbury;
> Tenth night, the White Horse in Fisherton Anger.[40]

Some vagrants actually lived in alehouses. A couple peddling cushions and bodices in the Southwest in 1633 said that their permanent abode was in one at Woodstock. Their day-to-day lives also centred upon the alehouse. Agnes Powell took up with Meredith Bassett after they met in

one in Somerset in 1618, and they continued to frequent them as they wandered around the region begging and pretending to be married.[41]

Alehouses were considered hotbeds of sin and disorder. In 1583 Philip Stubbes attacked them as dens of drunkenness, carousing and swearing. According to the barrister Cooke in 1648, they 'principally are the corrupters of youth, and the first rise of disobedience to parents is commonly from a tavern or a tippling-house'.[42] The authorities, in particular, were convinced that they fostered vagrancy and other crimes. A Buckinghamshire justice informed William Cecil in 1561 that alehouses were the 'stake and stay of all false thieves and vagabonds' in the county, while at Stafford assizes in 1622 it was complained that they were 'known to be occasions of many abuses and disorders, and increase of rogues'.[43]

Officials spent a great deal of time policing tippling houses. They licensed them, drew up detailed regulations, and suppressed them in times of poor harvests, so that barley could be used to provision the poor. Alehouse-keepers were supposed to provide room and board to anyone who was travelling 'upon honest occasions', but were only to take in persons for whom they would answer personally.[44] Most rules forbade taking in vagrants, but they were widely ignored. Essex tipplers were presented in c.1592 for harbouring rogues and vagabonds, who had allegedly stolen hay and farm tools from local inhabitants. In 1618 the inhabitants of Worle in Somerset complained of two alehouses that attracted 'many drunkards and other loose, vagrant and idle people, like caterpillars'. They allowed tippling, so that bloodshed resulted and 'honest people cannot sleep in their beds'.[45]

The problem was an intractable one. Staffordshire justices admonished an alehouse-keeper near Leek for lodging vagabonds in James I's reign, but his reply was that 'he would give entertainment at his house to the veriest rogue or thief that came out of Stafford gaol'. At Lancaster sessions in 1634 it was complained that Tatham was 'the most thievish corner in all the shire . . . the very receptacle of rogues', because of the great number of alehouses there.[46] On occasion, tipplers were accused of harbouring itinerant crooks and buying stolen goods. Two were presented at Richmond sessions in 1609 after their wives had allegedly purchased purloined items from passing strangers. A Longnor publican was reported in 1621 to harbour rogues, and himself to be a sheep-stealer and hedgebreaker; when his house was searched, stolen goods were found in a locked coffer.[47]

Contemporaries' reports of alehouse facilities were often negative. John Taylor, the 'Water Poet', visited the Rose and Crown in Nether Stowey in Somerset in 1649, much to his regret, for he found an absent hostess, a drunken host, no supper, spider webs decorating the rooms, and 'an Ethiopian army of fleas'. And he had no sleep because of bawling

children, howling dogs and restless pigs. Samuel Pepys and Izaak Walton had better experiences, but Pepys still had to do battle with fleas in his bed. Accommodation was certainly rudimentary in some hostelries: a Worcester butcher visiting Chester in 1609 slept on rushes on a cellar floor at the King's Head. Privacy was also at a premium. At the Tiger's Head in the city a couple, a single woman and two single men spent the night all in the same room in 1623, even though they denied knowing one another. An itinerant hooper who put up in a Somerset tippling house in James I's reign actually slept in the same bed as the host and his wife! The student of seventeenth-century travel who remarked that 'alehouse accommo- dation was in many places almost as primitive and unsavoury as the homes of the poor' was no doubt correct, but then to a vagabond any roof probably looked good.[48]

Vagrants also received lodging from persons who were often them- selves needy and who dabbled in illegal ale-selling. The poverty of these places is evident from their keepers, who were frequently widows. A family of Carmarthenshire vagrants travelling through mid-Wales in Elizabeth I's reign mentioned three widows with whom they had stayed.[49] Members of the poorer trades also took in vagabonds – a shoemaker in Chester in 1600, a cobbler in Wigan in 1630, and a Lancashire coverlet-weaver in 1634. In London cheap lodging-houses sprang up in the period in which six migrants might be stuffed into a single room, but in the provinces such establishments were still rare.[50]

Vagrants also received hospitality from officials, but often illegally. Constables were responsible for the relief and lodging of travellers, but some doubled as tipplers and took in vagabonds. One who kept an alehouse near Shrewsbury in 1577 allegedly harboured vagrants, abetted thieves and acted as a pawnbroker. When pursued by a woman at- tempting to recover some stolen goods, he warned her that 'he would lay her by her feet, for he might do so, being constable'. Alehouse-keeping constables who welcomed vagrants were especially common, it seems, in North Yorkshire. The Whitwell officer was accused in 1609 of lodging tinkers for ten days. It is understandable that a constable might open his doors to a stranger in the depths of winter in those remote parts, but what of the Sinderby officer (and alehouse-keeper) who allegedly permitted twenty vagabonds to sit drinking in his house at unlawful hours?[51] If the aim was to turn poachers into gamekeepers, it did not work.

Some vagrants stayed in gaols. From 1572 to 1575 the numbers in Winchester gaol increased during the winter months. They were possibly taking advantage of a clause in the vagrancy Act of 1572 that provided support payments to those in prison. In Nottingham in the early 1580s a gang of vagrants were reported to haunt the gaol, where the under-gaoler harboured them 'and other such good fellows'. Gaols even took in visitors

and passers-by. A Warwickshire vagrant who travelled to visit a woman in the Leicester lock-up in 1598 himself spent the night there, while an adulterous couple rambling around the East Midlands in 1606 passed one night in Northampton gaol. Early modern prisons were casually run, but to permit criminals to lodge in them was rather gilding the lily.[52]

As noticed earlier, vagrants often slept rough: in one in 5 cases in Cheshire between 1570 and 1600 and nearly one in 6 in Wiltshire from 1621 to 1638, although elsewhere the proportion was lower (see Appendix, Table X). They roosted in all manner of outbuildings, cellars, under market stalls, and out-of-doors in all kinds of weather. It must have been quite common to stumble across strangers squatting in strange places. A girl who went to inspect a sheep shed near her home in Cheshire in 1582 had a shock when she found five vagrants dining in it. One of them told her, 'pretty wench, be not afraid, here is nobody will hurt thee', but the authorities thought otherwise. Vagrants took cover in a great variety of out-houses, and especially barns. Harman described the barns they frequented around London, declaring that at one near Blackheath up to forty 'upright men with their doxies' assembled.[53] In Elizabethan Chester the city fathers took action against landlords who divided suburban barns and let vagrants lodge in them. Officials might regulate the owners, but they were hard put to halt the squatters. A Lancashire man arrested in 1577 said that he and his companion had spent five of the last seven nights in four different barns between Bury and Macclesfield, and in 1629 a Chester labourer admitted living for ten weeks in a barn near the Earl of Derby's bowling alley.[54]

If barns were not available, they holed up in other buildings. Brick-kilns were favoured in winter; those near Islington were the resort of London vagrants in the winter of 1582. A cobbler from the Forest of Dean, who slept in barns in Somerset in 1619, also put up one night in a church, while another man seized in the county five years later had spent the previous night in a straw-house.[55] Owners sometimes gave permission to lodge in outbuildings. But there were dangers to this hospitality, including theft in the middle of the night, conflagrations, and ever greater congregations of tramps. In fact, large numbers assembled in outbuildings, whether invited or not. A North Country pedlar couple who spent the first night of their honeymoon in a barn on the outskirts of Chester in 1609 shared it with a dozen others, including 'pedlars, tinkers and other wanderers'. In 1624 a Staffordshire woman was accused of taking in vagabonds and endangering the neighbourhood by letting them have candles in the stables.[56] The groups encamping in such places seem to have grown in size, as vagrant groups generally expanded. When a Tewkesbury attorney took refuge with a shepherd in Gloucestershire in 1637, he was startled to find thirty beggars huddled in the barns. In 1641 a Hertford-

shire village petitioned quarter sessions against a couple who harboured vagabonds 'sometimes to the number of 60, sometimes 40, and seldom less than 20, to the terror of most of the neighbours.'[57]

Some vagrants slept out-of-doors, no matter what the season. Katherine Frank was sent into Bridewell in January 1577 as a 'lier about in the streets under stalls', and a masterless Wiltshire weaver spent the night on Salisbury Plain in December 1612. Europe is thought by some historians of climate to have experienced a 'Little Ice Age' in the sixteenth and seventeenth centuries. Even if the weather then was no worse than today, anyone who slept outside in winter must have been pretty desperate.[58] In the country a favourite place to sleep rough was under hedges, which incidentally contradicts Tusser's argument that open-field villages were more likely than enclosed ones to attract persons who 'thievishly loiter and lurk'. Before a robbery in 1576 a suspected thief slept in a rye field near Broughton Hall in Flintshire, and afterwards hid under a hedge, while three vagrants who allegedly sheared sheep during the night in Somerset in 1616 slept under a hedge before the crime.[59] Haystacks provided refuge, too. A Cheshire man questioned in Warwick in 1584 had recently spent the night in one, and a soldier returning home from service in Scotland in 1655 slept in a haystack near Malton. Still more casual were two couples travelling through Wiltshire in 1614, who simply sat down and went to sleep under a tree as dusk approached.[60]

Cities were no more immune than country areas to rootless persons squatting out-of-doors. Elizabethan London sounds a great deal like twentieth-century Calcutta. Many of those who were observed earlier dying in the open spaces of the capital probably suffered from exposure. A Christ's hospital official described in 1587 how children like the Frank girl slept under stalls in the metropolis.[61] These were not exaggerations, judging by some entries in the overseers' accounts for St Margaret's, Westminster in the 1580s:

Item, . . . towards the relief of Rose Gawaine, a poor wench that lay in the street 4d

Item, to Elizabeth Whalley, a strumpet great with child and lying nightly abroad in the streets or privy house in Westminster and sent by the justices' warrant towards Nantwich 12d

Item, to Margaret Roberts for the taking into her house of Isabel Byrd, a poor diseased woman lying nightly in the streets great with child 2s

Item, to Joyce Bradford for the taking into her house one Margaret Bateman, great with child, which did lie abroad in the churchyard 12d

In 1605 City magistrates took action against masterless persons spending

the night in sheep-pens in West Smithfield.[62] When God's poor lived not only like animals, but *with* them, even the most Panglossian of optimists might be shocked.

CONCLUSIONS

It should now be clearer why vagrants seemed poised to wreck the social order. Besides having broken links with masters and families, they were rootless and transient, haunting alehouses and sleeping rough. They were ubiquitous, present all the year round in towns, and spilling into the countryside in summer. They camped almost everywhere – in fields and farm buildings; in city streets and suburban hovels; even on the doorsteps of Parliament and the monarch's court – and their assemblies probably grew in size in the early Stuart period.

Even if vagrants formed a small proportion of the total population, their mobility made them highly visible. Any single vagrant must have passed through dozens of villages and towns in the course of his travels, which might amount to 1000 miles a year in the early seventeenth century. Even if he did not tarry, members of the local community would have seen him and taken his measure. If he stopped to beg or steal, they might have had to confront him face to face – which, as is shown in a later chapter on begging, might be a disturbing experience. Yet there was worse to come, because in addition to tramping around the country vagabonds followed trades which further alienated them from the established order.

Chapter 6

Dangerous trades

Almost without exception, contemporary observers assumed that vagabonds chose to be unemployed. Robert Crowley denounced beggars in 1550 as 'such as do counterfeit' and who, 'having their strength to labour if they lust', should be made to work. Harrison castigated vagrants as 'caterpillars in the commonwealth', who 'lick the sweat from the true labourers' brows', while Thomas Adams asserted in 1615 that they would 'rather be sick than work'.[1] In fact, the majority of vagabonds had worked, or were still in employment. Their reputation for idleness was, of course, partly deserved. But that was because, as was shown earlier, unemployment was a growing problem and because begging was probably more lucrative than labouring by the early seventeenth century. Basically, commentators such as Crowley were objecting to the nature of employment among the poorer classes, rather than their failure to work. Labouring in the bottom jobs was undoubtedly a catch-as-catch-can existence – and that impermanence made the labouring poor suspect in the eyes of the authorities and liable to arrest as vagabonds. In addition, they worked in trades thought to be seditious or fraudulent, such as pedlary and entertainment. The evidence of vagrants' occupations suggests that the official concern was justified, for their involvement in these dangerous trades increased when the economy contracted in the early seventeenth century.

The evidence of vagabonds' occupations varies in quality, because officials were not required to list them accurately. Indictments recorded trades imprecisely, while parish constables rarely noted jobs, which was also true in London, probably because the volume of cases was so great there.[2] The best sources are the justices' examinations of vagrants, which not only list their occupations, but often provide details of training, where they had worked, and for whom.

The majority of vagrants could report work-histories: in Warwick, 1580–7, 77 out of 130, or 59 per cent; in Cheshire, 1601–30, 144 out of 262 (55 per cent); and in Reading, 1623–41, 114 out of 180 (63 per cent). These figures in fact underestimate the proportion with trades, because they include some persons dependent upon spouses and parents. Vagabonds' jobs ran the gamut from the professed gentleman to the rat-catcher and rag-picker: the 114 persons stating occupations in Reading named eighty or so different trades. But in general vagrants worked in lowly positions. Roughly a third were engaged in the production of food, leather goods, cloth and metal wares, and in mining or building; at least a quarter were servants, apprentices, journeymen, labourers and harvest workers; almost a fifth were petty chapmen, makers and sellers of 'small wares', entertainers and tinkers; and a tenth, soldiers and mariners. The remainder included a sprinkling of professionals – medical men, students, and clerics – and gentlemen (see Appendix, Table XI).

Gentlemen and professionals apart, this profile of trades is strikingly similar to that of the poor in Elizabethan towns – not a surprising resemblance considering vagabonds' mainly urban origins.[3] Few were involved in husbandry, excepting harvest workers and farm labourers. The leading industrial pursuit was cloth-making, accounting for one in seven occupations and one half of those engaged in production. The bottom of the work-force – apprentices, servants, labourers and journeymen – was more numerous than the figures suggest. When apprentices are counted separately from their individual trades, the proportion rises from a quarter to over a third and, in certain places, to over two-thirds. The other major group was a medley of tramping traders and artisans, which made up nearly two-fifths of vagrant occupations in Norwich, 1564–72, and close to three-fifths in Salisbury from 1598 to 1664. This group's substantial numbers resulted from being 'dangerous trades', which were supposed to be licensed, and the same was true of soldiers and mariners (Appendix, Table XI).

The trades of vagabonds changed in the early seventeenth century, with a fall in numbers employed in industries like cloth, and rises in the numbers of servants, apprentices, transient traders and artisans, and military men. There were no major shifts from one industry to another, nor from one sector to another, but a drift away from traditional industries is apparent. Why fewer vagrants came from leading trades is not immediately obvious. The crises in the cloth trade under James I and Charles I might have been expected to propel more clothworkers on to the roads, but with the exception of Reading that was not so. Even in Norwich, a major centre of production in the 1630s, clothworkers did not increase among vagrants (Table XI).[4] Instead the shift suggests a general shut-

down of manufacturing, reflecting the serious economic problems between 1620 and 1650. Another cause of change was the increased conscription from the late Elizabethan years. Finally, the rise in servants and apprentices is explained by the contraction in the chances for upward social mobility examined in Chapter 2. Thus the evidence of vagrants' trades confirms that opportunities were contracting in the early seventeenth century; and that, as a result, they were taking up less secure positions such as casual labouring, soldiery and entertainment, which had close links with vagabondage.

It is difficult to capture the mutable quality of finding a living on the road. The modern reader, even though he might hold just one or two jobs in a lifetime, is often convinced that his society is highly fluid by comparison with those of the past. That this view is questionable is shown by the work-lives of early-modern vagrants, which suggest that working at one 'regular job', which historians are coming to think was untypical of the population in general, was almost out of the question for the vagrant poor. In many instances the chopping and changing makes nonsense of the occupational categories in statistical tables. Henry Carre, arrested in Warwick in 1581, had recently served as a soldier in Flanders, before that was a serving-man in Buckinghamshire, and was now carrying a pedlar's pack. Still more changeable was a Wiltshire musician seized in 1605, who was 'sometimes a weaver, sometimes a surgeon, sometimes a minstrel, sometimes a dyer, and now a bullard', and who was accused of having 'no trade to live by'![5]

A good deal of discontinuity in employment was caused by harvest work, which was probably the most common by-employment of the poor. In June and July they laboured in the hay harvest, and in August and September in the corn harvest. Governments were not opposed to people travelling to take up this type of work. The labour and vagrancy laws actually provided for harvest folk to move around the country: a woman vagrant seized in Staffordshire in 1571 was released because 'she had taken harvest work in hand'.[6] A map of harvest workers' movements, were it possible to draw one, would resemble a modern road atlas, for they came from all corners of the country: a Northallerton man to Warwickshire in 1581; a Welshman to the London area in 1601; a Plymouth couple to London in 1614; a Staffordshire couple to London and Kent in 1623; a Cumberland pair to East Anglia in 1627; and a Montgomeryshire family to Hampshire in 1633.[7] They also came from a multitude of trades. John Hinden was a ship's carpenter in Plymouth before labouring in the hay harvest in 1614; likewise, a sailor travelling home from Bristol in August that year bought a sickle and reaped an acre of rye along the way. The work was unlikely to make one rich – Hinden claimed he made 14d a day, plus meat and drink, when building ships,

but only 3d a day plus food as a harvester – but it supplemented the income of the poor.[8]

Far more risky than harvest work was permanently taking to the road to get a living. Migrating from one place to another was hazardous, as we have seen. But in cutting loose to seek work there was a good possibility of ending up permanently vagrant, because of settlement restrictions, failure to find employment, or because a peripatetic trade was taken up. Resort to begging and crime might even be necessary. Work, begging and crime were far more of a continuum than the analytical historian might imagine. Any one vagabond, contrary to the literary stereotypes of specialist rogues, might engage in all three activities, all on the same day, simply because he had to. It is sometimes possible, however, to discern stages in the descent from working to scrounging and crime. Simon Sewell and John Cartrie were shoemakers who had served apprenticeships in the west of England, but left in the hard times of the 1620s, 'work growing scarce'. They had travelled extensively, doing journey-work for two years, before they were arrested in Essex in 1629 on suspicion of pig-stealing.[9] Here were rapid declines from apprenticeship, to day-labouring and crime. There were other possible variations. Some undoubtedly made successful transitions to other trades – for example, a former blacksmith turned tobacco salesman, apprehended in Leicester in 1624. The hard-up person might also combine a little work and a little mendicancy, but remain on the right side of the law. That was the way of a Merionethshire man who bought and sold skins 'up and down the country', as he reported to Caernarfonshire justices in 1620, but who also lived off 'the devotion of good people'.[10] Finally, a trade considered to be dangerous to the *status quo* might provide a living.

TRADERS AND CRAFTSMEN

A motley army of pedlars and artisans tramped the roads of Elizabethan England, and their numbers increased among vagabonds in the early seventeenth century. Street traders and craftsmen had their origins in the Middle Ages. In the seventeenth century the 'Cries of London' included thirty-seven crafts and commodities, and by the 1840s Mayhew found dozens on the streets of the capital. In country districts they continued to ply their trades into the twentieth century, while in the American colonies they were indispensable to survival on the frontier.[11]

A number of transient trades were so abhorrent to the authorities that they were defined as vagrants by statute. An Act of Edward VI's reign required pedlars and tinkers to carry licenses, and the vagrancy Acts of 1572 and 1597 included them among illegal occupations.[12] Although the words chapman and pedlar date from the Middle Ages, the sixteenth

century developed the epithet 'petty chapman' as a term of abuse. In 1604 the Edwardian statute was repealed, and pedlars and tinkers were omitted from a new vagrancy Act that year, but they were not left alone. There was sufficient hostility to pedlars to encourage a syndicate to seek a patent to license them in London in 1617.[13]

Chapmen carried a wide array of fancy goods, as the speech by Autolycus in The Winter's Tale (1610–11) indicates.[14] In reality, pedlars' packs showed great extremes of wealth and poverty. Some were prosperous, such as the Lichfield man who bought 5000 pins and a gross of lace, and who claimed that his purse contained £8 when it was stolen at a Chester fair in 1577. More indicative of the status of the petty chapman, however, was the bag discovered on Salisbury plain in 1618, which contained a piece of steel (needle) work, six girdles, five pieces of cloth, two leather purses, a piece of pink ribbon, some shoemakers' tacks, a knife and a bone comb.[15] But there was also a decidedly bottom end to the market, particularly those collecting old clothes and household goods. For example, Nicholas Mathews and his two sisters lived by gathering feathers and old metal, which they came to sell in Leicester in 1630. Some hawkers were little more than beggars, such as John and Pascha Guppie of Bodmin, he a saddler and she peddling 'thread and other small wares, by selling whereof they made some benefit for their living', who were arrested in Somerset in 1607.[16] Sales at this level were little more than bribes to be gone.

Pedlars found markets in all classes and many different locales. Some reported visiting country houses, where they sometimes made large sales.[17] But chapmen reached a wider market than the gentry and assisted, it has been argued, the 'great reclothing of rural England' in the period. In the country, according to Clement Armstrong in the 1530s, they went 'from fair to fair, from market to market', and were even found 'sitting on holidays and Sundays in church porches and in abbeys daily'. An order of the London Court of Common Council of 1602 said they 'walk up and down the streets hawking', 'come to men's or women's doors and into their houses or rooms', as well as setting up tables in the streets. In Norwich, it seems, they were invading the marketplace.[18]

Tinkers are an elusive group, less numerous than pedlars and generally poorer. It was a lowly craft, mending kitchen utensils and doing odd jobs, and it was in this period that the expressions 'to tinker' and 'tinkerly' took on the meaning of slip-shod work.[19] Having a tinker do a job was, again, rather like a bribe to go away. Tinkers were notorious for larceny, swearing and drunkenness, but they were not wholly shiftless. Some had served apprenticeships and were working in their meanderings. A Dorset man reported in 1620 that he was 'a tinker by occupation and bound apprentice' and that for two or three years he had wandered 'with his

budget and tools', while a year before a Hampshire bellows-maker stated that he had 'travelled the country these six years to mend bowls, dishes and bellows'. Even if worked at honestly, however, it was a poor life.[20]

The authorities disliked transient traders and artisans for a number of reasons. One of their sins was the violation of local economic monopolies. Hawkers in London were objectionable, according to the 1602 order, because they hurt 'the ordinary and honest tradesmen being shopkeepers . . . and impoverish others'.[21] Whereas formerly they had stood and sold at appointed times and places, now they roamed at will, some living in almost perpetual motion. London hawkers probably returned at night to hovels in the suburbs, and the better-off chapmen had shops and stalls, but others lived *en route*: Lawrence Wood, a Cheshire-born screen-maker arrested in Essex in 1635, had 'not been resident in any place certain for eight years'.[22]

Furthermore, itinerant tradesfolk were disquieting because they showed occupational solidarity. Groups of tinkers regularly turned up in Norwich between 1560 and 1630; in Reading in 1631 two pedlars referred to one another as 'brethren'.[23] They had extended kinship links, too, which included wives and husbands in the trade, but also children and siblings. Indeed, pedlars tended to travel in families.[24] Nevertheless, whether these transient workers had a distinctive culture is hard to say. 'Pedlar's French' was supposedly the cant vocabulary of the underworld, and it is unlikely that pedlars alone spoke it.

Finally, hawkers and tinkers had reputations for disruptive behaviour. The phrases 'a tinker's damn' and 'a tinker's curse' were not wide of the mark, judging by sessions records. A Teignmouth chapman who had 'a pot or two too much' in Wellington in 1618 was apprehended for 'railing and abusing' a woman, while a Southwark tinker arrested in Maldon in 1635 was 'drunk and swearing many blasphemous, profane oaths'. These high spirits were not always alcoholic in origin, judging by an apparently sober Taunton tinker arrested in 1613. When asked where he had travelled, the man retorted that 'he cannot bear a head to tell where he lies as he travels. And a death he does owe to God and that he must pay', but 'he will say no more, for any officer whatsoever does the worst they can'.[25]

Of special concern to officials were clothworkers, book- and pamphlet-sellers. William Cecil's opinion that 'people that depend upon making of cloth are of worse condition to be quietly governed than the husbandmen' reflected apprehension that in crises in the industry like that of the 1550s clothworkers might become vagrants, or worse. There was substance to these fears. Unemployed weavers were reported to be begging in the streets of Exeter and Devizes in the 1620s.[26] Correlations between

vagrancy and crises in the woollen industry are, however, weak. In fact, although the years from 1614 to 1660 saw crises in many centres, the numbers of clothworkers among vagabonds declined. One explanation is occupational mobility, because they turned to other trades: a Leeds clothworker seized in Derbyshire in 1660 reported that 'wanting work of his trade . . . [he] came into this country to seek for work at the coal-pits'. Another reason is that governments made special efforts to see that clothworkers received relief. The Privy Council ordered action in the west in 1622; when crisis deepened into quasi-permanent depression after 1629, it issued a Book of Orders ordering increased poor-rates, the regulation of corn prices and the raising of 'stocks' to create employment. Similar policies were pursued in the 1640s and 1650s.[27]

Colporteurs were liable to prosecution as vagrants, because governments attempted to regulate the publication and sale of printed materials. Licensing was permanently established in 1538; in 1556 the Company of Stationers was incorporated to act as a censoring and licensing agency. The system continued, despite violations like the Marprelate tracts, until 1695. It lasted even during the civil wars and Interregnum, although to less effect than previously. The chief aim was to check the publication of seditious and heretical works. Until recently far less was known about the distribution of printed materials than about their publication. Governments sought to avoid the necessity of policing the first by controlling the second. But proximity to the continent and secret presses at home made it necessary to regulate both. The death penalty was extended to anyone assisting the author of a seditious book in 1570; pedlars were forbidden to sell substantial works in 'the lanes of the City'; and a Star Chamber decree of 1637 ordered no selling of books by persons who had not served a seven-year apprenticeship with a printer, seller or binder.[28]

Hawkers of printed works were held in low repute. John Rastell described them as 'mountebanks [who] take up their standing in market-places, or void rooms meet for the concourse of people', where 'they set a stool to stand upon, or make a little scaffold for the purpose, from which they play their part'. They catered for popular tastes, judging by his list of titles:

> *News Out of India*, or *The Original of the Turkish Empire* or *A Powder to Kill Worms*, or *Merry Tales*, or *Songs and Ballads*, or *A Preservative against the Plague*, or *A Water to Make the Skin Fair and White*, or *Pins, Points, Laces and Whistles*.[29]

In official eyes the pedlars of such works were on a par with petty chapmen and tinkers. Ballad-sellers and singers, who are considered below, among entertainers, were further groups of 'publishers' to receive the disapprobation of governments. The colporteurs arrested do appear

to have posed threats to the state. Richard Cropland, seized in Leicester around the time of the Gunpowder Plot, catered for the recusant market. He was carrying books, but also pictures, jet rings and beads, and had links with the Spanish ambassador and with a Yorkshire recusant community. When Charles I's government collapsed in 1641, the flood-gates of publication opened. In April 1642 Bridewell officials complained of persons 'wandering, crying up and down ballads, pamphlets, and such like books' who could give no 'good account' of themselves, and arrests followed. Parliament and the Protector also sought to stem the tide. The Rump put Lilburne on trial in 1649 for publishing 'treasonable venomous books'; a London bookbinder was arrested in Hemel Hempstead in 1653 for publishing a libellous pamphlet (of which he was carrying 300 copies); and Nayler had his books burned for blasphemy in 1656.[30] But apart from blatant offenders, the torrent was basically uncontrollable. Here today and gone tomorrow, all types of hawker proved difficult to suppress, even with vagrancy laws.

MILITARY MEN

No occupational groups increased as much as sailors and soldiers among vagrants from 1560 to 1640 (Appendix, Table XI). In London they accounted for only 1.5 per cent before 1580, but rose to 12 per cent between 1620 and 1640; in Essex their numbers mounted from 9 per cent of occupations from 1564 to 1596 to nearly 20 per cent between 1597 and 1644; and in Doncaster their share among the transient poor given doles jumped from 28 per cent of the total in 1621–2 to 49 per cent in 1627–8.[31] Veterans worried governments because of their knowledge of weapons and the difficulty of reintegrating them into civilian life. Official action against vagabonds commonly coincided with or followed upon wars, as after Henry VIII's expedition to France in 1545 and the war of 1562–4 against Scotland and France.[32] Once wars began on the continent and in Ireland in the 1580s and 1590s, vagrants again received official attention. The unprecedented duration and scale of these conflicts arguably produced a new level of social disruption.[33]

   Peace was made with Spain and in Ireland early in James I's reign, but troops still posed a problem, especially when the country went to war on the continent in the 1620s and domestic troubles broke out in the 1630s. The Navy more than doubled its personnel between 1633 and 1658, and during the civil wars and Interregnum the numbers under arms were enormous, the army alone running to 40,000 c.1658. The forces were therefore a growing presence in the first half of the century, creating major difficulties for governments. A proclamation issued in 1627 complained of mariners who came to the Court to demand money. A year

later the Privy Council ordered Essex magistrates to appoint a provost-marshal to halt robberies by ex-soldiers.[34]

Troops were always likely to become vagrants, because they were chiefly recruited from the poor and criminal classes. Captain Barnaby Rich complained in 1578 that 'either they scour their prisons of thieves or their streets of rogues and vagabonds' in recruiting in London, while the Navy was said in the early seventeenth century to be a 'ragged regiment of common rogues'.[35] In fact, governments consciously recruited paupers and miscreants. Vagrants had been drafted since Edward I's reign, but under Elizabeth they became the mainstays of foreign expeditions, the Privy Council considering them 'such men as are fittest'. The governments of James I and Charles I held the same attitude. In a letter to Hampshire magistrates in 1624 Whitehall stated that the mustering of vagabonds to serve in Holland would result in 'the ease and benefit of the country, [which] will find it[self] being disburdened of many unnecessary persons that now want employment and live lewdly and unprofitably'.[36]

In theory all able-bodied men from 16 to 60 were liable to conscription. But the poor mainly went, because the better-off used money and influence to evade it. In *Henry IV, Part One* (1597–8), Falstaff reckoned that in pressing 150 men he had made over £300. Shakespeare's vision was not so far-fetched: William Lloyd reported receiving £3 10s in 1581 to go to Ireland in place of a farmer's son.[37]

Observers were aware of the dangers of filling the ranks with down-and-outs. They were bad soldiers, it was said, who were prone to desert and difficult to discipline. Moreover, the practice had political pitfalls, because soldiers might take part in rebellions.[38] But perhaps the major difficulty was the return to civilian life. Harrison wrote of those who, having served abroad, then 'shake hand with labour forever, thinking it a disgrace for himself to return unto his former trade' and became vagabonds. The principal problem was undoubtedly that conscription uprooted the young and unpropertied, who then had nothing to which to return.[39]

Because of their background, military men had greater potential for violence than most other vagrants. The greatest threats were mutinies, a number of which erupted, caused by unpaid wages and lack of food and clothing. In 1575 the Privy Council was upset by 1500 soldiers returning from Ireland who formed 'common routes . . . of roguing beggars by the highway side', while in the wake of the Portugal expedition mutinous veterans rioted in the metropolis (500 were reported in Westminster alone). Although the government scotched this uprising, it had to remain on the alert, because the wars continued until 1604. The expeditions of the 1620s produced similar disturbances.[40]

Even small numbers of vagabond troops caused disorder. John

Tompson was indicted at the Hertford assizes in 1602 for vagrancy and allegedly stating that 'if he were a soldier again as he had been, he would rather fight against his country than for it'. Stragglers harassed communities like Navestock in Essex, where five of them were caught begging in 1590, and warned that 'they would be revenged of them and that they would kill him that whipped them'. Similar disruptions occurred in Kent and Sussex, where troops committed thefts and burglaries in the 1590s and early 1600s, and in all places that saw their passage to the continent and Ireland. Few veterans, however, were found carrying guns or other weapons, which suggests that commanders were careful to disarm them when they were demobilized.[41]

Not all military men were genuine. Copland described vagabonds in Henry VIII's reign who 'do wear soldiers' clothing, and so, begging, deceive folk over all', while Harman attacked 'fresh-water mariners [whose] ships were drowned in the plain of Salisbury'.[42] Counterfeits can be discovered, but in the final analysis there probably was a real increase of troops among vagrants. That was in part because England's forces grew in size in the early seventeenth century. But the main reason was that they were drafted from the downtrodden. In addition, unlike on the continent, the standing army did not develop in England. Forces were raised *ad hoc*, which increased the likelihood of mismanagement and failure. It is no coincidence that the campaigns of Buckingham and Charles I were disastrous, for their forces were raised with a minimum of preparation. Armies levied in this manner were bound to produce vagrants.[43]

To solve the problem of veterans, governments allowed demobilized troops to beg on their way home, but this arguably increased vagabondage and provided no answer to the problem of reintegrating them. Then in 1593 an Act stipulated that parish rates should support soldiers disabled since 1588. It was continued in 1597, and another Act passed that year ordered justices to find work for veterans, again with public taxation. In 1601 the earlier legislation was substantially re-enacted: the maximum parish rate was increased, and a county treasurer was appointed to administer the funds, after which evidence begins to appear that pensions were paid. It remains to be seen, however, how effective the system was. Certainly during the civil wars and Interregnum the demand overwhelmed it, and no evidence has been found that veterans were employed.[44] In reality, many were left to shift for themselves, which meant continued problems. When caught stealing clothes near Mumford in 1621, an ex-soldier said he was 'very poor and sick, wanting means and money', after serving nine months in the Low Countries.[45] The direct effects of warfare were limited at home before 1642, but the problem of demobilized troops was clearly serious.

Performing artists have not always had a good press, and this was certainly true when the state regulated them through the vagrancy laws. A statute of 1572 included among vagabonds 'common players in interludes and minstrels' who were not patronized by the peerage or the Queen; fencers, who exhibited feats of sword play; bearwards, who trained and showed performing bears; jugglers; and magicians. A vagrancy Act of 1597 reiterated these provisions, putting these entertainers at risk for over 200 years. Later, in 1648, Parliament declared all players to be vagrants, while during the Protectorate a law ordered fiddlers and minstrels summarily to be branded.[46]

A wide array of performers turned up in towns and villages. An Oxford don and diarist noted that on one day in Charles I's reign the things to be seen in the city included

1. Plays;
2. Dancing upon the rope and vaulting upon the saddle;
3. Virginals and organs playing by themselves;
4. A Dutch wench all hairy and rough upon her body;
5. The history of some parts of the Bible . . .
6. The dancing of the horse at the Star [an inn].[47]

In the early seventeenth century the Master of the Revels issued licences to show a lion operating a turnspit; dromedaries and baboons; waterworks; a picture of the city of Jerusalem; an Italian motion, or puppets; pictures in wax of the King of Sweden (1633); and feats, or magic tricks, with feet as well as hands.[48] Formerly such performers had been retained by noblemen and royalty; now they passed the hat at public performances and earned wages for private ones. It was against these hired, 'common' entertainers that official opprobrium was directed. Entertainers corrupted youth, it was alleged. By attending plays, a proclamation of 1544 stated, the young were provoked to the 'unjust wasting and consuming of their master's goods, the neglecting and omission of their faithful service and due obedience', and the 'loss and hindrance of God's honour and the divine service'.[49] They also posed challenges to the state. Minstrels attacked unpopular persons and policies. Opponents of the Reformation employed the theatre to whip up seditious debate. Governments reacted by using the stage for their purposes, establishing censorship in 1543, and in 1551 the royal control of players through licences and patents.[50] Riots sometimes occurred when crowds gathered at shows – for example, in 1584 when mobs of 500 and 1000 battled near London theatres, and again when revellers led by a pipe and tabor fought all night in Walsall in 1610. Nevertheless, despite the occasional affray, Dr Bradbrook concludes that

'the record of grave disturbances at plays in the later sixteenth century is negligible, in relation to the number of performances'. Plague also was linked with plays, which were cancelled in London when deaths reached prescribed levels.[51]

Not all showpeople were vagabonds by law, because those patronized by noblemen and corporations were protected. Royal licences and the establishment of permanent companies were additional ways to escape prosecution. Those arrested were usually unlicensed, or conjurers and fortune-tellers suspected as confidence tricksters, or minstrels, who were itinerant and poor. The seemingly repressive vagrancy Act of 1572 was in reality a charter for the professional company. Frozen out henceforth were the unlicensed players, because the Act sought 'to stop poor strollers from pestering the country'.[52]

Minstrels, who included harpers, pipers and fiddlers, were also vagrants under the statute of 1572. They played wherever there was dancing, games and acting, and were unpopular with the authorities. The medieval Church banned them for promoting immorality, and sixteenth-century officials objected to them on similar grounds. Nicholas Bennet was seized in Wiltshire in 1614 for allegedly playing on Sundays, 'to the great dishonour of God'. Minstrel shows were also thought to be covers for thievery, Greene alleging in 1592 that music was helpful to pickpockets. Perhaps there was some truth to these aspersions: Richard Cokley, who came to a Chester fair in 1616 to do singing, dancing and tricks, was accused of taking a purse containing £5.[53]

Minstrelsy, too, was considered a cover for sectaries and recusants. According to a statute of Henry VIII's reign, songs and ballads were used by schismatics. An ecclesiastical inquiry in Durham diocese in the 1570s warned that popery and rebellion were spread by minstrels singing bawdy songs. The charge was not wholly absurd: in 1608 a man was presented at North Riding quarter sessions for harbouring a fiddler suspected of recusancy, and a Derbyshire piper was ordered to stand trial in 1616 in Nottinghamshire for carrying beads, crucifixes and books.[54]

All that is known about vagrant musicians suggests that they were poor. A man accompanying an unlicensed fiddler in Cheshire in 1577 was the son of a collier. He himself carried coals until age 20, but confessed he could now 'make no reckoning nor account of a certain or honest trade of life but has lived as a vagrant person'. The life of the petty minstrel was hard. Robert Dorey played one day until midnight for some milkmaids near Reading in 1623, and travelled the next day before sun-up to perform for 1d at a gentleman's house. John Parkins had purportedly served Lord Stafford, but was playing at fairs in Essex in 1634, and four years earlier had petitioned Stafford quarter sessions for poor relief.[55]

It was no coincidence that minstrels were poor and fell foul of the law,

because from the fourteenth century governments sought to suppress them. But it was Edward IV who rang the death knell of the petty minstrel by creating a gild with a monopoly over the profession. The tendency towards monopoly continued in the sixteenth century, when numerous towns organized musicians' gilds, or 'waits', to exclude strolling musicians.[56] Other forces working towards the isolation of the minstrel were cultural and social. In the later Middle Ages the upper classes began to prefer the new learned and lyrical compositions of the *trobaires* to the repetition of epics and popular songs of the minstrels or *joglars*. There was a social dimension to this parting of ways, because the *trobaires* were noblemen or bourgeois, while the minstrels were popular in recruitment. The second cultural development working against the minstrel was the rise of book-reading and the printed word. In the latter department the minstrel had a new rival, who ultimately stole his audience and whom we have already met, that is the licensed player.[57]

Ballad-singers were further casualties of cultural and political changes. Although not named in the vagrancy laws, they had the relevant characteristics. Like minstrels, they were transient, poor, and thought to be dishonest, immoral and seditious. From about 1570 the word ballad is a pejorative term. Both sellers and singers were considered criminals, their performances cloaks for larceny. Like Autolycus and Nightingale, the vendors and singers of ballads were sometimes difficult, shady characters. A Shropshire singer named Richard Rogers was ordered out of Norwich in 1600, and after he proposed marriage to a local widow was finally whipped. Another singer, Methuselah Flower of Tewkesbury, was hauled into Bridewell in 1642 as a rogue because he 'abused many in ill language and has not habitation'. Others were suspected of larceny, such as Walter Plummer of Southwark, who travelled in the Southwest in 1620 'carrying with him store of ballads to sing in his travels', and was stopped in Trowbridge fair.[58]

Singers also came under attack during the civil wars and Interregnum, when ballad-wars raged and governments were wary of popular gatherings. The House of Commons banned ballads from 1647 to 1656, and in 1648 the Provost-Marshal was ordered to seize singers and hawkers. The ubiquitous Flower was arrested again in 1654 in Bristol for 'singing of ballads, thereby contracting people together in a tumultuous manner', and a year later a Devizes man was despatched to a house of correction 'for singing of ballads contrary to the statute' at a time when Royalist plots were rife.[59] Officials normally looked askance at ballad-singers, but in such troubled times small provocation was needed to turn them against them.

Magicians and jugglers caused many of the same nightmares as other performers. Reginald Scot considered them to be 'deceiptful arts', like

cozening and witchcraft. Conjurers enjoyed a real vogue in the Elizabethan theatre. Scot's tract was the first to describe their tricks, but later publications show that the interest was ongoing. The art of legerdemain was literally 'nimbleness of hand'. According to Scot it included the three basic tricks of 'hiding and conveying of balls', 'the alteration of money', and shuffling cards.[60] From these manoeuvres the trickster progressed to more elaborate feats, some requiring machinery and assistants. They included 'to eat a knife, and to fetch it out of any other place'; 'to cut half your nose asunder, and to heal it again presently without any salve'; 'to cut off one's head, and to lay it in a platter'; and 'to thrust a dagger or bodkin into your guts . . . and to recover immediately'. These feats were actually performed, although not without risk. The head trick was successfully executed at Bartholomew fair in London in 1582, but a juggler who tried the dagger ploy in a Cheapside tavern was less fortunate: he was drunk and forgot to insert the requisite protective plate, and ended up stumbling into St Paul's churchyard to die.[61]

Like country fiddlers and ballad-singers, wandering jugglers lived on the edge of poverty and vagrancy charges. Richard Franckly, a Bedfordshire man arrested in Leicester in 1599, was a cooper by trade, 'but uses the art (as he says) of a tumbler', and was accused of vagrancy. Some transient performers defy classification. A Warminster man punished in Salisbury in 1607, 'having bells for his legs and using a kind of dancing', was probably a morris-dancer, but what should one make of an Edinburgh man 'using a kind of play upon bones and bells', who was punished in the town the year before?[62] England was evidently rich in itinerant entertainers, who evaded the licensing system if not the vagrancy laws.

ITINERANT HEALERS

This period saw increased regulation of medical practice, including the foundation of the Royal College of Physicians in 1518, to whom the government granted a monopoly over medicine in London and its suburbs; the incorporation of the Company of Barber-Surgeons in 1540, so that a seven-year apprenticeship was required to practise surgery and dentistry; and of the Apothecaries Company in the seventeenth century with similar powers. In the provinces the ecclesiastical authorities and the universities licensed physicians, surgeons and midwives. The new monopolies did not go unchallenged. During the civil wars and Interregnum critics attacked them on the grounds that licensing simply kept fees high. Despite state control, unlicensed healers remained popular throughout the period, a running sore to the monopolists. Among the charges levelled at them was vagrancy.[63]

Little is known about medical practice outside London and Norwich, licensed or otherwise, and transient healers are an entirely unknown quantity. Among vagrants they were an important professional group. Although church courts dealt with unlicensed practitioners, persons 'feigning themselves to have knowledge in physic' were covered by the vagrancy law of 1531. We also have the fascinating record of the Maidstone surgeon John Halle, who noted interlopers who visited the town between 1555 and 1564. Among them were a dozen or so itinerants, many of whom were from London, and who visited the countryside as well as towns. When they came to a new place, they drummed up business by publicity. One vagrant literally hung out his shingle in 1558, which stated that

> If any man, woman, or child be sick, or would be let blood, or be diseased with any manner of inward or outward griefs, as all manner of agues, or fevers, pleurisies, colic, stone, strangulation, impostumes, fistulas, canker, gouts, pocks, bone ache, and pain of the joints, which comes for lack of blood-letting, let them resort to the sign of the Saracen's Head, in the East Lane, and bring their waters with them to be seen, and they shall have remedy.
>
> By me, Thomas Luffkin.[64]

Transient healers came from a variety of trades. According to a statute of 1511, smiths and weavers were doing cures, although they lacked book-learning in medicine. The Maidstone intruders included a fuller, a shoemaker, a poulterer, a joiner and a sawyer. Why was it, Halle inquired, that 'so many rustical craftsmen leave their mysteries, and become physicians?' To look at the question from the other side, why were Halle and his fellow professionals so hostile to these nobodies? One charge against them centred on their violations of the new monopolies. By law physicians could practise physic and surgery, but surgeons only surgery, and both were supposed to be licensed. A vagrant named Mary Fen was reported to Warwick officials in 1587 as performing both professions without licence.[65]

Unlicensed healers were frauds in official eyes. Some were undoubtedly cynical swindlers. One admitted in Maidstone that he and two companions used the title of physician as 'a shift, mutually devised among them to get money'. But few willingly confessed to bilking patients. The issue of fraudulence was usually decided by reference to formal education. Halle attempted to show the ignorance and mistakes of his vagrant competitors, as when an itinerant physician's wife came to the town to purchase drugs but forgot some of their names. When the apothecary's wife asked her why the physician had not written out the order, she replied that he 'was a right Latinist, for he could write no English'. He had

convinced his customers in the Weald that he could speak Greek and Hebrew; the truth according to Halle was that he 'knew not a letter, or a "b" from a battledore'. In another instance Halle questioned a shoe-maker, who claimed to be expert in curing diseases of the eye. While admitting that he knew nothing about the nature of the human eye, even that he 'knew not how, or whereof a shoe was made', the man still insisted he could heal sore eyes.[66]

Such unorthodox healers harmed patients, the 1511 statute and Halle alleged. Robert Nichols came to the Maidstone area claiming to have been an assistant to the Queen's surgeon, and administered a purgation to a widow at Linton. She died within a few hours, whereupon he was arrested and imprisoned. When examined about his pretensions to heal, he claimed he could tell by the woman's complexion that her liver and lungs were rotten. But one official accused him of duping her, saying 'she was not sick, but thou told her so for thy filthy lucre, and she believed thee'. He was asked which medical authors he had read, and what different purgatives contained. When quizzed about what a spleen was, he replied that 'it was a disease in the side, baked hard like a biscuit'.[67]

The assumption was that itinerants used mobility as a 'tactical advantage' to cheat patients and to cut in on the licensed trade. Luffkin was asked, 'if you be so cunning as you are named, or as you would fain be esteemed to be, wherefore go you, and travel you from place to place?' Halle stated that 'no honest cunning man . . . will refuse to dwell and continue in some esteemed city or town'; nor 'run about here and there, through all the realm, thus like vagabonds, to deceive the unskillful people with their beastly doings'. Some were certainly mobile – for example an Oswestry healer who confessed 'many times to walk this country to his cures' in Warwick in 1581. Further alleged offences included theft, bigamy and diabolism.[68]

Despite their sins, there was clearly a market for the unlicensed transient. To Luffkin 'resorted all sorts of vain and indiscreet persons'; when the 'Latinist' set up in the Weald, there were 'people resorting to him far and nigh', and 'he was sought unto, and esteemed more a great deal than God'. One patient even threatened Halle with a dagger after the surgeon ridiculed the healer. That the public were prepared to make great efforts to see unorthodox healers is shown by a Worcestershire point-maker who travelled to a Somerset fair in 1610 after hearing that 'one White, which was very cunning in curing of sore legs', was going to be present.[69]

This lively market was based on a real need, which a statute of 1542 recognized by curbing the monopoly of the London surgeons and allowing any person to practise cures for external maladies and internal problems like the stone and agues. And it is possible that unlicensed

transients did some good. The Oswestry man and Mary Fen said they had 'helped many' with their physic and surgery, actually naming their patients in the West Midlands, while a Dorset truss-maker stated in 1629 that he had fixed many ruptures.[70]

Licensed healers were undoubtedly better read than unlicensed ones, but probably no better at curing many illnesses. The statute of 1542 remarked of surgeons that they 'oftentimes impair and hurt their patients, rather than do them good'. The approaches of many licensed practitioners were abstract and literary rather than practical. To test the shoemaker's knowledge, Halle asked him, 'What is an eye? whereof is it made? of what members or parts is it composed?', and Nichols was expected to define what a wound was, and what the natures of pepper and oysters were. Knowledge of general principles qualified one to practise under the new monopolies, but whether the patient profited greatly is doubtful. Licensed healers resorted to astrology, just as unorthodox ones did, while physicians fed their patients concoctions which included sheep dung and powdered mummies.[71] Halle's account shows how ambiguous was the position of the licensed monopolist because, despite his attacks upon the outlaws, he offered no alternative remedies to theirs. Instead he employed slander and libel to discredit them, and it was because men such as he had the ear of governments that unlicensed and transient healers were vagrants by law.

ERRANT CLERKS

Further vagrant professions included students and clerics, who can be treated together, since they were cognate occupations. Both had long histories as wayfarers. The early saints had tramped northern Europe converting the population and establishing monasteries; the mendicant orders were itinerant preachers, who begged in accordance with their vows of poverty; and students returned home in vacations and moved from school to school. In 1388 Parliament required university students who begged to carry testimonials from the Chancellor or suffer punishment in the stocks.[72] Sixteenth-century governments went still further, passing legislation which made students liable to arrest as vagrants. In Acts of 1531 and 1572 scholars were subject to serious punishments for unlicensed begging and vagrancy, and in a law of 1597 those who begged were labelled as vagrants, whether licensed or not.[73]

Learned itinerants were natural suspects, because of their education and travels to the continent: after the rebellion of 1569 a bill was proposed against disguised priests. A priest ordained under Mary was seized in Leicester in 1599 as a 'vagrant, recusant priest', and a 'dangerous wander-

ing popish recusant', and the occasion for the apprehension of the student Robert Constable in London in 1606 was a possible connection with the Gunpowder Plot.[74] In a later chapter it is shown that seminary priests were arrested *en route* to recusant centres.

Clerics and scholars experienced hard times in the seventeenth century. They were forced onto the roads in the Thirty Years War, the Irish rising of 1641, and by ejections of ministers in England in the 1640s and 1660s. They may also have become vagrants because of an unfavourable job market. The numbers matriculating at Oxford and Cambridge rose sharply between 1600 and 1630, and some historians have thought that unemployed clerks posed a threat to the social order.[75] Little evidence has been found of such alienation, but some certainly found it hard to secure livings and were forced to beg, steal and even emigrate. A preacher and minister born in Salisbury returned from Ireland in 1623 and wandered and begged his way to Somerset, where he was arrested for allegedly stealing clothing from hedges. The ex-vicar of Walton upon the Hill, arrested in Dorchester in 1629, was travelling all over Ireland and England 'to seek a place to serve in'. The clerical surplus also possibly led to less favourable treatment by the authorities. A student of Trinity College, Oxford, although homeless and penniless, received nothing in puritan Dorchester in 1631; another, from Magdalene College, Cambridge, was actually punished there in 1634, in spite of being sick and lame.[76]

WANDERING WIZARDS

Transient practitioners of white magic were subject to the vagrancy laws from 1531, when a statute included persons

> feigning themselves to have knowledge in . . . physiognomy, palmistry, or other crafty sciences whereby they bear the people in hand, that they can tell their destinies, deceases and fortunes, and such other like fantastical imaginations to the great deceit of the King's subjects.

Later Acts included similar provisions; in addition, there were statutes against witchcraft, which made it a felony.[77]

Those who practised magic were liable to prosecution in the church courts, but were also arrested by the civil authorities. Vagabonds overwhelmingly used white magic – finding stolen or lost goods and telling fortunes – rather than witchcraft, of which only three instances were found. There were some obvious benefits to being an itinerant wizard, because one could leave behind disappointed customers, although in general most cunning-folk were sedentary. It is rarely possible to discover much about wandering ones unless their customers became dissatisfied

or the authorities were sceptical. The evidence is therefore mainly of 'unsuccessful' or crooked white witches.[78]

A band of fortune-telling gypsies arrested in Yorkshire in 1650 provides a glimpse of how some transient wizards operated. Richard Smith, his wife Barbary and three others led a peripatetic existence, travelling to Northumberland from Herefordshire. The Brandsby constable alleged that they 'did tell fortunes to children and to others and asked them [for] money', which they denied. One woman stated that Barbary had promised her £60 in cash, three silver spoons and two gold rings that were buried, if she handed over half the cache, 1s 4d and some linens.[79]

Itinerant wizards were occasionally accused of fraud, but the authorities usually made the charge. To arouse clients' suspicions a wizard had to be blatantly crooked. A Kentish woman was caught cutting a woman's purse while telling her fortune in Somerset in 1625, but her previous customers had been well satisfied. In general, travelling wizards had no difficulty getting customers. A Caernarfonshire constable reported Harry Lloyd, a 'poor scholar', for practising there in 1636, but Lloyd had been working in the area for almost a decade. Eight years earlier he had lived in Tudweiliog with a couple whom he told he was a surgeon and a diviner, and 'that if any goods were lost he would tell how to come by them'. When he produced a linen sheet the woman had mislaid, his fame spread and many came to use his services.[80]

An itinerant wizard who was purportedly dumb was similarly successful in attracting clients in Craven in Yorkshire in 1652. During one week 'diverse from several parts of the country came to inquire, the wenches which husbands they should have and whence they should come, whether they should be widows . . . some men to inquire of stolen horses'. The man responded with signs in chalk and by mounting a stool and pointing it in various directions. Several reported 'that the said dumb man directed them very truly'. For his reward he accepted 1d, 2d, cans of ale, 'and of some, nothing'. Although a local husbandman thought the wizard only pretended to be dumb, he did not question his powers.[81] The success of fortune-tellers in drawing custom, and their clients' disappointment when the promised results did not materialize, show a real demand for their wares. But officials were more sceptical and to them a transient wizard, like many itinerant workers, offended on more than one count.

CONCLUSIONS

Although groups as diverse as apprentices and servants, ballad-singers, soldiers and students *prima facie* had little in common, if they were transient and/or out of work they were seen to endanger the state. To

those in authority these groups were far from innocuous. Those in the bottom labouring positions represented a large and vital part of the work-force. Pedlars violated gild restrictions, military men knew how to use weapons, entertainers brought together crowds who rioted, healers infringed state-sponsored monopolies, clerks were literate and un-employed, and wizards possibly associated with the devil. Elizabethan and early Stuart governments sought to control these groups through the vagrancy laws, but it is unlikely they wholly succeeded.

Part Three
Vagrants, society and the state

Chapter 7

The seminary of vagabondage

Begging cast the vagrant poor in a different role from working, and one that was no more comfortable. Rather than providing a service, however dubious in value, they in effect craved payment for doing nothing more than suffering and departing after the traditional 'God bless ye'. In addition, mendicancy brought them face to face with the public and the authorities at a time when, for three reasons, the relationship between supplicants and donors was an increasingly uneasy one. First, learned opinion, as we have seen earlier, was at best ambivalent and at worst hostile towards begging, often treating it as hypocrisy and theft rather than a sign of holiness. Secondly, the numbers moving about to solicit alms were increasing, particularly in the hard years between 1620 and 1650. Thirdly, the state poor relief system, which was the law of the land by 1600, seemed on the surface to have obviated the need for mendicancy. In this system, governments attempted to distinguish between worthy and false beggars, encouraging officials to relieve the first and punish the second. Although a tidy distinction in theory, it was unworkable in practice. Indeed it arguably fostered fraudulent begging by creating categories of deserving poor who were officially licensed to beg.

The literate élites castigated the able-bodied mendicant for being workshy and wicked, but they stopped short of completely rejecting him. Perkins attacked begging as the 'very seminary of vagabonds, rogues, and straggling persons, which have no calling, nor are of any corporation, church, or commonwealth'. But he and others would not refuse alms in case a person in genuine need were to perish, which could endanger the soul of the person who turned the beggar away, and provoke God's wrath. As the authors of a set of homilies published in 1596 stated, 'we are all God's beggars; that God therefore may acknowledge his beggars, let us not despise ours'. This ambiguous stance also arose from a fear that a wholesale casting out of beggars might encourage the decline of charity.[1]

The upshot was some allowance for mendicancy, which opened the door to frauds and outright vagrants.

THE BEGGAR'S BURDEN

Tudor tramps were 'analysed into species by the curious or scientific', as Tawney observed, but they still defy any simple (and therefore useful) classification. Some mendicants conformed to the literary stereotypes of the period, as will be shortly demonstrated. But not all beggars were legally vagrants and ultimately, because of almost infinite variations in their conditions, there were probably as many types of beggar as there were beggars.[2] Most of them were probably persons who received relief in their parishes from relatives, friends and neighbours, and who are largely unrecorded. In fact, local mendicancy was officially condoned in the poor laws, which usually limited it to the parish or hundred, and to those licensed by the local authorities. An Act of 1597 continued such provision where it involved 'relief of victuals', so that for most of the period local paupers who abided by the rules were left undisturbed.[3]

Yet even native beggars posed problems. The well-known census of Norwich's poor in 1570 was prompted by rampant begging among the town's 2300 paupers. In Warwick St Mary's in 1587 it was the 'disorder of beggars' that spurred Thomas Cartwright to instigate a similar survey there. And witchcraft accusations usually arose from the refusal of alms to a local beggar woman, who then cursed the misanthrope.[4] Thus ambivalent feelings about beggars were not confined to out-and-out vagabonds.

Itinerant, licensed beggars are rather better documented than local ones, because their condition was closer to vagrancy and, for that reason, their brushes with the law were more frequent. Basically there were four types of official licence. One was the letter or testimonial that students and military men were supposed to have; the second was a passport that convicted vagrants were to carry as they travelled home; the third was a licence to beg outside one's locality if the place were overburdened with paupers; and the fourth was a 'brief', which stated that the holder had suffered a calamity and was allowed to collect for his losses. The last might be issued by the Lord Chancellor, but local officials also provided them, as well as the other three. Proctors who travelled the country collecting for charity had papers similar to briefs. Three officials generally doled out alms to licensed beggars: the chamberlain in large towns; and constables and churchwardens in villages.[5]

Official charity to licensed and transient mendicants was significant and growing. At Leverton in Lincolnshire the local poor cost the parish £1 1s 8d in 1567, but another 16s 6d was paid to 'certain proctors of poor

houses, and others having licences to gather alms'. At Doncaster from
October 1627 to October 1628 such payments were seven times higher
than casual relief to the local poor, and the decade saw a rise in the
numbers relieved from 373 in 1621–2 to 597 in 1627–8. The town possibly
saw exceptionally large multitudes pass, because of its position astride
the Great North Road, but even small villages witnessed the passage of
large and growing numbers of licensed beggars. Barcheston, a south
Warwickshire village of only twenty-five households in 1670, relieved
close on 100 a year in the 1630s. In Upton in Nottinghamshire churchwardens gave doles to just 3 transients in 1608, but to 32 in 1632
and to over 130 in 1641.[6] Other Midland parishes relieved even
greater numbers and experienced similar rises, as noted earlier in
Chapter 3.

Some beggars contrived to live from casual alms. Agnes Cawsey's
husband was employed as a scarecrow in Bedfordshire, and they sometimes begged there. After his death, however, she became a full-time
mendicant, going from house to house in the parish, and then beyond
until her arrest in Essex in 1576. For the 1620s and 1630s the amount of
evidence for people – both Irish and native English – living permanently
on doles is quite staggering. A Salisbury couple apprehended in Dorchester in 1634 admitted 'wandering up and down the country, living by the
alms of good people' for two years, while a 20-year-old confessed in Essex
a year later that he had lived an itinerant life of begging since the age of 5.[7]
Some piled up considerable sums: a Yorkshire beggar had over £10 in his
possession in Exeter in 1566; others carried sums ranging from 21s to £5.
But the bulk of transient beggars never accumulated such wealth. When
searched, they usually had a few coppers, some articles of household
goods, clothing and pedlary.[8] Begging might have been as lucrative as
working in the early seventeenth century, but that is not really saying
much.

Many types of person became licensed and itinerant beggars. There
were Protestant refugees from the Palatinate in the 1620s; Irish ones, both
Protestant and Catholic, in the 1630s and 1640s; and also the victims of the
civil wars at home. But the demand for assistance was greater than that
generated by political and religious upheavals. Almost three-fifths of
those relieved in Doncaster in 1621–2 were listed simply as 'poor with
passes'; another quarter were soldiers and mariners; and the remainder
an assortment of cripples, students and convicted rogues.[9] Legally,
licensed beggars were not vagrants, but only the most legalistic mind can
treat the two groups as wholly distinct. It was commonly assumed that
many who carried papers were actually vagrant frauds, and there was
some truth to these assertions.

The distinction between true and false beggars almost guaranteed that there would be frauds, as did the licensing provisions in the poor laws. The result was a good deal of counterfeiting, which did nothing to enhance the image of mendicants. Proctors were one relatively upright group of legal beggars, who collected for institutions as diverse as prisons and university colleges. They carried letters patent stating the names of the sponsoring body and the collector, the length of time and the places in which collections were authorized, and an exhortation to local officials. Proctors are an elusive group, however, because they were rarely arrested and had few fraudulent imitators. Awdeley, referring to them as 'fraters', complained that they preyed upon poor women in markets. Harman noted that they 'carry black boxes at their girdle, wherein they have a brief of the Queen's Majesty's letters patents'. They were rarely bothered, he noted, because their licence was difficult to forge, its seal being the Great Seal, but one or two were arrested for abusing their licences.[10]

Disease and disaster generated licensed mendicants galore in this period. Parish records show endless processions of the deaf and dumb, blind, mad, shipwrecked, crippled, epileptic, and fire victims. The usual licence was the brief which, since it was issued by many authorities, was subject to frequent forgery. Fire was a common calamity, whole towns burning down in a matter of hours, because buildings were cheaply constructed of wood, and naked flames were the main sources of heat and light. A woman arrested in Leicester in 1606 reported leaving Tiverton after a fire in 1598. Peter Willis and his wife left Porlock after the town burned down in 1623, trekking to London with their children and his sister to stay with relatives.[11]

Injuries suffered in accidents must have been so common that they were hardly worth mentioning. In addition to fires, the population faced the perils of collapsing buildings and unsteady carts. Early industrial equipment was primitive and dangerous; miners were the most obvious group to suffer. A Cornish tinworker stated before Somerset justices in 1609 that he begged because of a disability incurred when timbers collapsed in a mine and five men were killed. Another tinner took his wife and five children with him to Bath in 1617, where he hoped to receive treatment for bruises sustained in accidents, and they begged food and lodgings along the way. But for all the genuine cases, there were undoubtedly some frauds. Harman described false collectors for fires as 'demanders for glimmer': they 'most lamentably demand your charity, and will quickly shed salt tears, they be so tender-hearted'. They never begged in their native shires for fear of detection, and carried wallets in which they stowed gifts of wool and cheese. They might garner six or

seven shillings a week, a princely sum for a wage-earner in the 1560s, and were mainly women.[12]

There is no doubt that fraudulent collections were a minor growth industry. In 1632 the Privy Council ordered that briefs should only be issued under the Great Seal, but Lord Keeper Coventry lamented in 1637 that the abuses continued. He reported authorizing no more than eight collections a year per county, yet 'a far greater number have been pressed upon the country'. The origins of the counterfeiting lay not in the Lord Keeper's office, but in the multitude of authorities who issued the documents.[13]

Some cases of fake documents which were detected show how lucrative fraudulent begging could be. One counterfeit beggar seized in Essex in 1583 had £5 in his purse. Even if such sums were rare, itinerant begging provided a living in the short term. John Lyning, *alias* George Harris, confessed to Bath magistrates in 1616 that he had recently collected 6s in Long Ashton, 12d in Batheaston, and 2s in Keynsham. Similarly, in a single day in 1622 John Bowden obtained 1s from a gentleman in West Pennard, 1s 6d from a churchwarden in Badtonsborough, and 6d in another parish. Three shillings a day was a handsome wage in the 1620s.[14]

The manufacture of false briefs was London-based, because of the specialized knowledge of royal seals. Forgeries could be purchased in the provinces, but they were probably made in the metropolis. Lyning, *alias* Harris, bought a pile from John Mason in the Nag's Head in Red Cross Street in 1615, and within a month had sold sixty between Reading and Bristol. He assured the examining justice that 'if he might have his liberty, he would find out 20 more counterfeits in the like case'. At this level, forgery was big business.[15]

But it was rare for a distributor to be caught peddling forgeries; rarer still for big fish like Mason to turn up in the records. Usually the small fry were arrested, because of their ineptitude. Bowden, for example, turned up again in Somerset in 1625 with the same story as two years earlier. He received 1s from a churchwarden in Shepton Montague after saying he was *en route* to Minehead to take ship for Ireland. But he was seen some days later in Bruton by the churchwarden's son, who knew that Bruton was not on the road to Minehead. Likewise, a greedy Warminster man petitioned for a brief in 1635, claiming a loss of £20 by fire, but his neighbours informed justices that his valuables were saved during the conflagration.[16]

Mendicants claimed to have myriad afflictions, some of which were genuine and some fraudulent. The latter are prominent in the literature of roguery, but that should not blind us to the fact that illness was pervasive. The catastrophic effects of plague, typhus and influenza have been

studied, but comparatively little is known about the lingering cases of lameness, blindness and deafness. Sickly and handicapped beggars must have been common sights in the streets and highways of Elizabethan England. In addition to the local sick poor, there were cripples travelling to Bath and Buxton for cures, and wandering blind persons. Parish records even in remote villages record their passage. In the town of Doncaster in 1621–2 nearly one in ten itinerants given relief was disabled or ill, and that figure does not include disabled military men. The movement into spa towns was huge: in Bath two parishes near the baths recorded almost a fifth of their burials as 'strangers' between 1569 and 1625.[17]

The rogue writers listed cripples in their catalogues of false beggars. Awdeley called them 'washmen' or 'palliards', who 'lie in the highway with lame or sore legs or arms to beg', and applied spearwort and ratsbane to the limbs. The first caused blisters that later disappeared; the second, incurable sores. Harman added a few embellishments and the term 'clapper-dudgeon' to the literature on cripples. Such dissemblers existed in real life – for instance, a man reported in the Southwest, who kept a lame arm 'so filthy that it smells very contagious' – but by the same token there were genuine blind and lame beggars who posed real problems.[18] On the road they might worsen and remain in the parish, which would be stuck having to support or, at least, to bury them. Villages sometimes reacted with hostility when cripples arrived in carts, or on the sledges used to shift them. Helperby in North Yorkshire purportedly takes its name from an incident when an old vagrant woman halted and could advance no further, and villagers shouted 'Help her by, Help her by'. Local authorities were no less determined to shift the disabled. In 1622 a pauper-catcher employed by a Southwark parish grabbed an old man who was 'not able to go, stand or speak', discovered that he formerly lodged in a neighbouring parish, and had two men carry him there.[19]

Invalids obviously received short shrift on such occasions. Between December 1582 and March 1583 Catherine Boland was shunted back and forth between a Northamptonshire parish and the city of Leicester, while officials fought over where she was born. In 1652 Mary Wooles broke her back when she fell downstairs in London. She was despatched to Bath after her legs gave way and her backbone began to protrude, but the authorities in Whiteparish returned her to St Bride's parish, which in turn returned her to Wiltshire, from where she was again posted back to London. The conveying of the disabled provoked some major disputes between communities. Hertfordshire officials ordered the county closed to 'cripples, diseased and impotent persons' in 1625, because they were a 'great and unnecessary charge', and villages

near Doncaster were at odds in 1635 over the cost of transporting invalids.[20]

Some authorities punished the genuinely blind and disabled, because that was the law if they did not possess licences. In Oxfordshire in 1572 an 'impotent woman' with a child was chastised for vagrancy, while Ellen Dixon, a blind woman, was whipped, stocked and sent away from Windermere in 1635. William Clay, who had 'no legs and is a vagrant and wicked liver', was incarcerated in Bridewell in 1640 and put to work making gloves.[21]

The wandering lunatic was dubbed an Abram-man or Tom O'Bedlam. Awdeley described him as 'he that walks bare-armed, and bare-legged, and feigns himself mad, and carries a pack of wool, or a stick with bacon on it, or such-like toy, and names himself Poor Tom', and Shakespeare used the character as a disguise for Edgar in *King Lear* (1605–6). The author of *O Per Se O* (1612) reported that Abram-men made marks on their arms with 'burnt paper, piss and gunpowder' to show they had been in Bethlehem hospital. They acted mad: 'some make an horrid noise . . . some whoop . . . some show only a kind of wild distracted ugly look . . . Some dance, but keep no measure; others leap up and down'.[22] According to Aubrey, 'they had on their left arm an armilla of tin, printed in some works', which they could not remove. He claimed they were not seen after the civil wars, but in 1675 the governors of Bethlehem published an announcement stating that vagrants wearing such plates and purporting to have been inmates were frauds; another observer reported seeing them in eighteenth-century Worcestershire.[23]

The origins of Tom O'Bedlam men are obscure. Aubrey thought they were licensed to beg, but no evidence has been found to support his opinion, and the governors' notice of 1675 positively refutes it. Bethlehem, founded as the hospital of St Mary of Bethlehem, was the major English lunatic asylum in late medieval and early modern times. From it originated the term Tom O'Bedlam; the name Abram-man may come from a ward in the hospital. It was a small institution, containing only twenty to thirty inmates in the early seventeenth century.[24] But if institutionalized lunatics were so few, why did they turn up wandering and begging? One answer is that Bethlehem's facilities were totally insufficient to care for all the country's lunatics; a second, that it was expensive to keep them there. The hospital was a quasi-private institution in which inmates, their families or parishes had to pay for their care; paying one's fees was indeed cited as their reason for begging. A cure was never certain, so that a family or parish might be burdened for years. Bethlehem's inmates in 1624 had on average been there for 6 years, and a substantial minority of almost a quarter between 14 and 20 years. Thus it is understandable that they were encouraged to beg; and that the majority

of the mad received extramural treatment from physicians like Richard Napier.[25]

Tom O'Bedlam men, or persons impersonating them, were arrested as vagabonds. The legal requirement that unlicensed mendicants be treated as vagrants covered the mad as well as the sane. Moreover, the treatment of lunatics, as Foucault observed, paralleled the institutionalization of the poor.[26] Hence the wearing of badges by madmen, just as cities badged their poor. Furthermore, lunatics were locked up in bridewells along with vagrants. A High Ongar man was despatched to an Essex house of correction in 1617 'for his disorderly life through lunacy', and the Norwich Mayor's Court ordered that 'Withers' wife, being distracted, is committed to bridewell' in 1633.[27]

The authorities sought to distinguish the truly mad from the fraudulent, which was not difficult in some cases. A Shrewsbury man confessed to London officials in 1578 that, having purchased a false licence for 2s 6d at the Griffin in Waltham Cross, he had gone about for five months 'feigning himself to have been in Bedlam this two years and a quarter for lunacy, and to beg for his fees'. Similarly, Francis Easterbrooke 'did at the first pretend lunacy, but afterwards confessed he was never in Bedlam' after his arrest in Wiltshire in 1618.[28]

But Tom O'Bedlam men were rarely such obvious dissemblers. It would be hard to prove that they were more disruptive than other beggars. Some may have acted strangely simply to attract sympathy and to present a convincing show. But some incidents involving obstreperousness were too unplanned always to be dismissed. After Sir Thomas Walsingham sent Bartholomew Bricket to Bridewell as a false lunatic in 1576 the man was punished for refusing to work, and a 'counterfeit Bedlam' refused alms by a Wiltshire man in 1614 threatened 'to beat him down with a crab-tree cudgel'.[29] It is conceivable, at least, that such cases might have been genuine.

Elizabethans had as much difficulty treating illnesses of the mind as those of the body. Medical practitioners normally left their care to the clergy, who were supposed to practise 'spiritual physic'. Although the use of observations and case-histories was on the increase, as in Napier's practice, madness was mainly treated with reference to humoral theory and demonology. Lunatics suffered from melancholy, or were possessed; the remedies included eating roasted mice, exorcism, beatings and, more sensibly, keeping patients calm.[30] When cures proved impossible, officials were often left to pick up the pieces, and they experienced great difficulties. That is evident from their dealings with supposedly 'fraudulent' cases. Matthew Childerman was discharged from an Essex house of correction in 1614 as a lunatic, but when incarcerated the previous year he was 'suspected to be but counterfeit'. A Cambridgeshire man placed in

the same house in 1627, because he was 'supposed to be some counter-feit', was later released *non compos mentis*.[31] Such contradictory evidence suggests that it would be unwise to accept the literary portrayal of all Tom O'Bedlam men as impostors.

Harman described beggars who pretended to be dumb as 'dummerers' and claimed they were mostly Welsh. They would not speak 'unless they have extreme punishment, but will gape, and with a marvellous force will hold down their tongues doubled, groaning for your charity, and holding up their hands full piteously'. For obvious reasons, the evidence of dumb beggars is heavily biased towards frauds. As with other types of false mendicancy, it could be profitable and achieve a certain level of sophis-tication. Two women were punished in Bridewell in 1560 for persuading a 14-year-old boy to act deaf and dumb. They had a scrivener draw up a letter of supplication to the Queen for a licence to beg under the Great Seal, with which they were taking between 1s 4d and 2s 4d a day.[32] As with false briefs, London was the main source of forged licences. Richard Beavan, arrested in Wiltshire in 1613, had bought his for 3s from a scrivener named Lightfoot in an alehouse near Tower Hill. It bore the signatures of the three masters of Requests, the seal of the same Court, and was a good counterfeit: Beavan had used it for almost six months in three different counties. But sham dumb beggars sometimes obtained permits in the provinces. John Gibb, 'a counterfeit dumb maunderer', purchased his from a schoolteacher in Marshfield in Gloucestershire.[33] Here, then, is evidence of successful fraudulent mendicancy, but it is impossible to say whether the fakes outnumbered the genuine cases.

Beggars suffered, or claimed to suffer from epilepsy, paralysis and syphilis. Phoney epileptics, or persons with 'falling sickness', received special mention in Harman's gallery of rogues as 'counterfeit cranks'. One of them, Nicholas Jennings, *alias* Blunt, provides one of the pam-phlet's most memorable portraits. Jennings went naked from the waist up, wore tattered remnants on the rest of his body and kept blood in a bladder to smear on his face (other cranks used soap to make their mouths foam). At night he returned to a comfortable home in the London suburbs, where he changed into perfectly good clothes. On just one day in 1566 he collected 13s 3½d, according to Harman.[34] In this instance the writer's statements can be corroborated, which has rarely been done when historians have employed material from the rogue literature. Jennings actually appeared before the Court of Aldermen in January 1567, that is, contemporaneously with Harman's publication and four months after the reported meeting with the Kentish gentleman. He was named only as Blunt, but the remainder of the description is remarkably close to Harman's. Blunt was ordered to be whipped at a cart's tail, 'having a picture of his own personage deformed in form and manner . . . as he was

wont to use, the same carried before him upon a long pole', and then put to hard labour in Bridewell.[35]

Jennings/Blunt was not the first to feign epilepsy. Miles Rose confessed to dissembling the disease in London parish churches in 1518. When he fell, people put silver cramp rings on his fingers, which English monarchs traditionally blessed for the purpose, and gave him twopences. Others feigned 'shaking palsey', a kind of paralysis. A boy named Robert Shakesbury appeared before the Court of Aldermen in 1548, and fooled them into believing that he had 'the palsey, or some other disease wherewith his body shakes, vexing sore'. But he was found out on a second appearance four months later, whipped and sent away.[36] Syphilis was one illness that even the cleverest beggar would have difficulty feigning, because it so ravaged the body. Vagrants who were infected in London were despatched to Bridewell, and then often transferred to St Thomas's hospital, Southwark, for treatment. A peculiar case of sham 'illness' occurred in the capital in 1560, when a woman 'feigned herself with a pack of clothes to be great with child' and was apprehended begging.[37]

The variety and versatility of beggars far outstripped the literature's stereotypes. According to one account of those living on the Isle of Anglesey in James I's reign, newly-wed couples were expected to go begging during their first year of marriage. They split up for the purpose, the men departing in sowing time to gather seed, and later tramping 'over all the country where they can reach' to collect corn during the harvest. Meantime, their brides paired off with old women – 'old impudent drab[s] . . . that can allege either kindred, alliance, nursery, or some affinity or other, with all men'. These female couples, known as *gwragedd cawsa*, travelled to solicit cheese, wool, hemp and flax. They were ubiquitous: 'you shall many a day see half a dozen or half a score couples of these at an honest man's door, using all kinds of rhetorical persuasions'.[38]

Another mendicant group in North Wales were milk-wives, old women who lived in cottages, sometimes two or three to a house, who 'walk abroad in the daytime, with their pitchers, under colour to gather some milk from house to house'. They begged, it was stated, not from need, but to 'know the humour of all men, especially the goodwife of every house'. Then they would 'devise news from all parts, and rip up all the neighbours' most secret faults, and have all the craft of the devil to glaver, flatter and insinuate unto fools'. They even provoked dissension among neighbours and persuaded children to pilfer food from parents, it was alleged. Some circumstantial evidence supports this literary account. Women were a key element among the poor in Caernarfonshire villages under James I, heading three-quarters of households and outnumbering couples and males in the adult pauper population by as much as ten to

one. In England women were also usually in a majority among the poor, but never to this extent, which suggests remarkably high levels of out-migration among North Welsh males.[39].

From the evidence examined here it is impossible to state whether the majority of beggars were rogues. Certainly there are numerous instances of deceitful begging which, whether they numbered 100 or 1000, could be (and were) interpreted to apply to all mendicants. But officials were almost in the position of creating a self-fulfilling prophecy. Because they believed that some paupers were worthy cases, who should be allowed to travel and collect alms, they opened the door to fraudulent, professional begging. Not surprisingly, considering the destitution experienced in the period, some of the poor seized such opportunities with both hands.

THE PITFALLS OF CHARITY

Notwithstanding statutory attempts to place mendicancy by transients under the control of officials, the public at large undoubtedly felt the main impact of the problem. The itinerant beggar could not be kept under permanent surveillance and, in the event, was unlikely to limit his supplications to the churchwardens and chamberlains. At any rate, there was a long tradition of charity to all-comers, even if contemporary observers were busy charting its decline; and there were goodly quantities of disposable wealth in the hands of prosperous gentlemen, yeomen and burghers. It is probable, as observed earlier, that most begging involved local persons who knew one another, and passed off without incident. Yet it has been seen that even local mendicancy incited official hostility and witchcraft accusations, and where itinerant paupers are concerned the evidence suggests considerable unease in relations between them and the public.

Some vagrant beggars got into trouble for importuning. A Derbyshire carpenter was banished from London in 1536 for 'resorting into men's houses without licence to ask his alms'. London householders complained again in 1601 about being 'continually troubled with relieving of beggars at their doors', and the Common Council ordered their suppression. But little could be done to stem the tide. In the 1620s mendicants were sent to Bridewell for hanging on people's coaches as they passed. Such aggression was not limited to the capital. An unemployed Lancashire man was arrested in Warwick in 1581 after he walked into a house uninvited and demanded something to drink 'for God's sake'.[40]

Beggars could be menacing and violent, even to the highest in the land. When the Queen went to Islington to take the air one evening in 1582, she was suddenly 'environed with a number of rogues', who were presum-

ably begging. Harman wrote of vagrants who, 'if they ask at a stout yeoman's or farmer's house his charity, they will go strong as three or four in a company; where, for fear more than good will, they often have relief'. Such incidents in fact took place. An Essex woman was confronted with three vagabonds in 1611 who told her that 'if she would not open the door and give them beer, they would have beer and something else'. That was an unpleasant, but by no means unique, encounter. Another dangerous beggar was Stephen Martin of Filey, who was branded in York in 1649 after forcibly entering a house, assaulting a young gentlewoman, and declining to depart until she gave him something.[41]

The beggar's by-employment was assumed to be theft, as in the nursery rhyme

> Tinker, tailor
> Soldier, sailor
> Rich man, poor man
> Beggar man, thief.

Thomas More considered that thievery was the only alternative to begging for the dispossessed; Brinkelow protested in 1546 that the new owners of monastic lands were so stingy that thousands were driven 'to rob and steal, to get food for us and our poor wives and children'.[42] Mendicants stole from the very persons who relieved them. A Stroudwater vagrant, given lodgings in the stables of a Wiltshire man in 1623, rose at 4 a.m. and left with farm implements and clothing. A pauper woman provided with shelter near Alford in 1634 departed in the middle of the night with a pile of bed linen and clothes, which she sold at an alehouse.[43]

Other beggars walked into houses and lifted what they pleased. Jane Powell of Cound admitted stealing a Bible from a Shrewsbury house in 1622, where she came 'to crave an alms', while a Faversham man who begged in Sussex in 1625 carried off meat and a loaf of bread from one house.[44] They also pilfered clothes from gardens. That was evidently on the minds of three women who came to the gate of a Hertfordshire yeoman's house in 1590, two of them soliciting doles while the third sneaked up on a hedge. An itinerant weaver received alms in a Wiltshire village in 1617 and proceeded to clear a hedge of its contents. Harman reported that upright men staked out burglaries in the course of begging. That was possibly true of a Somerset labourer charged with breaking into a house and stealing a long list of goods in 1623, who claimed he was only there to crave relief.[45] It is unlikely, however, that all such thefts were premeditated. More likely, beggars turned up hoping for the best, whether legally gained or not.

The public understandably refused to succour beggars. The main

motive for rejecting them was probably fear. A Southampton landlord turned away a man in 1577 who 'came lately out of trouble from London', and an Ashford woman rebuffed a vagrant girl with a newborn baby in 1604 'for fear of sickness'. Not even kinship necessarily guaranteed a warm reception, judging by the experience of a Dorchester woman in 1608. She escaped gaol before Chard assizes and made her way to her husband's kinsman, but he refused to aid her until she camped in the near-by fields.[46] The 1630s saw determined official efforts to stem the rising tide of itinerant paupers. Buckingham officials reported that 'the inhabitants will not relieve strange beggars' after restraining their own poor from begging and making a by-law against vagrants. About the same time, as was seen in Chapter 5, puritan Dorchester showed little tolerance for sturdy mendicants, even university men.[47]

Refusals of charity triggered abuse from mendicants. When a gentleman refused him alms, an Irish sailor prophesied in Maldon in 1573 that the man's ear 'would breed a scab before Easter day', while a vagrant travelling from Plymouth to Gravesend 'fell to railing with many foul speeches' when he was turned away in Wiltshire in 1613. Some beggars were provoked to violence when spurned. A Southwark cripple was locked up in Bridewell in 1605 for cursing those who rejected his supplications, and for hitting a constable in the face with a clog.[48] Others turned to theft. A servant and her mistress decided to become thieves in Somerset in 1613 because, they said, 'so many misers were abroad, of whom, if a poor body asked a piece of bread for need, they would not give it'. But menaces and uproars were not always the work of alms-seekers. A Yorkshire beggar had the temerity to enter uninvited the house of Isaac Terry in Chartham in 1606, which the landlord found presumptuous. He ordered the man to go to the door, and when he did not move quickly enough, Terry threw him out.[49]

CONCLUSIONS

Thus in some measure the ambivalent feelings about transient beggars expressed in the literate élites and the poor laws were shared by the public. Yet the public response was not wholly negative. The Southampton innkeeper who denied lodgings to the supplicant in 1577 still gave him 6d to see him on his way, while the girl turned down by one Ashford resident in 1604 was relieved by two others.[50] Despite official hostility and numerous frauds, there was evidently a good deal of residual public sympathy for the itinerant beggar, and it lasted for centuries in the countryside, judging by Flora Thompson's description of Lark Rise in the 1880s.[51] Nevertheless, it seems that distrust of the mendicant, including local ones, accelerated considerably in the early

modern period owing to a more critical opinion of idleness, rising
numbers of itinerant poor, and state intervention to separate the deserving from the reprobate. Ironically, the attempt to assist the worthy ones
through a system of licensing aggravated the problem of the unworthy by
encouraging deceptions. The long-term solution – a Welfare State without such means tests – is still a utopian dream.

Chapter 8

The underworld uncovered

The opprobrium directed against vagabonds arose in large measure from the crimes they committed above and beyond illegal begging. To what extent, however, was there an underworld of vagrant crime, as the literate classes thought and later historians have believed? And if it existed, how extensive was it, how was it organized, what crimes did its members perpetrate, and how great a threat did it pose to the established order? This chapter attempts to answer these questions, chiefly from the justices' examinations of vagrants, a source which is well suited to the task. Unlike the literature of roguery, which was largely fictional, examinations recount the real-life criminal activities of vagrants. Furthermore, in contrast to other judicial records such as indictments and presentments, which are terse and uninformative, vagabonds' depositions yield a wealth of detail of suspected crimes, their organization and execution.

The results of the investigation suggest that the extent of organized, professional crime among vagrants has been exaggerated. A dangerous minority were alleged to have committed serious offences that included burglary, fraudulence, highway robbery, assault, sectarianism, sedition and counterfeiting, and these misdeeds are analysed here. In cataloguing the crimes of those examined, however, it should not be assumed that the list is exhaustive. The misdemeanour offence of vagrancy, which involved the majority of vagabonds, is not considered here; nor is illegal begging, examined in the previous chapter. These considerations need to be borne in mind, for they help to explain why vagrancy was ultimately a more intractable problem than the crimes of the underworld.

REALITY OR ILLUSION?

The expression 'Elizabethan underworld' was coined by Professor Judges in the 1930s, and since then the notion of an anti-society of rogues has

persisted in historical studies.[1] Vagabonds, according to one recent study, were 'highly organized – far more efficiently organized, indeed, than the forces of law and order'. They had divisions of labour, demarcated areas of operation, systems for disposing of goods and for training recruits.[2] Another authority suggests that vagabonds often travelled in gangs of 40 to 50 members, with recognized leaders, their doxies and the rank and file.[3]

These interpretations are misleading. Based largely upon literary sources, they exaggerate the underworld element among vagrants. Examination by justices is one possible criterion for underworld membership, since suspects were frequently questioned about more serious crimes than the misdemeanour of vagrancy. By that standard a minority of vagabonds were suspected of underworld involvement. Thus in Wiltshire the number punished as misdemeanants surpassed those examined by 2 to 1 between 1603 and 1620, and almost 5 to 1 between 1621 and 1638.[4] Another indicator of the hard-core element among vagrants is the number of repeat offenders, which can be calculated for early seventeenth-century London, where prior offences were at times regularly noted. There, rates of 'recidivism' worsened, rising from 1 in 4.6 in 1602 to 1 in 3.4 by 1631, but still involved a minority.[5] The evidence examined here suggests that elements existed that were suspected of more serious crimes and were repeatedly arrested, but that they comprised at most a third of vagrants.

In addition, the evidence adduced to show that vagabonds were organized in gangs is unconvincing. One study cites a letter from the Recorder of London to Burghley, which describes a school for pickpockets near Billingsgate in 1585. This is an interesting case of a school for crime, but it does not demonstrate that the thieves worked together in gangs after graduating.[6] The letter from the Somerset justice Hext to Burghley in 1596, which purportedly states that vagrants travelled in bands of forty to fifty, turns out to say nothing of the sort. Instead it reports *one* instance when '40, sometimes 60 [*sic*]' gathered weekly in a remote hay-house.[7]

How should we define a gang? Is it simply more than one person, or several? As was shown in Chapter 4, most vagabonds were accompanied by at least one other, groups of three or more increased their proportion of the total in the early seventeenth century, and the Irish and gypsies travelled in extended families. Groups of vagrant youths numbering several members also frequented the streets of London, and gangs of burglars, highwaymen and gamblers are examined shortly. Troops of forty members or more were quite exceptional, but it has been seen in the last chapter that a handful of rogues might wreak havoc in a community. Clearly, the question of gangs depended on a person's point of view.

To someone who was alone, two or three vagabonds might be a gang.

There is limited evidence of hierarchies among vagrants. A London vagabond told Kent officials in 1597 that he was the 'Lord of Rogues', but what that meant is unclear.[8] To people living in a society obsessed with hierarchy, it was natural to assume that criminals had leaders and followers. Evidence of solidarity among vagrants is also scarce. They occasionally referred to one another as 'brethren' and 'walk-fellows'; when Cranfield's steward met thirty of them in Gloucestershire in 1636, he found they 'will admit no strangers to come amongst them'.[9] Gypsies, the Irish and certain occupations also stuck together. But gangs were fluid in membership. They broke up to avoid capture, when members were arrested, and when disputes occurred among members.

The clearest sign of cohesion among vagabonds is their canting vocabulary. Harman recorded over 100 phrases and words, Professor Judges noted over 300 in the literature of roguery, and Francis Grose's *Classical Dictionary of the Vulgar Tongue* (1785) listed thousands.[10] Vagrants were caught using canting jargon, or admitted knowing it. Two women seized in Essex in 1580 were overheard speaking 'Pedlar's French', which was synonymous with canting, and other vagrants confessed to knowledge of it. In her deposition before Dorset justices in 1613 Mary Roberts used cant expressions like 'glimmer maunderer', 'dumb maunderer' (a counterfeit dumb person) and 'fakers' (makers of false passports).[11]

The origins of cant are obscure. Harman stated that it first developed in the 1530s, but there are many earlier references dating from the *Liber Vagatorum, c.* 1509, which listed over 200 words.[12] There is also disagreement about the etymology of the word. Some authorities trace it to the mendicant orders and the whining manner in which they and later secular beggars solicited alms. Others, however, think it was taken from the Latin and French words for chanting and singing; still others, that it has an Irish or Gaelic origin.[13]

How far English vagrants employed cant is difficult to establish. The rogue writers reported that it was in general usage by Elizabethan times, and later dictionaries show its vocabulary increasing. It is possible that vagabonds learnt cant from childhood, but knowledge of it was not confined to them. Greene and Dekker were not of the poor, and yet knew some words, and a vagrant claiming to know it in 1590 had reportedly lived in aristocratic households.[14]

Why should vagabonds use a jargon, and how far does it suggest they formed a 'subculture'? Professions, clubs and friends are known to develop special vocabularies, a tendency which the author of *A Manifest Detection* observed in 1552: 'always you must consider that a carpenter has many terms, familiar enough to his 'prentices, that other folk understand

not at all; and so have the cheaters'. Thus they might refer to illegal matters in public without fear; the frequency of terms relating to illicit gains, hiding-places and officials confirms this practical origin. False dicers, for example, used cant 'to the intent that ever in all companies they may talk familiarly in all appearance, and yet so covertly indeed that their purpose may not be espied'. Some vagrants denied knowing cant, and refused to confess where they had learnt it. But if Pedlar's French was supposed to help avoid detection, it was possibly counter-productive, since justices were on the look-out for it.[15]

The cant vocabulary of vagabonds, like its successors the hanging terminology of the early eighteenth century and the tramp slang of the twentieth century, suggests the existence of a marginal group.[16] Nevertheless, it is unknown how standardized canting was. It is unlikely that all vagrants used the same cant; the dictionaries listed the jargons of 'the special tribes of gypsies, beggars, shoplifters, highwaymen, foot-pads, and all other clans of cheats and villains', so that lists of cant words are probably compendia.[17] It is doubtful whether Pedlar's French represented an alternative ideology. It provided a means of communication, but its parameters were quite narrow.

CRIME IN THE UNDERWORLD: AN OVERVIEW

Masterless men who were examined by justices were principally arrested on suspicion of theft (45 per cent) and vagrancy (16 per cent) (see Appendix, Table XII). For a third major group, numbering 23 per cent, the reasons for their apprehension are unclear, while a fourth, counterfeiters of passports and licences to beg, accounted for 5 per cent of cases. The remainder included misdeeds ranging from homicide to fraudulence, but none accounted for more than a few per cent. Fraud and immorality each accounted for 2 or 3 per cent; the crimes of sedition and religious dissent were similarly few. In some instances, such as drunkenness, offences were non-civil ones, but perpetrators were probably also suspected to be repeat vagrancy offenders, which was felonious under many statutes.

There are great difficulties in comparing the alleged crimes of itinerants with those of the criminal population generally. Nothing is known about the suspected wrongdoings of non-transients who were examined. By the indictment stage it is rarely possible to distinguish itinerants charged with offences other than vagrancy, because the evidence provides only a person's name, occupation, dwelling place and alleged offence. The one comparable set of data, the assize indictments for the Southeast, 1559–1625, relates to a later stage in the legal process at which formal charges were made. Nevertheless, broad comparisons can be made between indictments and examinations. As one might expect, suspected

vagrants were more numerous in examinations (10 per cent higher in most places). In indictments, theft accounted for between 63 and 81 per cent of offences, while in examinations 45 per cent. Crimes against persons – homicide, infanticide, assault and rape – varied between 6 and 20 per cent among criminals generally who were indicted, while among masterless men they were just 0.4 per cent.[18] More numerous among vagabonds were fraud and passport abuses; cases of immorality, religious and political offences, are too few to yield meaningful comparisons.

The general picture is that among the criminal population generally and in the itinerant underworld the most common alleged crimes were against property, especially theft, but that transients were suspected of fewer crimes against persons. Vagabonds were no angels, but their alleged infringements were no more dangerous to property or life and limb than those indicted at assizes. That is to be expected from a group whose crimes usually originated in their status rather than their actions.

The masterless were, however, suspected and convicted of crimes to a greater extent than settled persons. The reasons for arrests were unclear in nearly a quarter of instances, as noted, and about half of the alleged thefts involved suspicions without an information being laid, which means that in nearly half of the 1604 examinations studied it was uncertain whether a crime had been committed, apart from that of status. In many instances itinerants were questioned about every piece of clothing on their backs without being charged, and they sometimes were incarcerated without charge – for example, the 581 persons 'sent in' to Bridewell in 1624–5.[19] There was a long history of blaming wanderers for crimes, and they were more likely to be indicted than local persons. They might have been guilty more often than the locals, but in reality the latter were more likely to receive neighbourhood sympathy, including that of the grand jury.[20] But whatever the degree of the law's bias against them, there is no denying that masterless men included a hardened minority, accounting for as much as a third of the total, who stole, assaulted, occasionally murdered, and attacked the Church and state.

PROFESSIONAL CRIME

It is impossible to determine how many vagrants made a full-time profession of crime. The extent of professionalism is overstated by the rogue writers, who were catering for a market in which a full-fledged criminal was more exciting than an amateur. It is also exaggerated in judicial records like indictments, which list persons' misdeeds but provide no information about their activities when they were not committing offences. Examinations counteract these misrepresentations by showing that the transient poor passed through various stages in becoming

criminals, and that they engaged in many other subsistence activities besides crime.

Professional crime nevertheless existed. Fraudulent beggars made a living at it, as the last chapter showed, and there are further signs of lives of crime. Some families produced more than one generation of criminals, suggesting long-term involvement outside the law. William Judkin, for example, had been in Northampton gaol before coming to Warwick in 1584, where his daughter was in prison. Of Joan Bennett, Derbyshire justices wrote in 1669 that 'her father and mother at the time of her birth were wandering beggars, and that she herself has for 20 years last past been a wandering beggar'. Family crime also appears among pedlars, many of whose kin were arrested in addition to themselves. This phenomenon is not always explained by direct occupational links, for many of their relatives were non-pedlars; rather, by the fact that they practised illegal occupations and were accompanied by family members.[21]

Another sign of professional crime among vagabonds is the use of aliases and nicknames. A Somerset woman punished in Wiltshire in 1610 called herself Mary Welles, *alias* Farwell, *alias* Cross, *alias* Andrews, while a burglar arrested in 1627 was 'known by three surnames, Hownell, Jacob and Gryner'.[22] They also adopted names that included Fine Mary for Mary Anderson, Black Jane for Jane Williams, and Jack a Chester for John Storey (who actually came from Newcastle-upon-Tyne). The professional element is sometimes obvious in their pseudonyms: for example, a forger of passports named Dick Skoler, and a 'creeper in at windows' called Little Tom.[23]

Thieves

According to the literature of roguery, itinerant thieves were highly organized. They met accomplices in safe alehouses and forests, staked out territories, specialized in certain types of theft, and carried special tools for jobs.[24] Elizabethan England was certainly plagued with thieves, who cut purses and picked pockets, lifted goods from market stalls and sneaked into the houses of rich and poor alike. Leonard Worrell, himself a gaol-bird, alleged that 100 felonies were perpetrated each week in London under James I, many by thieves. In *The Court of Conscience* (1607), another author described a scene in which

> Cheating thieves and cutpurses . . .
> Traversing the City all the streets along.
> Besieging every crowd in every place.
> And will undo a man before his face.[25]

They lifted anything that was not nailed down. In the country they made off with swarms of bees, feathers from beds and the backs of

chickens, even herds of livestock. One vagrant was arrested in early Stuart London while cutting the gold from a gentleman's scarf as he stood in the street. Others were caught cutting buttons off a gentleman's cloak on Tower Hill; pilfering three cloaks from Lady Montagu's house; taking lanterns off doors; and even the Queen's plate.[26] Theft was common partly because of the trusting natures of citizens, who received wandering beggars into their houses, and in alehouses slept next to total strangers. They left their houses unlocked, had few facilities for securing possessions, and carried valuables in purses and pockets that were easily picked in crowded streets. Their trusting way with their wealth helps to explain their outrage when they were robbed.

London, in particular, was likely to attract gangs of thieves because of the great concentration of wealth there. The author of A Manifest Detection reported in 1552 that they had divided up the capital, one taking St Paul's, and others, Westminster Hall, the shambles in Cheapside, and Southwark. One of the best-known accounts of metropolitan crime, the letter from the Recorder to Burghley in 1585, listed forty-five 'masterless men and cut-purses, whose practice is to rob gentlemen's chambers and artificers' shops', and named eighteen inns or 'harbouring-houses' where they holed up.[27] The Bridewell Court Books corroborate these remarks. One inmate reported in 1576 that cutpurses gathered every Saturday night in a barn at the end of Tothill Street, Westminster. Another pair frequented an alehouse in Warwick Lane, and yet another gang met in a barn near Lambeth marsh 'with diverse whores'. Two years later a cozener sent to the hospital named nine others who haunted the Three Footstools in St Katherine's near the Tower, while a year later a pair of 'roguish boys' reported that the Blue Boar in Thames Street was a refuge for cutpurses and harlots.[28] These examples suggest that, far from being isolated in a criminal quarter like post-Restoration Alsatia in Whitefriars, bands of thieves existed in many parts of London. According to Worrell, some had apprentices, and 'live by the same in great pride and excess of expenses'.[29]

Pilfering gangs were not confined to London. Five of them were alleged to be plying their craft in the Midlands and the North in 1610. They included three couples who cut purses and picked pockets at fairs. One of the male partners, Roger Crook, always carried £5 to secure the release of his female confederate should the need arise. Couples like this resemble the rogues and upright men with their doxies and morts in Harman's descriptions. But there were other types of gang as well – for example, six adolescents who broke into shops at night to steal sweets, and who cut purses in the daytime in Chester in 1617.[30] One reason why thieves did not work in gangs larger than a few members was the risk of detection. Harman suggested that upright men split up into small groups, and

vagrant thieves denied knowing one another and dispersed to avoid capture. At Stebbing fair in Essex in 1616 a gang of pickpockets was reported, and one member actually apprehended, but the rest fled and 'could not be taken'.[31]

The rogue literature pictured transient thieves as skilled specialists. Horse-thieves, for instance, were 'queer birds', 'priggers of palfreys' and 'priggers of prancers' in Pedlar's French.[32] A few horse-rustlers crop up in the records, but they rarely stuck to one type of beast. Hugh Tunnicliffe was accused of stealing seven heifers, five cows, five oxen and four bullocks, as well as eight horses, in Chester in 1597, while in Essex in the 1620s livestock thieves also made off with geese and sheep.[33] Further evidence of specialist crime appears in the Recorder's letter of 1585, which describes a Fagin-like character who 'procured all the cutpurses about [London] to repair' to him, and set up a school 'to learn young boys to cut purses', whose lessons are described in some detail.[34]

The literature also described thieves called 'hookers' or 'anglers', who carried staffs 5 to 6 feet long with holes about an inch from their ends. At night they inserted hooks, reached through open windows and purloined clothes and linens. Harman recounted one occasion when a hooker robbed three men of their covers and left them sleeping in their shirts. This type of thief turns up in examinations. A blacksmith accused of lifting clothes near Crewkerne in 1615 carried such a stick, which he claimed was for fishing, and a masterless man was similarly described in 1622 as carrying 'a staff with a crooked nail . . . to crook clothes from hedges and out of windows'.[35]

Examinations show that the techniques of the vagrant thief were highly diverse. Some used the tried and true method of mingling with crowds: thus a Lancashire woman suspected of picking pockets at Midsummer fair in Chester in 1610, who said that she stood near her intended victim 'for that she was thrust upon him by press of people'. But the ploys were not always so obvious. The same year Wiltshire magistrates heard about a vagabond woman who made 15s a day stealing chickens. Her ingenious method was to enter farms and drop corn as she went, so that the birds followed. They were soon killed, dressed and sold.[36]

Like hookers and anglers, some thieves carried special tools. A man seized in Warwick in 1581 on suspicion of stealing an ox carried a metal file, presumably to cut chains. But tools aroused suspicions and might be incriminating: a Newark woman alleged to be cutting purses in Leicester in 1614 tossed her scissors into a butcher's stall before her arrest, but a vagrant caught red-handed in London in 1621 had 'many cutpurse-knives found about him'.[37]

The itinerant thief's greatest problem was the disposal of loot. Rustlers drove beasts to distant markets as fast as possible – horses were desirable

prey, because they could be ridden – and sold them to unsuspecting buyers. But if market officials grew suspicious, the animals might have to be unloaded privately at knock-down prices.[38] Concealing stolen goods *en route* was hard because they were often heavy and bulky, so that some thieves chose to bury the booty. Others attempted to conceal it on their persons, and they must have presented odd spectacles, trundling along with bulging bags, wallets and clothes. An Anglesey man arrested in 1575 had sheets stuffed into his breeches, while Joan Earle, *alias* Jugg, had tied a bunch of clothing between her legs, under her skirt, when apprehended in Warwick in 1587. The bulk was sometimes literally staggering: for instance, the Somerset woman found toting thirteen pairs of woollen stockings and 25 feet of canvas in Warminster in 1627. Such loads were bound to arouse suspicions, as well as to encumber the thief. Smaller items were safer, better bets, especially cash, which was difficult to trace. A Northamptonshire woman searched in Leicester in 1616 carried money 'in the hair of her head'; a rag-collector arrested near Salisbury in 1637 had secreted a brass pot under his hat.[39]

Burglars

Itinerant criminals included burglars in their ranks, although ordinary thieves outnumbered them by fifty to one in examinations. They were likely to be organized in gangs because of the nature of the work, which required members to reconnoitre the premises, carry out the break-in, watch out, help carry off the loot and dispose of it. Burglary possibly also involved bands because of the risks. To break into a house at night was a felony, and after 1576 it was no longer subject to benefit of clergy. Furthermore, burglars who tried to rob the rich might encounter armed resistance from masters and retainers.[40] Break-in gangs usually numbered at least two members, sometimes as many as six or seven, and in one instance as many as forty. The last, led by Stephen Hales and Thomas Burley, operated in the Midlands in 1595. It was alleged to number between twenty-four and forty members, and also engaged in banditry. But gangs were not normally permanently together on the road. The Hales/Burley band broke up into units of three to nine after a crime.[41]

House-breaking rings had a complex web of relationships, judging by one involving sixteen persons in southwest Wiltshire and east Somerset in 1606. Six men were named as suspects, whose base was the house of Philip and Denise Trivett in Stourton. In addition, four other members of the household knew of the thefts, and the comings and goings of the burglars. The Trivett couple acted as receivers of the booty and harboured the villains, but the gang was further suspected to employ two Somerset widows as fences, and a weaver and a dyer to remake stolen linens. The

last two were perhaps ignorant of the alleged break-ins, but the other fourteen had, at least, indirect knowledge of them.[42]

Burglars had to have considerable expertise, because they needed to gain entry and rob houses while the occupants slept, or were absent. In such a dangerous line of work they were best advised to pursue the big prizes, but the wealthy usually had better defences than the rest of the population. Hence the use of keys and other instruments to pick locks, the 'black art' as Greene dubbed it. In the literature the lock-picker was a 'charm', and he who watched out, a 'stand'. Charms had 'such cunning in opening a lock, that they will undo the hardest lock . . . even while a man may turn his back'. A member of a gang that allegedly robbed the Bishop of Chester in 1603 carried a key called a 'grass', which it was stated 'will open any lock'; a Worksop labourer seized in a barn belonging to the Earl of Newcastle in Charles I's reign had a picklock in his possession.[43] Where entry was impossible with such instruments, other devices were employed. A Wiltshire gang in James I's reign always avoided houses with dogs, and burrowed their way in through thatching. When Ellen Thornton and her children were starving in Yorkshire in 1649, she stole seven cheeses by forcing a window and pushing her son through it. Others gained entry through holes or cracks; some, more crudely, simply broke windows. The prize for originality must go to the Burscough tailor, who swam the moats of unsuspecting Cheshire gentlemen and carried away £10–£15 worth of linens at a go.[44]

Violent burglaries were not unknown. The Hales/Burley gang assembled two dozen men armed with bows, arrows and guns when they robbed the Spencers in Warwickshire. A house-breaker named Hampshire Will and an accomplice tied up and threatened to murder the families they despoiled in Berkshire and Oxfordshire in 1623.[45] Gangs might pull off three or four break-ins a fortnight, but fewer if they went after big fish like the Spencers. It was a risky line of work. One young man involved in burglaries around Reading in the 1620s ended up 'hanged about the Duchess of Lennox's plate'.[46]

Mobility was important to all thieves, but burglars enjoyed less than most because of the need for reconnaissance and the disposal of loot. Hampshire Will and two confederates spent six weeks reconnoitring houses around Henley-upon-Thames and Reading in 1623, and sized up at least a dozen. But that was dangerous, for villagers began to notice them: a man they robbed in Arborfield remembered seeing Will, who was tall and carried a rapier, in an alehouse before the break-in. The booty had often to be fenced locally because of its bulk, so that malefactors might be observed by officials, as well as the receiver's family and servants. The testimony of servants was instrumental in the arrests of both the Stourton gang and Hampshire Will.[47]

Because of the limits on their mobility, house-breakers chose their territories carefully. Both the Stourton band and Hampshire Will seem intentionally to have operated near county boundaries, so that they could slip from one jurisdiction to another and fence their gains in another county without travelling great distances. The Stourton burglars were harboured in Wiltshire, but mostly sold their spoils in Somerset. Fencing goods and robbing close to home was dangerous. Hampshire Will was captured after attempting to sell his plunder in Reading; that is, in the county where three of his four recent break-ins had taken place, and no more than 10 miles distant from them. The Stourton band were shrewder in heading for Somerset after a robbery near Warminster, and might have escaped had one member not run into the vigilant Somerset justice Edward Hext. They too, however, had run great risks in robbing only a dozen miles from their base.[48]

The burglar's difficulties in fencing his takings is illustrated by an incident when Hampshire Will and an accomplice robbed a widow in 1623. After tying up the woman and her servant, the pair made off with

> seven pewter platters; a pewter salt-cellar; a pewter tunnel [?funnel]; four spoons; a brazing basin; a brass chafing dish; a brass pot; a brass kettle; two gowns; five 'kerchiefs; a neckcloth; two coifs; two crest [head?]-cloths; five aprons; three pair of cuffs; two hats; a pair of sheets; a smock; a pair of shoes; two girdles; a silver ring; 8d in cash; a dozen live chickens; three gallons of wheat; half a bushel of nuts; a wallet; a hemp bag; a quarter [probably 28 lb.] of flax; and two apple pies

which were the proceeds from just one of four break-ins in seven to eight days.[49]

Unless they stole cash, or themselves consumed what they took, thieves had to sell their booty. Sometimes they exchanged it in alehouses for board and lodgings; more often they sold or pawned it, usually obtaining a fraction of the value. For all his ingenuity in swimming moats, the Burscough tailor received only 8s for £10 worth of linen. The efforts of the petty thief fetched no more than a few coppers: the Bible theft in Shrewsbury in 1622 netted its perpetrator but 6d, while the receiver had 6s 6d from the resale.[50]

Fences were thick on the ground, probably because the crime was a misdemeanour, even if the goods were known to be stolen.[51] In addition to the Trivetts, the Stourton housebreakers reportedly used six receivers in east Somerset. Not all of them were full-time in the business, for two (a Bruton dyer and a Wincanton weaver) were contacted to re-work a piece of cloth. Others probably dealt in stolen goods as a sideline.[52] Women, often widows, were commonly fences, and so were alehouse-keepers. The first appear in examinations more frequently than the second,

although in one instance the person was both. Women and widows may have been attracted to receiving as a way of getting pin-money.[53] For alehouse-keepers it was the opportunity, as well as the income. They saw many people come and go, and were subject to a high degree of temptation. Transients paid bills with stolen goods, or offered them to landlords at low prices. How were tipplers to know the items were stolen, they might protest? In 1619 a Somerset ale-seller bought a brass kettle for 6d from an itinerant bellows-maker, which the man said he received in Wiltshire 'for work that he did there', but which, it later turned out, he was suspected to have pilfered.[54]

Of course, alehouse-keepers did not always receive vagabonds and their loot in innocence. Wiltshire rogues were reported in 1613 to spend Christmas at the Rose near Salisbury which, together with a house next door, were 'places both of receipt for such people and such things as shall be stolen by them in their thievish wanderings'. The Leopard's Head in Ware boasted facilities in 1626 that might have astonished James Bond. The plunder was buried behind the kitchen door and under the buttery stairs. The lady of the house could allegedly 'convey any man from chamber to chamber' undetected, and had hidden five deserters from constables, and another fugitive for a fortnight. There was no equivalent hideout within 100 miles, it was stated.[55]

Cony-catchers

Fraudulence was central to the Elizabethan conception of vagrancy. In the literature of roguery the vagabond was as likely to be portrayed as a cozener, or cheat, as an ordinary thief. That was because frauds made livelier reading than common larceny, especially deceits involving gambling, which was fashionable among the upper classes. In law fraud was the intentional misappropriation of another's property by fraudulent means. It is not always clear, however, whether offenders were considered as larceny cases, which might involve felony charges, or as cheats, which was a misdemeanour.[56] Bowling and cards were outlawed under Henry VIII, but the statute was a dead letter. The King himself continued to gamble, Elizabeth I is reputed to have played with loaded dice, and among the aristocracy the stakes outstripped the inflation of the 'Price Revolution'. Gambling was also popular among the populace, some of whom were prepared to impoverish their families in losing large sums. It was that kind of person who was the mark of the cony-catcher.[57]

Cheats were examined by justices, but were not as ubiquitous as the literary evidence suggests. Two gangs, above all, appear in the early Stuart period, whose members fluctuated but were linked by the Kemp or Kent family. Philip and Thomas Kemp appeared at Midsummer fair in Chester in 1618, telling officials a number of stories, but they were almost

certainly there to gamble. They were later accused of cheating at cards in Somerset in 1622, and were sought in Reading a year later for the same offence under a Chief Justice's warrant.[58] The second syndicate included Allen Kemp, William and Robert Lee, and Richard Bush. Although Allen cannot be definitely linked to the earlier pair, the surname is unlikely to be coincidental in this specialized line of thievery. He was involved in bilking a Wiltshire clothier in 1631, and was accused with the Lees and Bush of cheating a Worcestershire man in Leicester two years later. The other three were veterans by then, since they had been arrested seven years before in Reading as suspected 'cheaters, or cony-catchers'.[59] A third gaming ring included William Vincent, *alias* Hocus Pocus, and Archie Shocke, who were accused of cheating at tic-tac, a form of backgammon, in Reading in 1625.[60]

It would be erroneous, however, to portray all cheats as full-time professionals. Some were part-timers who normally lived honest lives with their families. And the membership of syndicates was fluid. Four members of the Kemp gang were said in 1631 to have 'known each other for a long space and [to] have been fellow gamesters together for these many years'. Yet at least ten others took part in the gang's frauds and appear in the records on just one occasion each. Furthermore, the Lees and Bush played on their own before working with the Kemps, and while Vincent teamed up with Shocke in 1625, he later appeared in Norwich with another partner 'to show feats of legerdemain'.[61]

The techniques of the crooked gamester are difficult to discover, because they naturally protested their innocence and would anyway be loath to disclose trade secrets. The *Manifest Detection* described how 'some pinch the cards privily with their nails; some turn up the corners; some mark them with fine spots of ink', as well as pricking holes in them. Sometimes the 'cony' was placed with his back to a mirror; at other times onlookers were strategically placed to see his cards – for example, a woman who pretended to sew, signalling his hand to confederates by the speed of her needle. Dice were loaded by hollowing and altering the length and surfaces. In that line of cheating the skill was in the introduction of good and bad dice, first to encourage the victim by letting him win at low stakes, then to take everything he had at high ones.[62]

The cony-catchers were Londoners almost to a man. Cheating probably developed there because gambling for high stakes was common in the capital. The City authorities issued a proclamation against card-sharpers and cozeners in 1571, and one of the professed aims of the rogue writers was to alert unsuspecting provincials to London's dangers. What they did not grasp was that Londoners worked in the provinces, as well as at home. Two allegedly playing with false dice in the Southwest under James I were compared to 'the fox that will never prey near home'. The

Kemp gangs had Gloucestershire connections, but Londoners were prominent in the Chester meeting of 1618, in the Bush/Lee band, and among gamblers in Reading in the 1620s.[63]

Cony-catchers presented themselves as gentlemen, but such claims were often fictitious. Those whose status can be identified included a weaver, an embroiderer, two surgeons, a chapman, two husbandmen, two tailors, and a man who lived from his wife's bone-lace work. There was occasionally evidence of higher status, or at least connections. A man seized in Leicester in 1616 with dice and counters bragged that he had served a peer of the realm, another claimed to be married to the daughter of the steward of Windsor castle, and yet another was said to be a gentleman with £80 a year income from lands in Wales. Shocke stated that he lived at Court with Sir Thomas Dishington, while his partner Vincent said he was 'the King's Majesty's servant'.[64] Although these statements deserve to be treated with scepticism, they are rare enough among vagrants possibly to have some authenticity.

Cheats were distinct from the mass of vagabonds, but similar to burglars, in going for major trophies. John Smith and six confederates were alleged to have taken £15 from a Cirencester man in Bristol in 1609, and Allen Kemp and others were supposed to have cheated the Worcestershire gentleman of £18 in Leicester in 1633. The best record belongs to those who conned a Wiltshire clothier in 1631. Besides the £15 they had from him, they had allegedly taken £14 or £15 from another man in Bristol, and £30 from a man in Twyford. These were princely sums, sufficient to support a labouring family for three or four years.[65] Cheats who worked in ones and twos were not as successful as bigger rings. Smith and his companions took £15 from their Bristol victim, but when the band broke up and he worked with just one other, the proceeds diminished to £3 and 30s. That was a *per capita* decline, and by the 1620s Smith was reduced to informing on other crooks.[66]

Cony-catchers often gathered at fairs to find victims. A Shepton Mallett cheat admitted in 1609 that he and seven others travelled to a number in the Southwest; similar syndicates appeared at fairs in Leicester in 1616, Chester in 1618 and Bristol in 1632. These events offered regular meeting-times, but above all fat prey. Mobility was intrinsic to the trade outside London, some cheats travelling from Cornwall to Cheshire. Unlike burglars, however, they had no need to tarry once they had made their killings.[67]

Various other transient sharpers were at work in the period. One common ploy was to sell 'silver' and 'gold' chains and rings, which on inspection turned out to be gilded copper. The trick disappears from the record after 1602, possibly because of loss of faith in cramp rings as cures for epilepsy.[68] Another common deceit involved a low level of counter-

feiting, literally with 'counters', pieces painted to resemble money. A Leicester tailor was sent to Bridewell in 1578 after taking £3 from a Wakefield man with such a device; an accomplice reported sixteen others working at the game in London alone. A lackey incarcerated a year later did not bother with painted tokens, paying his bill in a victualling house with 'gold' that turned out to be a piece of an orange. Still others swindled people with forged documents above and beyond the false 'briefs' discussed in the previous chapter.[69]

Highwaymen

Robbery was theft aggravated by violence, or 'putting a person in fear', and was a felony. Highway robbery was also felonious, and from Henry VIII's reign it ceased to be subject to benefit of clergy; it was another crime with upper-class associations. It had a long pedigree going back to periods of lawlessness in the Middle Ages; nor was its gentlemanly aura new in the seventeenth century.[70] 'Martin Markall' distinguished two types of highwayman in 1610 – 'high lawyers', gentlemen who 'ride on horses well appointed, and go in show like honest men'; and 'padders', who robbed on foot and, having 'no other help but a pair of light heels', hid in forests until the hue and cry passed. Both wore false beards and hair; it was the padder who ordered victims to 'stand and deliver!'.[71]

Examinations of highway robbers are not plentiful, but those extant suggest that padders were more common than high lawyers. In general, it seems one was far more likely to meet a sailor or tailor than a gentleman among highwaymen. Like burglars and cony-catchers, they worked in gangs, but also sometimes alone.[72] The Hales/Burley band were clearly in the big time. Over eighteen months they were alleged to have committed thirty robberies in the Seven Hundreds part of Gloucestershire alone. They were accused of taking £300 from the Ludlow carriers, and to have attacked a troop of twenty Berkshire clothiers who were carrying over £1000. Similar gangs were reported in the Southwest, West Midlands and East Anglia in the 1590s.[73]

Highwaymen preyed upon travellers in out of the way places, especially forests and heaths. The author of *Le guide des chemins d'Angleterre* (1579) warned, 'prenez garde à la plaine de Salesbury, lieu fort dangereux à cause des voleurs et brigands qui y font leur repaire quasi journellement'. Other dangerous spots included Finchley Common, Gad's Hill, Hounslow Heath, Maidenhead Thicket, Newmarket Heath, Shooter's Hill, Watford Gap, the forests of Wyre and Sherwood, and Stone Gate near Grantham.[74] Examinations suggest there was good reason to beware of such haunts: twenty-one persons were reportedly robbed on Newmarket Heath on one afternoon in 1595, and three Londoners stripped a

poulterer of his goods in a coppice near Sidcup in 1598.[75] Few Robin Hoods were encountered in these perilous places, and highwaymen were usually prepared to use violence. The Hales/Burley band were armed with pistols, staves, and bows and arrows, while the Londoners who robbed the poulterer threatened him with cudgels.[76]

In sum, professionals organized in large gangs existed, although they formed a small fraction of itinerant thieves. More typical was the amateur lone wolf, or those with an accomplice or two, whose methods were typically of the grab-and-run school. Nevertheless, vagrant thieves were a problem – seemingly omnipresent, at times employing ingenious methods to fleece the public, using mobility as a tactical weapon and, when organized in gangs, dangerous menaces.

CRIMES AGAINST PERSONS

It is impossible to determine what proportion of vagabonds had weapons. A small fraction were reported carrying them in examinations, most commonly knives and cudgels, but occasionally more lethal ones. A masterless man caught near 'a very dangerous passage' in Kent in 1596 had a pistol charged with four bullets,[77] while a Cambridge vagrant was locked away in Bridewell in 1641 after 'running into men's houses with a prong and truncheon to their terror'.[78] It would be misleading, however, considering the limitations of the evidence, to underplay or to stress the dangers presented by armed vagabonds. All classes of society were likely to go armed. The poor, if anything, were less violent than the rest. The list of aristocratic violence is so extensive that it could be 'indefinitely re-peated'; in Essex, crimes of violence in fact diminished as one descended the social ladder; and, as noticed earlier, those transients examined by justices were suspected of committing rather fewer crimes against persons than criminals indicted at assizes.[79]

Itinerants used force during burglaries and highway robberies, and when they were refused alms. Otherwise the ordinary citizen was un-likely to be the object of assaults from them. No rapes or infanticides involving vagabonds have been discovered, although one suspects some hapless girls must have killed their babies. Homicides are so few that it is difficult to generalize about them. One involved seven 'wandering rogues' who were incarcerated in Stafford gaol in 1621 after allegedly breaking into a widow's house and killing her son. Another murder concerned a Gateshead soldier who told Yorkshire justices in 1642 that he had killed a man eight years earlier.[80] The most frequent examples of random aggression come from London, where it was possible to be assaulted by vagrants. For example, Thomas Oliver tried to pull a gentlewoman from her coach in 1606, while William Mouseley and

another 'threw dirt and stones and other rubbish at the Lady Slingsby, being at a draper's shop in Cheapside' in 1630.[81]

Assaults commonly occurred when officials arrested vagabonds. When a Stafford gentleman seized a couple in 1614, the woman beat him on the head 'with a great stone', while her mate bit him on the thumb. London experienced a rash of such incidents in 1630, including a vagrant who attempted to stab a Bridewell governor, and five who beat up an assistant provost-marshal in Southwark.[82] Vagabonds also uttered menaces and threatened to wound. A man arrested in a North Riding town in James I's reign threatened to return and burn it down, while Richard Rogers offered to 'rip up' a constable's belly at Queenhithe in 1621.[83]

But vagrants could attack one another as well. Two homicides involved children who accompanied them; other clashes arose over property and personal matters. One woman was accused of stealing the clothes off the back of a fellow vagabond in Warwick in 1587, and a Lancashire woman was beaten by four other vagrants near Chester in 1598 after she refused to share the proceeds of her begging.[84] Masterless couples did not always enjoy harmonious relationships either. A pedlar and his 'pretended wife' got drunk in a Wiltshire alehouse in 1609 and accused one another of being bigamists. When he beat her, she 'in her rage offered to stab [him]', and reported him to the constables for carrying false papers. Quarrels were also triggered by the eternal triangle: when a soldier went drinking with an acquaintance's wife in Leicester in 1634, the two men fell to blows, and one produced the inevitable knife.[85]

CRIMES AGAINST THE STATE

Religious and political

Attacks upon the established order in religion and politics were as scarce among vagrants as in the criminal population generally. But where such activities are concerned, their number is less important than their intentions, and how far they succeed. The Gunpowder Plot was a near success, even though it involved a handful of conspirators, and it took just one disappointed man to assassinate the Duke of Buckingham. Governments reacted to such threats by extending the statutory definition of treason, proscribing religious dissidence, and treating seditious words in the same manner as seditious writings.[86] The transient poor posed a problem because of their mobility. They lashed out at both temporal and spiritual authorities, spreading discontent after the break with Rome. With the country unsettled in religion for another 150 years, no government could afford to countenance such dissidence. Itinerants also undermined the state by coinage frauds and false passports. Not surprisingly, then,

state action was stepped up against them, particularly during religious/political crises.[87]

Mobility was useful to all types of religious dissident, from seminary priests under Elizabeth I to George Fox the Quaker. For recusants it was essential to keep in touch with the strongholds of the faith on the continent and to maintain a steady supply of priests. The authorities saw links between popery and vagabondage: the Bishop of Lincoln wrote to a local magistrate in 1622 describing vagrants as devotees of 'popery and blind superstition'.[88] There were essentially two kinds of itinerant recusant, the traditional believer who was unlikely to have direct contact with foreign Catholics, and the new believer who was. A Lancashire sawyer arrested in Warwick in 1582 is a prime example of the first sort. His method of attending the established church was to walk in and out without taking part in services. His reason was that 'his father and mother brought him up in the time of King Henry VIII, and then there was [an]other order, and he minds to observe that order and to serve the Lord God above all things'.[89]

Of greater concern than the likes of the sawyer were recusants with foreign connections. They included seminary priests but also laymen educated in Catholic countries, and carriers of relics and books. Priests went *incognito*, disguised as merchants, gentlemen and students. John Gerard travelled as a gentleman, on horseback.[90] The movements of recusants suggest that England was as porous as a sieve for those travelling abroad, but that inside the country the risks increased. A major centre in the Northwest was the city of Chester, through which English Catholics passed to Ireland. But the south coast and East Anglia were probably the main avenues for recusant travel to and from the continent.[91]

Radical Protestants also tramped the roads. Some early members of the Family of Love sect were wandering artisans, spreading the word in their travels. Parliament reacted by passing an Act in 1593 against 'seditious sectaries and disloyal persons . . . [who] go about to move or persuade any of her Majesty's subjects . . . to deny, withstand and impugn her Majesty's power and authority in causes ecclesiastical'. The statute lapsed under James I, but itinerant sectaries were still arrested. Dorothy Kennell was imprisoned in Bridewell in 1620 by the Court of High Commission 'for taking upon her in private houses to read a parcel of Scripture, and to expound the same and to pray extempore'.[92] After 1640 it must have seemed as though the bowels of Hell had opened to release the hordes of tramping radicals: in Wales alone in 1648 there were reckoned to be 800 itinerant preachers; in 1656 the Wiltshire grand jury presented 'many evil spirited people which do wander about spreading many evil and dangerous opinions to the dishonour of God' during an apparent outbreak of

Ranting.[93] Such prophets were probably a far cry from the vagrant poor in wealth and status, just as were most recusants, but ironically enough they gave the genuinely uprooted a bad name.

Officials also seized transient visionaries with no clear sectarian affinities. One vagrant was sent to Bridewell in 1575 for 'holding certain foolish opinions, thinking that he should be fed only by angels from heaven', while another announced in Leicester in 1623 that he was a 'convertite'.[94] Others were simply irreligious or anti-clerical. The Dean of Westminster despatched William Whetston to Bridewell in 1606 'for a vagrant, turbulent fellow and . . . railing in the church against preachers', and Thomas Beck was incarcerated in a Staffordshire house of correction in James I's reign for speaking 'reproachful words against God's ministers'.[95]

Itinerants were thought to spread sedition and rebellion. Of their actual involvement in uprisings there is limited evidence. During the Pilgrimage of Grace a wanderer carried the news of the risings around the North, and others did likewise in southern parts. An insurrection reportedly planned in Suffolk in 1569 was suppressed, it was claimed, by a round-up of 13,000 masterless men. Tramping artisans were also supposed to have disseminated propaganda for the abortive Oxfordshire uprising of 1596. The closest thing to a rebellion involving vagabonds, however, was the riot of demobilized soldiers in Westminster after the Portugal expedition. Vagrants were more likely to irritate than instigate in a political crisis. Thus a Chesterfield man apprehended in Bridgeward shouting 'Arm, Arm, Arm together, a mutiny and tumult' on the eve of the first Civil War, who was drunk and a vagrant.[96]

More common than open rebellions were seditious outbursts of this kind. The law of sedition covered the monarchy, members of the government, judges and the Church. Truth was no defence, publication unnecessary, and the death of the person slandered no bar to prosecution. The criminality of seditious words was 'comparatively new law' in common-law courts, but the crime remained a misdemeanour except when the monarchy was involved. Then it could be treason.[97] Vagabonds occasionally articulated general attacks upon the *status quo*. The message was usually that the meek had not inherited the earth and that only radical changes could improve things. A Ripon labourer was arrested about 1600 after saying 'he would make the highest the lowest' and 'would cause all Kent to be plucked out by the ears'. Still more specific in his attacks was a Dorchester sieve-maker in 1631, who allegedly said of lawyers and clerics 'that they had got all the riches of the land into their hands and were grown so proud that they will not vouchsafe to speak to a poor man'.[98]

Transients also voiced vague prophecies and threats. One spread a rumour in Poole in 1586 that a Catholic armada of 600 ships and 500,000

men was going to invade the country, which 'would have Sir Francis Drake, for that he did spoil the Indies'. Another, a 'plain, duncical country fellow', was sent to Bridewell for 'fabulous dreams, and one that undertakes to prophesy of matters of state' in the aftermath of the Gunpowder Plot.[99] Monarchs and officials were common targets of abuse. Two female inmates of St Thomas's hospital were transferred to Bridewell in 1560 for speaking 'lewdly and in naughty manner and lewd communication as touching the Queen's Highness'. The scurrilous attacks continued under the early Stuarts. Robert Wood allegedly called Charles I a knave in Dover in 1634, and during the crisis of 1641 a vagrant was locked away in Bridewell for 'speaking words against the King and Queen'.[100]

Vagabonds calumnified local officials as well as the mighty. When an itinerant couple were halted by a Somerset parson in 1623, the husband was said to have reviled him 'with very foul and outrageous words, and withall kneeled down and prayed that the devil might confound him and all his'. When they did not abuse magistrates, they were insolent and uncooperative. A tinker sent to Leicester in 1626 by Northamptonshire officials was described as 'ill-conditioned and very saucy in his language'. Refusals to co-operate with justices were dangerous, for if one were found 'mute of malice' and guilty of a felony, the punishment was *peine forte et dure*, or pressing to death, and some vagabonds went down this perilous path.[101] Nevertheless, all told, vagrant sedition and dissent were running sores in the body politic rather than major causes of crises.

Counterfeiters

Coin-clippers presented a threat to the state by ruining its monetary system, and they, too, were itinerant. The offence was a serious one following statutes of 1415 and 1553, which made it treason to clip and to counterfeit respectively. Some measure of transiency was inevitable for these criminals, because they had to distribute their product. Two seized in Leicester in 1628 had journeyed from Scotland and were on their way to London; another taken in the town in 1634 had come from Edinburgh to dump counterfeit farthings. They also had to travel to secure materials, as in the case of a Settle gang who purchased silver in Lancaster in 1648.[102]

Another form of fraud posing a direct challenge to the state, and of great importance for vagabonds, was the false passport. The genuine article was required of a wide range of itinerants, and it was almost a licence to beg. The papers usually stated that the holder had been shipwrecked, or was a soldier returning from service. They additionally requested that he be permitted to pass unmolested, and be given lodgings and relief on his way. The holder was normally allotted a period in which to travel, and his papers were to be endorsed by magistrates where he

passed. A good example was in the possession of Meredith Bassett, arrested in 1618 in Somerset, a copy of which survives. It stated that he and five others from Devon were on their way to Spain in a ship carrying tin and kersies, when they were 'by tempest cast away and lost'. They were rescued by an Ipswich ship and disembarked at Dover, where the mayor issued passports to Bassett and another man, allowing them two months for the homeward trip 'by reason they have not been in good health, but are weakened by sickness which they lately sustained'.[103]

Counterfeit passports grew so common that the system became a nonsense. The vagrancy Act of 1572 ordered that frauds be punished, and by 1580 JPs showed no surprise at discovering vagabonds with false papers. One justice simply wrote out a genuine version and sent the offender away.[104] That ersatz passports were readily available is also suggested by their prices, which were low compared with the benefits their holders might reap. In the 1570s and 1580s they ranged from 2d to 4d, and in the early seventeenth century, from 6d to 1s.[105] Some vagrants carried more than one set: a man taken begging in Salisbury in 1620 had two, one saying he was from Colchester, and the other, from Fetter Lane, Holborn (he actually lived in Wotton-under-Edge in Gloucestershire). There was even some do-it-yourself forgery of passports. When a Truro labourer returned from Somerset in 1619 and was denied a settlement by the town, he wrote himself another pass and returned to Somerset to beg.[106]

False papers could be purchased almost anywhere. Some vagrants bought them in London, but because passports were easier to forge than charitable briefs, the metropolis enjoyed no monopoly over this kind of literate crime. Some counterfeiters were themselves itinerant. One called Tom Whiting, reported in 1581, made a 'mark with white chalk like unto a whiteing' where he passed, so that potential customers knew he was in the vicinity; while a Staffordshire man arrested in Wiltshire in 1619 bought his from a forger who 'wrote them abroad, out of any house, upon his knee'. Between Bristol and Salisbury, two vagabonds stated in James I's reign, there were at least a half-dozen counterfeiters working, which meant on average one about every 10 miles.[107]

Making a passport required considerable skill: Wiltshire sessions rolls include one written in Dutch.[108] The forger had to know the names of local justices or to invent likely sounding ones. They had also to vary the handwriting in endorsements, which were supposedly made by different officials *en route*, and to possess a good deal of equipment: pen, paper, ink and seals. They achieved high levels of proficiency, so that for every forgery detected dozens probably went unnoticed. Davy Bennett, reported in Essex in 1581, was supposed to be able to counterfeit any seal: 'if he sees it in wax, he will lay it before him and carve it out in wood very

perfectly'. He also forged magistrates' handwriting perfectly, 'for that he writes sundry hands'. Another carried a list of knights and JPs in various shires, 'to know whose names might fitly be used of the same counties in his counterfeit passes'.[109]

Since forgery required literacy, the crime was mainly the preserve of the middling sort. Pedlars, shoemakers and soldiers counterfeited passes, but more often the miscreant was a priest, clerk, scrivener, school-teacher or student. An Irish sailor seized in Essex in 1573 had his from a teacher in Brentwood, while a counterfeiter in Pilton in Somerset was variously described as the minister and schoolmaster in the parish.[110]

Vagrants used false papers with near impunity. One examinee re-counted how two of them received soldiers' pensions from three counties simultaneously, and how a Reading man regularly collected alms in four shires. Endorsements were no doubt genuine in some instances, showing that officials had been duped.[111] Forgers and carriers of false passports were normally only caught when their documents contained gross errors. John Medcalfe had the misfortune to encounter a Wiltshire justice interested in palaeography, who analysed the document line by line, comparing words in the endorsements with the text, and concluded it 'plainly to be perceived that all the writing therein to be one man's hand'. Obvious mistakes with geography also landed frauds in trouble, as when James Dunn told a Wiltshire JP in 1614 that he had come from Ireland via Swansea and Cardiff, but his papers placed the last town in Cardiganshire.[112]

CONCLUSIONS

It would be hard to prove that the vagrant underworld of this time was more dangerous and better organized than criminals in earlier and later periods. In the late Middle Ages gangs numbering forty to fifty members had kidnapped and murdered gentlemen, judges and churchmen. In London during the Augustan age, as Jonathan Wild's revelations show, organized thievery flourished.[113] Contrary to the literary sources, it was not the Elizabethan underworld's organization, specialization, or direct threat to the established order that made it so obnoxious. It is admittedly possible, as we have seen, to discover examples of the stereotyped qualities of the underworld in the examinations of masterless criminals. And no one can deny that some were the dangerous rogues that the literature depicted. Fundamentally, however, the literature's taxonomy is superficial and its amusing stories trivial. Vagrant crime was protean rather than specialized, ranging from illegal begging to burglary. Most of it also lacked gang-style organization. But those very qualities made it more difficult to suppress, compared with Wild's former confederates,

who were easily rounded up after he turned informer. Furthermore, transient crime was enduring, because the demographic and economic preconditions fostering it lasted for over a century, as was shown in Chapter 2. Officials might break up this gang or that, but they were largely helpless to control the conditions that led the vagabond to commit his depredations. It was not, however, for want of trying, because, as the final chapter seeks to demonstrate, governments were remarkably inventive in attacking this intractable problem.

Chapter 9

State policy: from *Utopia* to the penal colony

Vagabonds posed new and perplexing problems to early modern governments, above all the policing of persons without settled ties. The medieval system of frankpledge, whereby every resident of a jurisdiction was legally responsible for every other, was useless when it came to dealing with itinerant strangers. Responsibility for them was *ipso facto* uncertain.[1] Returning them to their home parish perpetuated the principle of community obligation, but it ignored the fact that many had no settled base. There was the additional difficulty of determining the extent of their crimes if they were rootless. Were they just masterless, or had they lifted the missing sheet from Goodwife Smith's hedge, or burgled the squire's mansion? Were they possibly disguised priests? Generally, how was it possible to control the throngs of transient poor? To the challenge of disorder by vagabonds governments responded in ways that significantly extended state authority and raised thorny constitutional issues. Before examining that response, however, it should first be established that the authorities were capable of enforcing controls over vagrants.

THE ENFORCEMENT ISSUE

English local government has often been saddled with a Dogberry image, in other words the impression that, because of negligence by lesser officials, Parliament's statutes were 'frequently honoured as much in the breach as in the observance'.[2] Because Tudor and early Stuart governments lacked a standing army and full-time police forces, they are assumed to have been weak compared to continental regimes.[3] JPs and constables were unpaid, part-time officials who were useless in major crises and might even, like Dogberry, turn a blind eye to vagrants.[4]

Local government's image of indolence and impotence has some claim

to accuracy. The administration of justice depended upon circumstances, above all the will of the enforcers. Thus local authorities sometimes acted quite independently of Parliament and Whitehall – for example, those towns which regulated labour in the 1550s and early 1560s before the Statute of Artificers was passed, and the many which took action on poor relief before statutes ordered it.[5] They also sometimes refused to obey royal commands, especially where their purses were involved. Early Stuart JPs, it has been observed, 'put their own pockets first, their county second and the interests of the crown third'. They sometimes refused to collect taxes, even for local purposes, while constables were often loath to enforce social and economic regulations that affected their neighbours.[6]

Policy was most likely to be effective when rule-makers and enforcers were in agreement. Hence the difficulty of making enclosure legislation stick, for those supposed to implement it were themselves likely offenders. The regulation of the poor presented fewer obstacles, and the vagrant poor fewer still. In Essex, village élites proved keen to police paupers, because of puritan hostility to disorder, a widening economic gulf between themselves and the destitute, and their identification with the interests of county magistrates.[7] How typical these places were remains to be seen, but they are unlikely to prove wildly eccentric where lowland England is concerned.

Regarding vagrancy, local officials were not as idle as is often assumed. Their Dogberry image arises largely from the silence of the records. Most vagabonds received summary trials and punishment at parish level, so that unless clerks and JPs diligently kept constables' presentments, or a vagrant was examined by a justice, the records would disappear. It is no coincidence that the best documentation resulted from the search campaigns of 1569–72 and the 1630s, when Whitehall leant on officials to make regular reports; from justices' examinations; and from major towns, where records were often better kept. Many village constables were probably illiterate and made only verbal presentments.

Instances of constables' negligence are not wanting. One in East Grinstead was indicted in 1605 for punishing a vagrant 'very slenderly, as with a whip taken out of a hedge', and in 1610 a Kentish officer was alleged to have permitted a begging ex-soldier to escape, saying 'he could not endeavour to follow him because the weather was very hot'.[8] Higher officials complained bitterly about subordinates. An anonymous report of 1586 raised the question 'why there is so great a number of rogues and thieves in all parts of this realm', and blamed jurors and justices. They were lobbied, it alleged, by the 'basest and most ignorant sort of common people', to acquit notorious rogues; they even allowed illiterate malefactors benefit of clergy. Of fifty to sixty committed for trial, only twenty were condemned as felons, and less than ten actually hanged.

Justices and judges were bribed to reprieve condemned rogues, and constables winked at passing vagrants. Such allegations are not unique. In the early years of James I's reign one observer claimed that three-quarters of London's thieves and vagabonds escaped arrest altogether.[9]

By itself, however, anecdotal and denunciatory evidence is insufficient to prove that officials did their jobs badly, or well. Specific cases might be untypical, and *ex cathedra* pronouncements often lack supporting evidence. The historian needs to know how well enforced the laws were in general, but such documentation is difficult to find. One instance of a spectacular piece of negligence relates to Elizabethan Montgomeryshire, where a true bill listed 259 places, surely most of the county, which had failed to arrest vagabonds. But elsewhere the Dogberry problem appears less staggering. In James I's reign thirty parishes in northwest Staffordshire were ordered to return presentments of vagrants whom they had punished. Thirteen provided lists of names, eight reported that none had entered their parishes, another eight made no returns, and one admitted that it had no constable.[10] In early seventeenth-century Wiltshire, moreover, twenty-six out of twenty-nine hundreds made presentments of vagrants, and individual returns survive for roughly a third of the shire's parishes. In Essex and Lancashire during the 1630s, although petty constables were reluctant to report their neighbours' misdeeds, they willingly arrested vagabonds.[11] If 80 to 90 per cent of parishes reported to JPs and one-third to one-half can be shown to have been executing the law, then there was some 'default of justice'. But these figures make no allowance for illiteracy and lost records, and they do not support the view that constables were utterly dilatory.

There is plenty of evidence that towns regularly apprehended vagrants. Chester, Colchester, Leicester, London, Norwich and Salisbury all have records of arrests for long periods in the late sixteenth and early seventeenth centuries. In the countryside the documentation is less plentiful, but still suggests that officials were capable of regularly dealing with offenders – for example, at Marston Trussell in Northamptonshire, where constables recorded passing ninety vagrants a year on average from 1616 to 1674.[12] Considerable parish evidence also survives after an Act of 1597 required that records be kept. In some places it is limited to the years immediately after the statute's passage, but in others enforcement was sustained for decades: in Bisley in Gloucestershire from 1598 to 1617; in Crondall in Hampshire from 1598 to 1622; and in the Essex parishes of Hornchurch from 1598 to 1684, Great Easton from 1598 to 1634, and Canewdon, 1598 to 1620.[13]

That governments were capable of effective action is also shown by the special searches mounted under Elizabeth I and Charles I. Petty constables made presentments to high constables, who then passed certifi-

cates on to JPs and sheriffs, who in turn forwarded them to the Privy Council. Notwithstanding this lengthy chain of command, substantial numbers of reports survive in the State Papers, Domestic: from almost half the English counties, including details of 742 vagrants, for the campaign of 1596–72; and from 39 of 52 English and Welsh shires, reporting nearly 25,000 arrests between 1631 and 1639.[14] The Caroline round-ups, in particular, are striking evidence of state action, encompassing the remote north – Westmorland sent the most detailed reports; Lancashire's arrests were among the highest nationally – as well as the south. Any government that successfully goads its servants into apprehending numbers of this order, even allowing that a fair share might have been recidivists, deserves to be taken seriously.[15]

MODEST PROPOSALS

The vagrancy problem inspired a number of proposals to remedy it, and almost invariably they involved state action, whether in direct management or in patronage. While a few projects were half-baked and others just designed to enrich the 'projectors', many were serious and probably influenced policy.[16]

Vagabondage first received detailed analysis in Thomas More's *Utopia* (1516), which identified unemployment and crime as related problems and offered remedies. More showed great insight in raising the question why thieves, despite capital punishment, still abounded. He came up with the answer that no punishment 'is sufficient to restrain from acts of robbery those who have no other means of getting a livelihood'. The fundamental causes of crime, he argued, were economic – unemployment, exploitation and poverty. His solutions were revolutionary for the time: to stop executing thieves, which was a punishment out of proportion to the crime; instead, to pass legislation against depopulation, and to employ the idle in husbandry and cloth manufacture. Later generations made but limited advances upon this shrewd analysis.[17]

The development of such ideas into legislation was the work of Thomas Cromwell and his circle in the mid-1530s. In poor-law drafts they planned a national council to employ vagabonds in building highways, harbours and fortifications. Labour was to be compulsory, but those who worked were to receive 'reasonable wages', meat and drink, and medical care. The scheme would be financed by public taxation.[18] A draft bill of 1536 shares some of the humanitarianism of *Utopia*. It accepts that some persons became vagrants after masters wrongfully dismissed them, that others were spoiled by parents, and still others reduced to beggary by accidents and illness. But the bill also contained harsh elements. It blamed some vagabonds for being unemployed 'through their own default',

defined vagrancy in terms that included all the able-bodied dispossessed, and provided that those refusing to work should suffer capital punishment for third offences.[19] The proposal also included some distinctly authoritarian features. The council in charge was empowered to make 'laws', and to enforce its will upon the officials responsible for implementing the plan with 'distress, fines, amerciaments, *tortures* and imprisonment, or otherwise as to them shall seem to be most expedient', pain of death excepted. No wonder that a House of Commons made up of men who might be liable to such penalties balked at the bill and passed a watered-down version.[20]

Numerous plans to employ vagrants were hatched in the Elizabethan and early Stuart period as the problem worsened. Among the most imaginative were the proponents of fishing fleets. In 1580, Robert Hitchcock, an Oxfordshire gentleman, published *A Politic Plat for the Honour of the Prince, the Great Profit of the Public State, Relief of the Poor, Preservation of the Rich, Reformation of Rogues and Idle Persons, and the Wealth of Thousands That Know Not How to Live.* His aim was to root out 'that loathsome monster idleness (the mother and breeder of vagabonds)'. The idea was to create a fleet of 400 herring boats on which vagrants would be 'set on work, and labour willingly, and thereby prove good subjects, and profitable members of the common weal'. These 'Flemish busses' would employ 10,000 men, nearly 5000 of them vagabonds, and would benefit the realm to the tune of £200,000 a year from the sale of herrings alone.[21] The result of the plan is unknown, but the idea was revived at least three times in the early seventeenth century and came to fruition in 1632 with the establishment of the Fishery Society. Whether any vagrants were employed in fishing schemes is unclear.[22]

From Elizabeth I's reign plans were also mooted to remove the poor, including vagabonds, to greener pastures overseas. One advantage of colonies, Sir Humphrey Gilbert urged in 1583, was that 'a great number of men which do now live idly at home, are burdenous, chargeable, and unprofitable to this realm, shall hereby be set on work'.[23] Later proposals for colonies usually presented them as safety-valves to relieve over-population and social tensions at home. For example, there was a plan for an Irish plantation in 1619, the title of which – 'A Religious and Easy Course Offered for the Transplantation into Ireland of the Superfluous Multitudes of Poor People Which Overspread the Realm of England' – virtually tells the story. The idea was to deport 'idle or disordered beggars', as well as 'poor married couples who fill every place full of children'. Thus 'civilized England shall be disburdened of its worst people'.[24] The fate of this project is unknown, but governments of this period did use colonies as dumping-places for undesirables, as will be shown in the next section.

The aims of more than one Jacobean scheme were fiscal. Leonard Worrell offered a project to the King that would relieve England's poor and vagrant populations, thus saving £300,000 a year; enrich the monarchy to the tune of £130,000 a year; and help 4000 'decayed gentlemen' (was Worrell one?) to incomes of £100 p.a. The project lacked more detail. The author wrote of employing vagabonds, catching felons and encouraging the use of seacoal, but he was no ordinary mountebank. Writing from a London debtor's prison, he also related that he was a six-time loser – four times bankrupt and twice robbed by cutpurses – and concluded that 'this shall be the most famous and honourablest account both for your Majesty and [the] commonwealth and benefit of the poor'.[25]

Not all projectors were so desperate, or self-deluded. Two schemes actually got off the ground, and may have made money for the principals. *Stanley's Remedy: Or, the Way How to Reform Wandering Beggars, Thieves, Highway Robbers and Pick-pockets* was published in 1646 but actually dates from James I's reign. It seems to have been designed to persuade the authorities to permit Stanley and his associates to take over Bridewell in 1605. Like most projectors he had a way with figures, reckoning that vagrants cost the country £90,000 a year. If they were all employed and stopped from begging and stealing, a total of £365,000 (£1000 a day) would accrue. Besides plagiarizing part of the tract, Stanley made a hash of the Bridewell deal, as will be seen later in this chapter.[26]

Abraham Williams and some associates were another group to attempt to make money out of the vagrancy problem. In 1617 they wrote to the Lord Mayor informing him that they had been granted authority by the King to put a halt to 'daily abuses, daily [sic] committed by such as under habit of pedlars and petty chapmen do abound in all parts of this kingdom'. Their stated aim was to 'suppress the multitude of idle vagabonds' by licensing pedlars, but in fact they were trying to practise some economic blackmail. In effect, Williams and his confederates were asking the City to pay them, or they would license more pedlars in London.[27]

During the civil wars and Interregnum further plans were floated to cure vagrancy. The impetus was partly that censorship was in abeyance, but the hard times of the late 1640s and the idealism aroused by the puritan triumph also contributed.[28] Samuel Hartlib, the German social and religious reformer, put forward a number of proposals. He observed that the child was the father of the man, and recommended that to solve the problem of vagabondage pauper children should be educated in workhouses. He probably influenced the short-lived London workhouse, and his ideas were well designed, if they were excuted, to make some impression.[29] Peter Chamberlen devised similar though less detailed plans in *The Poor Man's Advocate* (1649). He criticized the existing

bridewells and suggested a new regime of 'houses of labour', which would employ all the able-bodied poor, not just offenders. He and Hartlib thus sought to expand the provision of work for the unemployed as a means of checking vagrancy. However, both writers retained harsh attitudes towards vagrants and beggars.[30] In sum, it is hard to detect much progress in these and the other proposals that followed More's analysis. And ultimately, whatever the detailed plans, action was left to governments.

INVENTIONS OF ABSOLUTISM

The authorities were resourceful in developing institutions with which to attack vagrancy. The multiplicity and occasional ferocity of the means employed in the battle underline the seriousness with which they viewed the problem – and its fundamental intractability. Why otherwise use martial law against vagrants, as was done? Provost-marshals were military in origin, subalterns to the Earl-Marshal, and possibly replicas of the French *prévôts*. They date from Henry VIII's reign and were originally appointed to discipline the armed forces. But they were also deployed against civilians: in the execution of rebels after uprisings in 1536, 1549 and 1569, and finally against vagrants. The poor law of 1536 authorized the Knight-Marshal to take action against beggars in the King's court, and the law was evidently enforced, for a marshal arrested two men 'begging for their fees' in London in 1537. The office was again used against non-combatants in 1556, when the marshal of the Irish army was ordered to proceed against 'suspects, vagabonds and all idle and masterless folk'.[31]

Under Elizabeth I and the early Stuarts the office of provost-marshal became a paramilitary force with wide powers. When the country was again embroiled in continental wars after 1585, marshals were widely appointed. The soldiers' riot of 1589 in Westminster, in particular, triggered the extension of martial law, and the officers were soon dealing with all kinds of disorder. The Privy Council ordered the lord-lieutenant of Cheshire to appoint a marshal in 1595 to apprehend vagabonds and 'prevent all unlawful assemblies, especially [of] suspected persons'.[32]

Notwithstanding twenty years of peace under James I, the government continued to use martial law against civilians, further increasing its rigour and coverage. A proclamation of 1616 ordered the City of London and justices in six surrounding counties to appoint provost-marshals to round up masterless men. If any resisted, the officers were empowered under the Great Seal 'without delay to execute them upon the gallows, by order of martial law'. Although no examples have been discovered of such executions, that these extreme measures were contemplated in peacetime

shows how far martial law was becoming accepted in government circles.[33] Earlier, in 1603, marshals in London were authorized to supervise all kinds of traffic and lesser officials. When the poor of the western shires rioted in 1622 during a trade slump, the government appointed a marshal to punish them.[34]

The provost-marshals unquestionably gave a fillip to local law enforcement. JPs in Elizabethan Essex found them so useful that they opposed the termination of the appointment, and in London marshals played an important role in arresting vagrants.[35] In the 1630s reports from various shires reveal their effectiveness, officials stating that vagabonds were 'well cleared', 'well avoided' and 'very few of late', because of their presence. Judging by two Hertfordshire hundreds in 1633, the marshals won hands down when it came to catching vagrants: of 136 taken, they had apprehended 95, while parish officers just 41.[36] The provost-marshals were effective because, unlike constables and JPs, they were full-time and well paid. They also went mounted outside towns, covering much larger areas than local constables. They were of higher social standing, too, than lesser officers, gentlemen and esquires actually serving in the Elizabethan period. Riding through the countryside with a clutch of deputies armed with pistols, carbines and staves, they must have been quite awesome sights.[37]

Some notable officials took exception to the use of martial law. The Kentish lawyer and justice William Lambarde attacked it as a 'new invention' in 1591. If jurors did their duties and reported negligent constables, he declared, and the foolish public did not relieve vagrants, 'we should be able of ourselves to rid us of all that vermin much sooner than could 20 provost-marshals'. His animadversions were based upon a commitment to the common law as against 'imperial or Roman law'; to local institutions as opposed to those created by government fiat.[38] Furthermore, the City of London had sufficient doubts about the legality of the office to consult learned opinion in 1596. One citizen challenged the marshal's authority on grounds of trespass, won the case and received damages in King's Bench. The Earl of Essex, the Earl-Marshal, also expressed reservations about the institution's use in peacetime. He thought its powers of summary justice infringed upon the tradition of due process: 'it does agree with her Majesty's merciful and excellent government not to let her subjects die *sans replique*, as the Frenchman terms it, while her kingdom is free both from invasion and rebellion'.[39] In some measure, however, the Earl was splitting hairs. The vagrancy laws, as will be demonstrated below, gave the power of summary justice to every constable in the land, although admittedly not the power to execute summarily.

Not all the weapons for dealing with vagabonds were so novel.

Licences to beg and passports, counterfeits of which were discussed earlier, originated in the fourteenth century. They were intended to restrict labour's mobility and hold down wages after the Black Death. A statute of 1388 required passports, or 'letters testimonial', of servants leaving masters, able-bodied pilgrims, wandering beggars, university students and persons returning from abroad (perhaps aimed at soldiers and mariners). Tudor and early Stuart governments kept the requirement, even though labour shortage was rarely a problem, because of their preoccupation with public order, and extended it to further itinerant groups. An Act of Henry VII's reign stipulated that military personnel had to carry such papers, and Acts of 1531 and 1563 ordered persons begging outside their localities to have them. Another statute of 1572 added a variety of entertainers, pedlars and tinkers to the list.[40]

The able-bodied, transient poor were all expected to have valid papers. The poor law of 1536 exempted servants for one month after their service ended, but required them to obtain a testimonial stating the date of their departure. Later legislation, including the Statute of Artificers of 1563, provided that those who failed to carry passports were to be punished for vagrancy, and these provisions were enforced for a further century, whatever the state of the labour market.[41] In addition, the passport was used to control the movements of convicted criminals, including vagabonds. An Act of 1572 stated that persons leaving gaol were to have a licence from two JPs, if they wandered to 'beg for their fees', or simply travelled home. Another in 1597 laid down that convicted vagrants were to carry papers stating their birthplaces or last residences, that they had been chastised for their crimes, and their destinations.[42] Despite widespread fraud, the passport was the only effective method of controlling the movements of the vagrant poor.

Badging was another procedure that governments devised to check vagabondage. It involved wearing a badge, or 'token', to indicate one's status as a convict or authorized beggar. The origins of the practice are obscure, but it may have developed from the badging of those other 'deviants', the Jews, with yellow crosses.[43] Whatever the case, the institution became common during the Renaissance. In England the purposes were penal and administrative, that is, to punish convicted vagabonds by holding them up to ridicule and to limit the numbers and movements of beggars. The penal element was prominent when London's Court of Aldermen ordered a vagrant to be banished in 1516 'with a letter "V" of yellow woollen cloth fastened upon his breast'. The punishment prefigures the branding of vagabonds, but was also a bureaucratic device to distinguish genuine beggars. In 1515 York officials ordered those unable to labour to wear tokens upon their shoulders.[44] Badging was applied to the entire country when the poor law of 1563 required that

licensed beggars wear 'some notable badge or token' on the breast or back of their upper garments. When poor relief became a statutory obligation for parishes in 1597, there was further incentive to badging those receiving relief. London officials commanded in 1600 that anyone receiving pensions 'shall every day openly wear a badge of lead upon their left sleeve', and if they refused, relief was to be suspended. Whether or not such arrangements were generally applied, however, remains to be seen.[45]

As noticed earlier, governments mounted special searches or man-hunts for vagrants, which took on new dimensions under the Tudors and early Stuarts. The Statute of Winchester (1285) had required regular round-ups of felons in towns, and there were frequent searches for vagrants in London from 1514 and about the same time in some provincial towns. But national campaigns were seemingly first instituted under the Tudors.[46] The vagrancy Act of 1495 ordered them in all the towns and villages of the realm, as did a proclamation of 1511 and another of 1530. The poor law of 1536 also commanded officials to conduct nightly and daily 'privy or secret' searches for 'all rufflers, sturdy vagabonds and valiant beggars', and a new Act in 1610 established regular swoops for the first time. Justices were to send out warrants twice a year to constables to hold nightly searches for vagrants, and then at petty sessions they were to examine the results. The procedure was followed in Wiltshire, and a similar system was employed in the great Caroline round-ups.[47]

How the searches were organized is seen in a set of orders from Devon in 1569:

1) That every fortnight between 5th November and Christmas a strong night watch and search be held in every parish in the county, followed by a day watch;
2) That local officials and keepers of lodgings for travellers examine lodgers' names, dwelling places, destinations and reasons for travel, and bring any suspicious persons before a JP;
3) That rogues born outside the realm be taken to a port and sent away;
4) That JPs reassemble at a later date to certify the results of the searches to the Privy Council, as well as any 'matters of great importance' that had happened in their localities.[48]

And how such provisions worked in practice is shown by a Shrewsbury example of 1571. In addition to local constables, two or more of the 'most substantial parishioners' were to scour each parish for vagrants. Eleven such bands of 'watchers and searchers' were formed, each headed by a captain and numbering 125 men in all, which also ranged beyond parish bounds in the manner of provost-marshals.[49]

The motives for the great national searches of 1569–72 and 1631–9 were

primarily political, for both occurred in unsettled times. Traditionally the rebellion of 1569 has been presented as the crucial element in the first set, but in reality the campaign began almost a decade earlier. It originated in attempts to shore up the established order after the mid-Tudor crisis. At the beginning of Elizabeth's reign proclamations controlling dress were issued which, for detail and frequency, are unmatched by other periods. Proposals to Parliament in 1559 contained swingeing attacks upon social mobility, and the revival of the slavery Act of 1547 to suppress vagabonds. A proclamation to the mayor of York in 1561 ordered the city to keep watch on a number of fronts, including servants and labourers, middlemen, alehouses, livery and maintenance, rumours, riots and unlawful assemblies, as well as vagrants. Searches for vagrants may have begun in Wiltshire in 1560, and were definitely under way in Essex from 1564.[50]

The Caroline campaign was no less the product of crisis. The government's difficulties included disastrous wars against France and Spain, from which military men returned disgruntled and idle; the assassination of the King's leading minister; harvest failures and food riots; massive immigration by hungry Irishmen; riots in the forest and fens provoked by royal policies; depression in the cloth industry; and trouble among the top people in conflicts between the monarchy and 'Country' gentlemen.[51] The Book of Orders of 1631 was the government's response. As in the 1560s and previous Books of Orders, local officials were handed hefty briefs: eleven directions covering the control of the corn trade, masters and servants, apprenticing the poor, relief for the impotent, and another eight concerning the methods to be employed. Vagrancy, of course, figured large in the Orders of 1631.[52]

Government attempts to check vagrancy included further innovations, besides martial law, that departed from the common-law traditions of trial by jury and oral testimony. Summary justice, which was widely utilized, was a significant move away from trial by jury. The Act of 1383 had ordered vagrants to be imprisoned to await trial, but Tudor and early Stuart legislation with one exception put their 'trials' in the hands of constables and justices out of court. Henry VII's statute of 1495 abolished committal to gaol and authorized officials 'by examination' to punish vagrants for three days in stocks; later laws modified the procedure only slightly. The Act of 1572 continued the practice of summary justice, while altering it. The statute sent offenders to gaol to await the Gaol Delivery, and made second and third offences felonies, but trial by jury was not mentioned. Conviction was to be based upon 'inquest of office' by justices, or the word of two witnesses. In 1576 a new Act specified that trial by jury take place for further (felonious) offences; that passed in 1597 returned the power of summary justice to constables, while the 1610 statute had JPs judging cases in special sessions. In addition, dangerous

offenders could be banished from the country by justices at sessions according to the Act of 1597, and from 1604 they could also be branded on the justices' orders, although they were entitled to a trial if accused of felony.[53]

The extension of powers of summary justice worried legal theorists and MPs. The author of a 'Discourse upon the Commission of Bridewell' suggested that the London hospital's powers of summary conviction violated chapter 29 of Magna Carta. MPs also voiced fears about the procedure in the early seventeenth century. They specifically opposed granting it to JPs in cases of unlicensed alehouses, drunkenness, absence from church and swearing. They feared that justices might abuse their authority for financial gain, but also thought that summary justice oppressed the 'free subject' and was contrary to Magna Carta.[54]

Examinations of suspects were a departure from the principle of oral testimony, but historians are divided about the procedure's constitutional significance. One authority considered it an extension of the prosecution's power, because it allied the magistrate with the accuser. The JP 'becomes an inquisitor as well as a judge', gathering information in the manner of the police, deciding whether there was sufficient evidence for the case to go to court, and then judging it. In such a system there were few safeguards against a self-interested or corrupt magistrate, particularly if judgements were summary, as some MPs noted. On the other hand, it is argued that the Marian statute did not require that examinations be conducted under oath, so that suspects could not incriminate themselves. And at no point did English examination procedure involve a revamping of criminal law in the manner of continental reforms with their development of 'inquisition process' and use of torture.[55]

There is no simple way of resolving these interpretations, because one cannot read the minds of the law-makers. It is possible, however, to see both summary justice and examinations in their historical context. As regards the first procedure, it undoubtedly made sense to hard-pressed governments. Few sixteenth-century states had enough gaols to incarcerate vagrants while they awaited trial; nor a large enough judiciary to try them. The authorities indeed cited the inconvenience of administering the law in the traditional way. The Act of 1495 referred to the 'great charges that should grow to [the King's] subjects for bringing of vagabonds to the gaols' under the legislation of 1383. In London in 1579 it was decided to judge suspects summarily in Bridewell, 'without tarrying for any delay of sessions at the Guildhall, which to the governors should be troublesome and to the house very chargeable'.[56] As well as providing a short-cut around the courts, summary justice suited the interests of the urban oligarchs and village notables who dominated local government. It granted them the authority to police their inferiors almost at will, and thus

to control the pressing problems of destitution and disorder, in addition to obviating costly and time-consuming court appearances.[57]

As stated in Chapter 1, examination procedure sprang from the growth of state authority to deal with new crimes, including vagrancy. From the thirteenth century European law became more severe. With the introduction of Roman law and inquisition process, examinations and torture were used to discover the innocence or guilt of the defendant and the identities of confederates.[58] In England inquisition process developed in an attenuated form. Ordinary justices did not administer torture, and pre-trial examination under the statute of 1555 was not determinative. But examinations were determinative in some instances – for example, in a vagrancy Act of 1531 – and they were recommended for use in discovering accomplices in felony cases. Thus Dalton wrote that if in an examination 'a felon brought before a Justice of Peace accuses others, it is sufficient cause for the Justice to grant out his warrant for the rest'.[59]

A final procedure to be altered in vagrancy legislation was bail. As in other late medieval statutes that made offences imprisonable, those relating to labour and vagabondage prohibited bail. The intention was apparently that imprisonment should be punitive, which perhaps represents the germ of the bridewell idea.[60] All told, then, the English state did not import inquisition process wholesale from the continent, but it still developed revolutionary new procedures for dealing with social and political crimes like vagrancy. Perhaps most remarkably, it gave the power of summary justice to officials in every parish in the land, which they eagerly took up. Who would judge that to be an insignificant extension of state authority?

RETRIBUTION

Punishment, like crime, has its origins in society, and the growth of rootless elements necessitated new forms of penalty. Some penal systems emphasize redress, that is, the obligation of the offender to compensate his victim. Thieves must make restitution, the families of persons harmed are compensated, and miscreants do penance or pay fines to propitiate God and the victim. But where the evil-doer is too poor to pay a fine, or the offence is not committed against a specific person, which was true of vagabondage, redress is no longer an appropriate form of penalty. Instead some form of retribution, involving 'loss or suffering', is usually inflicted, and early-modern England saw a significant increase in such punishments.[61]

The retributive punishments of vagrants were of two basic types. By far the more common was corporal, of which the range was great and expanding; a second involved loss of freedom. The period from the

mid-fourteenth to the early seventeenth century witnessed a remarkable growth of corporal punishment in statute law. Stocks, which were used in medieval gaols, were ordered to be built in every town by the Statute of Labourers for the detention of runaway servants and labourers. According to another Act of 1388, they were to be locked in them if they carried no testimonials, and until they produced sureties that they would return to service. Then in the statute of 1495 vagabonds and beggars were to be set in stocks for three days and nights with a diet of bread and water, and for six days for a second offence. So what began as a detention place for masterless men became a means of punishing them.[62] Stocks and whipping posts were commonplace in sixteenth- and seventeenth-century towns and villages, standing in marketplaces or on village greens. The York authorities ordered four new pairs of stocks erected in 1588 for the punishment of rogues and beggars; in 1630, according to John Taylor, the 'Water Poet', London and its suburbs had sixty sets of whipping posts, stocks and cages, and eighteen gaols.[63]

Whipping was a sixteenth-century development. The poor law of 1531 stipulated that vagrants be 'tied to the end of a cart naked and be beaten with whips' around the town or village, and until their bodies were bloody. Then the ferocious Act of 1572 required them to be flogged, as well as having their ears bored, while in 1597 a return was made to the practice of 1531.[64] Whipping, probably the most common penalty for vagrancy, was the creation of an authoritarian patriarchal society, which considered it 'the only reliable method of controlling both children and adults'. It was therefore natural for officials to flog the masterless, who were rebellious inferiors.[65] Whipping also enjoyed wide currency because it was the most efficient way of dealing with vagabonds. To hold them for trial, or send them to a house of correction, was expensive and troublesome, whereas a sound thrashing and a passport saw them off to become someone else's troubles. Whether the punishment alleviated the problem is doubtful. In fact, it probably worsened it by keeping vagrants perpetually on the move.

Branding and ear-boring were statutory punishments from the late fourteenth century. A labour statute of 1361, for instance, declared that fugitives were to be branded in the forehead with an 'F' for their 'falsity'. But there is no evidence that the penalty was executed, nor the provision of the slavery statute of 1547 that vagrants be branded with a 'V' on their breasts.[66] Ear-boring was introduced in 1572, when a statute was passed requiring all vagabonds to be 'grievously whipped and burned through the gristle of the right ear with a hot iron' an inch in diameter. That sentence was apparently executed upon six vagrants, two of them women, in Essex in 1574. Under James I branding became common practice. By an Act of 1604 incorrigible rogues were to be 'branded in the

left shoulder with a hot burning iron of the breadth of an English shilling, with a great Roman "R" upon the iron'. Male vagabonds were regularly punished in this manner at quarter sessions in the North Riding; women were usually let off with a whipping, although in Essex in 1614 one was branded for vagrancy. The punishment was partly intended as a means of identifying repeat offenders. The Act required that the mark be 'so thoroughly burned and set on upon [sic] the skin and flesh, that the letter "R" be seen and remain for a perpetual mark upon such rogue during his or her life'. JPs examined suspects' bodies for the marks when they took their depositions.[67]

Further forms of corporal punition included hair-polling, the pillory, the ducking-stool, ear-cropping and hanging. No statutory basis has been found for the first three, although they were used at least once against vagabonds. Hair-cropping was a punishment administered to London prostitutes and bawds in 1384, and was utilized against vagrants there and in Southampton from the early sixteenth century.[68] The pillory was employed against fraudulent dicers and beggars in the late Middle Ages. It first appears as a penalty for vagrants in 1520, when the Court of Aldermen commanded 'a new engine to be made' in Cheapside, to which a bevy of them had their ears nailed. They also had papers placed above their heads stating their offences, and were made to stand there for four hours. Two women seized in the City in 1534 were similarly ordered to wear such papers and to be 'set upon a cucking stool', while two others were banished in 1537 under threat of losing their ears.[69]

Vagrancy was a felony for repeat offences in the Acts of 1536, 1547, 1572, 1576, 1597 and 1604. In practice it seems offenders were mainly hanged under the first two Elizabethan statutes. Three males and a female were executed at Middlesex sessions in 1575–6; another was ordered to die in Warwick in 1582; and still others were hanged for consorting with gypsies, which was felonious by a statute of 1562.[70] It is impossible to state what proportion of vagabonds were executed. The vast majority received chastisement from the constable's whip. Between 1603 and 1638 Wiltshire constables reported punishing 982 vagrants in this manner as opposed to 143 who appeared in Gaol Delivery calendars. Only 64 of the 143 were then committed for trial as felons, indicted or convicted, so that at most 6 per cent were hanged.[71]

It would be wrong to conclude that punishments were not harsh, simply because they were not fatal. Floggings could turn into murderous affairs, and undoubtedly fostered class hatred and authoritarianism.[72] Torture was against English law but was occasionally covertly administered. The rogue writer Thomas Harman, who was a Kentish JP, casually described an incident when a pretended dumb beggar was hanged by his wrists until he confessed.[73] But with a catch-all definition of vagrancy and

constables holding the authority summarily to judge and punish, torture was hardly necessary.

Retributive punishments also included loss of freedom. The vagrancy laws of 1383 and 1388 provided for offenders to go to gaol. Imprisonment also cropped up in the Acts of 1576 and 1597, but few places had sufficient space to incarcerate more than a few dozen at a time. The statute of 1495 specifically complained of the expense and trouble of gaoling vagrants, while in Warwick in 1581 a vagrant soldier, his wife and child were stocked for three days and then released, 'because the gaol was pestered with many prisoners, above 50'.[74] Vagabonds were also sent to bridewells, which are examined below, but even there they mostly received summary punishment. So it was probably mainly suspected felons who were imprisoned for the purpose of awaiting trials.

Compulsory labour was another form of loss of freedom. The Act of 1547 placed convicted vagrants in slavery for two years, and that of 1597 despatched them to serve in galleys, but no evidence has been found that either provision was enforced. The same is true of enactments in 1536 and 1597 stating that vagabonds should be put to work.[75] But in an Act of 1572 more detailed arrangements were developed. First offenders were re- leased to serve a householder in lieu of corporal punishment, and for second timers the term was two years. Those provisions were in some measure invoked, judging by local records, although it is doubtful whether the sentence was as common as the corporal varieties.[76] Com- pulsory labour was also the *raison d'être* of the bridewells, but how far they fulfilled that function will be shown to be doubtful. It was probably mainly enforced through placing the young in service.[77]

Two final forms of retributive punishment involving loss of freedom were impressment and transportation. The legal background to both is complex. Neither was utilized exclusively for vagabonds, and neither was a common statutory punishment for the offence. But both were used to rid the country of them, and it is probable that thousands of paupers, especially the young, were exiled overseas from 1560.

Impressment began in the reign of Edward I, and outlaws were taken for military service from Edward III's reign.[78] It was seen in Chapter 5 that Elizabethan and early Stuart governments drafted vagabonds for cam- paigns, and that impressment escalated in the second half of the sixteenth century. The practice continued under the first two Stuarts, and while precise figures are lacking for the total numbers press-ganged, they must have amounted to thousands, because vagrants accounted for a major share of armies.[79]

In theory, all recruits were 'volunteers', but in reality the option was between that and possible trial as a felon. Faced with Hobson's choice, many took the opportunity to escape the chance of hanging. A Lincoln-

shire vagrant was reported willing to serve in the Low Countries after being told in Norwich in 1627 that 'if he fails, he stands committed to bridewell'. Likewise, Nicholas Haselwood was imprisoned in a Hertfordshire house of correction in Charles I's reign, where he was to be flogged until he paid a fine of £10. If he could not pay, the only escape was if a captain took him as a soldier, or he was sent 'beyond the seas'. Sometimes the choice was seemingly not even offered – for example, when twenty-three men in Bridewell were 'appointed for her Majesty's service in Ireland' in 1598, and when more were sent to the Low Countries the following year.[80]

Impressment had a dubious constitutional position. Conscripting seamen had been accepted since the reign of Richard II, but the army was another matter, especially for overseas missions, which was against the common law. However, that obstacle was overcome by commissions of array and by statute, although doubts persisted: Sir John Smythe informed men mustered in Essex in 1596 that a proposed 'press' of 1000 men was illegal.[81] The Long Parliament passed an Act in 1642 that limited the use of impressed men to their native counties, but whether that statute arose from concern for the subject's liberties is questionable since it still allowed conscripts to be sent elsewhere in case of an invasion.[82]

The transportation of vagabonds dates from Elizabeth I's reign, although it only came into full spate later. A hint of a move in this direction came in the 'Book Devised to Set the Poor on Work' issued by the London Common Council in 1579. It recommended that, to avoid Bridewell becoming 'over-pestered' with vagrants, the governors should see 'that owners or masters of ships be entreated to receive such into their service', but nothing seems to have come of the proposal at the time.[83]

The statutory authority for transportation was a vagrancy Act of 1597 which provided that dangerous rogues should be banished overseas. Then a Privy Council order of 1603 exiled them to Newfoundland, the East and West Indies, France, Germany, Spain and the Low Countries, although in practice most were sent to the American colonies.[84] The whole business was of dubious legality, because many who were sent were young and poor rather than the hardened rogues described in the official documents. Again, in principle the authorities gave offenders the choice whether to go, but as with impressment the decision was often made under duress. Others were kidnapped outright – 'crimped' or 'spirited' from the streets – and never saw a judge or jury.[85]

The first reference to transportation comes in 1607, when an apprentice dyer was 'sent to Virginia' from Bridewell for running away with his master's goods. Thereafter there was a steady flow to the New World. The deportees were usually indentured for service, as in the manner of

apprentices at home, with a colonial master. It is impossible to determine the total numbers or to distinguish vagrants who were misdemeanants from convicted felons and children spirited away.[86] Yet even the scattered data suggest that several thousand were removed in the seventeenth century. In London the first major shipments took place from 1619 to 1622, when about 300 London youngsters were shipped to Virginia. Bridewell also exiled hundreds to Bermuda and Barbados, and simply 'to sea', particularly during the Interregnum.[87] But the provinces were also affected. A Hampshire correspondent wrote to the Virginia Company in 1627 that 'there are many ships now going to Virginia, and with them, some 1400 or 1500 children, which they have gathered up in diverse places', while in the 1630s Kentish officials summarily shipped the poor to the colonies. In 1653 two ships sailed to collect 400 Irish children; back in London in 1656 several hundred prostitutes were banished to the West Indies to boost the birth rate there.[88]

Transportation understandably provoked fears and opposition. A man with a commission to transport young women to Virginia and Bermuda caused panic in the West Country in 1618, Hext reporting that forty 'poor maidens' had fled one Somerset village alone. There was also resistance a year later to the first major transportation in London. In 1620 the Common Council ordered that parents refusing to allow their children to be taken were to have poor relief cut off. Later a revolt occurred among the children held in Bridewell, some protesting 'their unwillingness to go to Virginia', but they were sent, just the same, by Privy Council order.[89]

As with conscripts, the alternatives often amounted to Hobson's choice: to risk a life of temporary servitude in a strange place, or to rot in a house of correction and possibly stand trial as a felon. William Benny, described as 'a vagrant, a nip and common guest [therefore triable as a felon] that takes no warning', still refused a trip to Virginia, but to many others the chance to escape incarceration must have been attractive.[90] Officials held out carrots as well as sticks to reluctant transportees and their families. Generally, they were promised 'good education and future maintenance' in the colony, and material rewards were also on offer. In 1620 the Virginia Company proffered an allowance of £3 each and £2 for clothing for 100 London children. Boys were to be apprenticed to the age of 21 and girls until marriage. Then they were to be 'placed as tenants upon the public land with best conditions', including a house, stock of corn and cattle, and half the profits.[91]

Life in the colonies rarely measured up to the rosy picture painted by the Company. The attempt rapidly to settle Virginia between 1618 and 1624 was a disaster. It has been estimated that, although 3500 to 4000 immigrants arrived in that period, the total population rose from just 1000 to 1500. The London children suffered badly. Of the ninety-nine sent in

1619, few survived to adulthood, and another sixty-six sent in 1619–20 suffered similar fates. An indeterminate number died on the way and at least five were killed in a massacre by Indians in 1622.[92]

Those who survived were probably worse off than they had been in England. Only two or three of the 300 Londoners sent in 1619–20 enjoyed any material success in later years. For most, servitude was harder than in England, because with labour in short supply their masters reduced them to virtual slavery. At home the normal term was a year, but in the colonies it was seven. If they committed crimes during their terms, these could be extended for a further seven years. Servants were bought, sold and inherited as chattels. They received exiguous wages because a substantial part of their pay went to cover their passage.[93]

Conditions in early Virginia were perhaps unusually harsh, but it is difficult to be sanguine about the prospects of the vagrants (and others) sent overseas. After the first years of settlement few received grants of land; masters in the southern colonies continued to exercise almost complete control over them. When conflicts occurred, servants might sue masters, but the courts normally protected the latters' interests.[94] In the event the policy removed troublesome, surplus people from England, but it and the other retributive punishments can hardly be interpreted as progressive.

BRIDEWELL: A PROTO-PENAL INSTITUTION THAT FAILED

Potentially the most revolutionary of the institutions developed to police vagabonds was the bridewell, or house of correction. In the medieval period itinerants had traditionally received hospitality in monasteries and almshouses, but after the Tudor dissolutions they were imprisoned in a new kind of 'hospital', which sought to reform them through work. The bridewell, it has been observed, is the prototype of 'the reformative policy of modern penology'. Its regime belies Foucault's argument that the prison idea, with its regimentation and its aim of moulding the malefactor's soul, only developed in the late eighteenth and early nineteenth centuries.[95] Although bridewell failed in its reformative programme, degenerating into another gaol-like institution, it provides further evidence of the extremes to which the authorities were driven in their anxiety about the vagrancy question.

With the chartering of the London Bridewell in 1553 vagabonds began to be incarcerated with the purpose of reforming them. Gloucester, Ipswich and Norwich founded similar institutions in the 1560s, and there was a further spate of foundations after an Act of 1576 ordered the establishment of houses of correction in all counties and corporate towns.[96] Further statutes in 1597 and 1610 required the setting up of

bridewells, and more were established: Devon and Norfolk each had four in 1598, Hertfordshire seven by the early 1620s, Sussex five before 1642, and Warwickshire three by 1635 and six by 1701, although it is unlikely they all had continuous existences.[97]

The bridewell was novel, because it sought to transform the vagabond's character. 'The mean[s] to reform beggary is to fall to work', London's city fathers declared in their suit for the former royal palace in 1552. The poor of all conditions might be employed there: children 'unapt to learning' who were masterless; the 'sore and sick' after they were healed, so that they would not beg and wander; prisoners acquitted at quarter sessions; as well as the idle able-bodied. The rationale in the Act of 1576 was that in houses of correction 'youth may be accustomed and brought up in labour and work, and then not like[ly] to grow to be idle rogues'. Sir Edward Coke thought bridewells a definite improvement on gaols: 'few are committed to the House of Correction or Working-House, but they come out better'.[98]

Notwithstanding these reformative purposes, penal elements were also present. A plan for a Westminster bridewell in 1561 declared that one aim was the 'repressing of the idle, sturdy vagabond and common strumpet', and the statutes of 1576, 1597 and 1610 all listed punishment as one intention of the houses. The bridewell regime did terrify vagrants, who begged instead to go to gaol, according to Hext.[99]

The Somerset justice was probably correct, for inmates were disciplined in the bridewells. The usual routine was a whipping, followed by incarceration and hard labour. In Bury St Edmunds the rules stated that all prisoners 'without fail, at their first coming into the said house, shall have put upon him, her, or them, some clog, chain, ringle, or manacle'. Anyone who was stubborn or unruly received further punishment, including 'thinner diet and harder labour, until he or she shall be brought to reasonable obedience and submission'. A first refusal to work was punished by four stripes and fettering, a second by six stripes, and a third by referral to justices as an incorrigible rogue. Anyone persistently using 'unchaste or unchristian speeches or behaviour' was to receive three stripes. But officials employed incentives as well as chastisements. Inmates in the Bury house who worked willingly received additional rations between meals, the amount depending upon how well they applied themselves. If they refused to work, their food allowance was cut.[100]

The houses had detailed procedures to maintain discipline. The sexes were separated in the Westminster plan. And the day was regimented: in Norwich the prisoners worked from 5 a.m. to 8 p.m. in summer, and from 6 a.m. to 7 or 7.30 p.m. in winter, with half an hour to eat and fifteen minutes to pray. Dress and diet were regulated, too.[101] Provincial bridewells were simple in plan, a matter of a few rooms, but London's

resembled a modern prison with its many chambers. They also had small-scale bureaucracies. Most houses had just one or two officials, but in larger towns the staff was more considerable. In Norwich there were about ten, including four directly running the place, while London had thirty, most of whom were full-time with families living on site, making a total of perhaps 100 persons in 1631. In addition, the governors met on the premises at least once or twice a week. Before 1620 only six to eight attended, but after that thirty were commonly present. When the comings and goings of constables, warders and marshals are reckoned on, the London house was a hive of activity.[102]

Officials used proto-bureaucratic methods, including records of inmates. The Bury St Edmunds keeper was to note the dates they entered and left, their ages, height, colour of hair, complexion, descriptions of clothing, places of birth and last abode, by whose warrants they were incarcerated and released, and any distinguishing features. The Bury records have unfortunately disappeared, but ten volumes of them exist for the London Bridewell for sixty-three years between 1559 and 1659. Admittedly by the standards of modern prisons the numbers in the bridewells were small, provincial ones having no more than ten to twenty inmates at a time, while in London they rarely surpassed 150.[103] Nevertheless, running these institutions was time-consuming and expensive. Accounts for London in 1631, which include little information on inmates and expenditure, still ran to thirty pages of foolscap, and the house's revenues that year were over £1300. Provincial institutions had modest budgets – for example, Bury St Edmunds, which spent just £20 in 1630–1 – but even a small house involved dozens of items of business each year, even ignoring time taken up with the prisoners.[104]

The bridewell programme involved the employment of vagabonds, and statutes ordered that stocks and equipment be purchased. In London in 1631 the house had resident sixteen craftsmen, who kept 106 inmates at work, its own mill and a hemp-house. Only a dozen persons were employed in the Norwich house, but 1000 were said to be put to work outside, whereby the city saved £3000 in poor relief.[105]

But the high hopes for the bridewells were largely dashed, mainly because of bad management. The local authorities often skimped on finance. To attack vagrancy and its causes would have required hundreds of thousands of pounds, so that most institutions' budgets were insufficient. The plaster was too small for the sore, as the author of a memorandum of 1595 noted: 'the number of such vagrant poor within every shire, if they be all taken up, will be over large for one common receipt, or house of correction, and for the masters, governors of the said houses, to oversee and correct'. The necessary bureaucracy would be expensive, as would the materials to be worked upon, and so the richer

parishes would refuse to participate. That was a perspicacious assessment, for raising sufficient funds proved a major difficulty.[106]

Badly paid, the private contractors who increasingly ran the bridewells used them for personal gain. In 1600 the London governors complained that the lessee of the corn mill had converted it to grind malt for his own brewhouse. The most spectacular misuse of a bridewell occurred in the capital five years later, when the group headed by Stanley – 'sometime an Inns of Court gentleman, afterwards by lewd company . . . a highway robber' – took over the house with the support of the King and City magistrates. He promised to put 500 vagrants to work, but the scheme was a disaster. He never employed more than 100, and after seven months the inmates were starving and neglected. Meanwhile, Stanley had turned the place into a bawdy house with its own brewery. That episode was outrageous but not unparalleled, and the bridewell's slender resources, combined with corruption and neglect, resulted in frequent calls to sessions to bail them out.[107]

Because of such problems, the houses of correction lost their original purposes of employing the willing poor and correcting the unwilling. By the early seventeenth century they dealt overwhelmingly with offenders: of over 900 persons sent to London's Bridewell in 1600–1, over half were described as vagrants, a third were immorality cases (whores, mothers of bastards, bigamists), and the rest were runaways and thieves. Only seven were described as 'poor apprentices', who were apparently there for training in a craft. The pattern was similar in the provinces, judging by evidence from Essex, Norwich and Wiltshire.[108] Thus one plank in the bridewell's programme collapsed near the start, which supports E. M. Leonard's conclusion that houses of correction were developing into lock-ups. They were, in fact, increasingly described as 'prisons' – denoting a common gaol rather than a modern prison – and the inmates as 'prisoners'. Sometimes the houses were built next to the local gaol, and had gaol-keepers as masters. In Caroline Ilchester 'the poor suffered in fetid incommodiousness with the wicked', because the house of correction and gaol were under the same roof.[109]

The bridewells failed to employ significant numbers of vagabonds, because they dismissed them soon after punishment. Critics were aware of the tendency. One wrote in 1619 of vagrants 'whom the houses of correction cannot reform, for they only whip such as be sent unto them, and after chastisement enlarge them to follow their former lewd courses'. Likewise, the Court of Aldermen complained in 1631 that vagrants were released from Bridewell without examination or punishment, much less reformation through work.[110] The issue of whether to keep or release offenders was critical. To incarcerate and employ them required great expense, while to let them go meant that they returned to crime, as

another critic observed in 1595. The problem proving insoluble, bridewells took the cheaper route.[111]

Not surprisingly, the houses developed many of the problems of gaols. Bridewell corrupted the good and made the bad worse, a London hospital official stated in 1587, because persons genuinely in need were 'packed up and punished . . . with rogues, beggars, strumpets and pilfering thieves'. The author of the memorandum of 1595 similarly noted that 'many such people being for the most part of lewd disposition kept together within one place, the one will infect the other'.[112] Efforts were sometimes made to separate the innocent and the wicked, but it is doubtful that such measures were generally taken. When Sarah Hancock went on a rampage in the Dorchester bridewell in 1634, shouting filthy abuse at other inmates, 'the boys of the house were present and heard all her talk'. As Chamberlen stated in 1649, houses of correction were 'more apt to make men (from being poor) to become vagabonds and beggars'.[113]

Bridewells were prey to further problems associated with lock-ups, including fraternization and crime. In Chester's in 1613 the master got drunk with two visitors, who proceeded to help an inmate escape down a rope, while at Devizes in 1637 the keeper was alleged to have released a man 'to go abroad . . . for to earn some monies against Christmas'. A tip to the gaoler gained people admittance to most gaols in the period, and in London it became fashionable to attend the whippings of prostitutes in Bridewell. Slack management led to blatant abuses: at Hertford assizes in James I's reign the master of a bridewell was accused of harbouring a rogue and stolen goods; in London in 1630 a governor of Bridewell was accused of fathering a child on an inmate.[114]

Conditions were hard in the houses, which encouraged the prisoners to be difficult. Although the better-off ones might obtain a decent living-standard by paying fees, most were down and out. A woman in the Dorchester house complained that 'they could not sleep for fleas and lice'. Prisoners understandably escaped and rebelled as a result. They went out of windows on ropes and bed-linen, deserted work-details, and broke out of stocks. Organized rebellions were rarely reported, but seven female prisoners were punished in London in 1620 for disobeying the matron, filling the latrines with straw and defiling their rooms 'like beasts'.[115]

Things were not improved by the harsh treatment that prisoners sometimes received. In London the matron examined girls to determine whether they were virgins. If they were not, they were punished and kept with the 'common whores'. Males had their heads shaved.[116] Beatings were regularly administered and on occasion got out of hand. Prisoners were sometimes thrashed to extract confessions. Joan Albiston, a beggar suspected of theft in 1560, 'would confess nothing, although she was well punished'; a month later she was discharged with a sore leg. Thomasin

Latimer entered Bridewell in 1560 'for relief of necessity' and was described as a 'sore labourer', but was 'unreasonably beaten by the matron of this house in such sort as we were ashamed to behold the same'.[117]

A wide range of persons was empowered to commit people to bridewells, which led to cases of alleged wrongful incarceration. A Wiltshire widow petitioned the King in 1618 for the release of her son from the Devizes house, where she claimed he was wrongfully sent by his master and had spent nine months in 'want and misery'. Even worse was the plight of a butcher's apprentice sent to Gloucestershire on an errand, and who met a stranger who gave him a letter to deliver in Devizes. When it was opened, the boy was arrested and sent to the local bridewell, where the master nearly beat him to death.[118]

To one authority the powers of the London house were of questionable legality. 'A Discourse Upon the Commission of Bridewell', probably the work of a barrister in the 1590s, raised doubts about the governors' authority. He argued that a provision in the hospital's charter empowering them to arrest and imprison vagabonds conflicted with the provision in Magna Carta that no free man could be arrested and imprisoned without a trial by jury, or by the law of the land. He further questioned their authority to examine and punish vagrants, which he suggested was given to JPs by Act of Parliament but not to the governors.[119]

The bridewell idea retained some currency until the birth of the prison in England. Similar institutions continued to be established to check vagrancy by employing the poor, including the London workhouse of 1649, the Colleges of Industry of Bellers and Cary in the 1690s, and the many workhouses set up in the eighteenth century. The latter, at least, differed little from the bridewells and shared many of their problems. By the early 1800s some poor law reformers were calling for their abolition.[120]

CONCLUSIONS

The proliferation of institutions to combat vagabondage, together with the limited success that some like the bridewell enjoyed, might suggest that governments were helpless in the face of the problem. That conclusion would be a questionable one. It ignores the fact that thousands were apprehended and punished for vagrancy, that thousands more, in all likelihood, were sent into exile abroad, as well as the possible deterrent effect that state action had upon others. Furthermore, it turns a blind eye to the very real extension of state authority implicit in the policies of Parliament and the Privy Council. To grant powers of arrest, judgement and punishment to parish constables, as well as to chartered bodies such as Bridewell, was a major constitutional innovation, and just one of many. That fact was not lost upon contemporary legal observers. Rather,

the evidence of state policy again suggests that governments were faced with a formidable social problem; so formidable that they were prepared to breach the traditional bounds of the constitution.

Conclusions

After 1660 vagrancy policy changed. The penal element declined and settlement laws redefined the transient pauper. Henceforth instead of being punished as a vagabond, he was removed to his place of origin where he received statutory relief, which kept him from becoming a permanent itinerant. Signs of a changing policy are evident in parliamentary debates in 1656, when a committee of the House proposed to define a vagrant as anyone straying more than 10 miles from his dwelling place. Opponents protested that 'by these *terminis generalibus*, any man may be adjudged by the justice to be a vagrant'. One member further observed that 'for aught I know I myself may be whipped, if I be found but 10 miles from my own house'.[1] Such questioning of a rigorous policy was almost unheard of before the mid-seventeenth century.

Of course, Parliament continued to pass vagrancy laws after 1660, but they added little that was new. Furthermore, the Privy Council took limited interest in vagabonds, apart from continuing to conscript them for military service. Later round-ups were mostly local in inspiration and regular constables' presentments of vagrants largely ceased.[2] Whipping declined, too, and in its place developed a system of passing without punishment, in which the convicted were basically paid to return home. Eventually the local authorities lost interest in that expensive and time-consuming business, and from the early eighteenth century began farming it out to contractors.[3]

While historians have been aware of the shift in policy after 1660, they have not examined the reasons for it in any depth. The traditional explanation is that state control generally declined, because the Great Rebellion ended paternalistic government from the top. Shorn of its judicial powers, the Privy Council could no longer enforce its will. The result, according to one constitutional historian, was that 'government by the propertied classes in their own interest took the place of government by the Crown in what it held to be the national interest'.[4] Lipson argued

that the political crisis of Stuart absolutism opened the door to capitalism: 'under the influence of changed political conditions the State moved steadily in the direction of *laissez-faire*, and the capitalist classes did not hesitate to challenge its right to dictate to them'.[5] Professor Hill suggests that the 1640s and 1650s wrought a 'revolution in government', since the old state was restored only in its non-essentials after 1660. The result was an exceptionally free society, at least for the propertied.[6] These hypotheses are suggestive but inadequate, for they do not show the linkages between alterations in policies and political and economic changes. The concluding remarks of this book will attempt to establish these connections in the evolution of vagrancy policy.

Perhaps the key development was that demographically and economically England became more stable and prosperous from the mid-seventeenth century. The long-term growth in population that had begun in the early sixteenth century ceased in the 1650s, and the total hovered around five millions until the early 1700s. In addition, in contrast to the preceding 150 years, the period after 1650 experienced a levelling off in consumables' prices which, combined with stagnant population levels, resulted in 'a moderate, long-term increase in disposable income for many wage-earners', amounting in the case of building-workers to almost 50 per cent from 1650 to 1750.[7]

Labour was in greater demand, as well as being better paid, because the century from 1650 to 1750 saw recovery and expansion in the economy. In agriculture higher productivity was achieved through root crops and grasses, improved drainage and larger units of production, and England became a regular grain exporter.[8] Foreign trade experienced sustained growth, possibly trebling in value; internal trade flourished, too, judging by the expansion of transport facilities. Growth was also the order of the day in industry. If statistics were available for the entire period, it has been suggested, 'they would show that the latter decades of the seventeenth century were marked by brisk industrial advance', followed by a slower rate of increase up to 1750.[9]

By whatever index is used, therefore, economic prospects brightened from the mid-seventeenth to the mid-eighteenth century, which led to a demand for labour that was largely absent before 1650. A further indicator of the change in conditions was the tendency to migrate over shorter distances. The great majority of the population continued to shift residence at least once or twice during their lives, but long-distance subsistence migration waned, and by 1700 was confined to 'a rump of three or four groups of itinerant poor' – the Scots and Irish, gypsies, pedlars, entertainers and military personnel. This more localized pattern of movement was partly connected with improved employment opportunities.[10]

But the new situation of the vagabond was the work of policy as well as

demographic and economic conditions. The settlement laws, in particular, mitigated the problem. Although it is true that paupers were still shifted from pillar to post in disputes over settlements, at least now they were less likely to become permanent vagrants. Indeed it became easier to secure a settlement after 1662, when a new Act required forty days' residence to establish one, while for most of the sixteenth century the rule was three years, and from 1597 one year.[11] Local restrictions on settlement were also more arbitrary before 1662. Statutes, by-laws and manorial custom were used against immigrants in many places, the authorities demanded securities and poor relief contributions of newcomers, and paupers were turned into vagrants.[12]

By the mid-seventeenth century the distinction was becoming established between vagrancy and settlement problems. Justices increasingly required parish officials to accept persons who earlier would have fallen foul of the vagrancy laws.[13] The Act of 1662 implicitly guaranteed parish relief to the migrant wherever he or she went – that at any rate was how JPs increasingly treated disputes about residence – which helped to diminish vagabondage. The settlement laws also probably assisted the mobility of labour. As one authority has written, the 1662 statute represented an effort 'to meet, though in a very hesitant and restricted way, the growing demand for the mobility of labour'. Previously the testimonial system had aimed to control masterlessness and vagrancy; migration by legal means was not even considered, much less condoned.[14]

Wage-earners' opportunities for movement increased further under an Act of 1697, which established that a certificate-holder could not be removed until he was a charge on the poor rate. Prior to that statute officials often interpreted the presentation of a certificate 'to save the parish harmless' as conferring the right to remove the bearer forthwith. Local evidence suggests that the able-bodied poor seized the chance to move after 1697: in Birmingham the number of poor-law migrants rose sharply.[15] All told, the settlement legislation probably helped to alleviate vagrancy, first by ensuring that the migrant who fell on hard times was relieved in his last parish; secondly, by restricting long-distance migration, which had traditionally given rise to the problem; and thirdly, by providing a legal mechanism for migration. Admittedly the system produced bitter wrangles in which paupers were harshly treated, but that is still a far cry from saying that it did not work.

Parish poor relief also mitigated vagrancy by removing the need to wander. The provision of relief increased in the seventeenth century, even when population growth petered out after 1650. It mainly consisted of a weekly cash dole, but housing, fuel, clothing, victuals and medical care were also provided. And it was not only the 'impotent' who received succour. Elizabethan and early Stuart censuses of the poor show that the

able formed 80 to 90 per cent of the total, and while not all were given assistance, many were. Half of the 700 petitions for aid at Warwickshire quarter sessions from 1625 to 1680 came from able adults with families, and the bench usually ordered parishes to pay them weekly doles. Widows, children and old men were still probably the most common recipients of regular relief, but the able-bodied also figure in overseers' accounts, especially in *ad hoc* payments, which could make up a quarter of expenditure. They were additionally granted the right to have cottages built on wasteland under an Act of 1597.[16]

Expenditure on poor relief rose tremendously in the seventeenth century, far outstripping price inflation and population growth. Andrew Willet reckoned in 1614 that it was between £30,000 and £40,000 each year; for 1650 it has been estimated at between £188,000 and £250,000; and in the last quarter of the century the guesses ranged from £600,000 to £1 million p.a.[17] More realistically, a Board of Trade survey produced figures of £185,000 for outdoor and £165,000 for indoor relief in 1695, or a grand total of £350,000, which represents a tenfold increase over the early seventeenth century. That level of increase seems plausible. Without rising to the levels of the exaggerated estimates, it squares well with complaints about rising rates and with the next credible figure of £690,000 a year in the mid-eighteenth century.[18] Furthermore, long-term rises of that magnitude are also evident in parishes in Hampshire, Lincolnshire, Shropshire, Somerset and Warwickshire.[19]

Poor relief was a powerful element in controlling disorder among the needy. Quarter sessions and parish records show that local government was responsive to short-crises such as harvest failures, trade slumps and epidemics. In seventeenth-century Hampshire and Warwickshire relief expenditure was increased at such junctures. At the beginning of the nineteenth century Cobbett proclaimed that 'the poor man in England is as secure from beggary as the king upon his throne, because when he makes known his distress to the parish officers, they bestow upon him, not alms but his legal dues'. Even in 1700 that statement was substantially correct.[20]

In addition to poor relief, other forms of state action dampened vagrancy. Impressment probably increased, considering that the country was at war for almost half the period from 1688 to 1756, with 200,000 men under arms in the reign of Anne alone. During the Napoleonic Wars naval impressment became 'a large-scale business, demanding extensive organization', which must have absorbed considerable numbers of vagabonds, too.[21] So did the colonies, since between 100,000 and 150,000 persons emigrated to the Americas from 1660 to 1700. Most of them were young able-bodied males who had formed the mass of vagrants before 1640, as was shown.[22] The facilities for locking up vagabonds also

increased in the period. Most counties had regular gaols by 1700, and the numbers of houses of correction were rising. Even if those places did not employ or reform offenders, they at least got them off the streets. The Corporations of the Poor established in many towns from the 1690s probably had the same effect.[23] Changes in the law, finally, played some part in the decline of the offence. Itinerants who were tried for misdemeanours before 1640 might fall foul of capital statutes after 1688, because these mounted in number from 50 to 200 between then and 1820.[24]

In conclusion, the development of the vagrancy laws suggests that those who ruled Tudor and Stuart England were able to make effective responses to serious social problems. Thus it cannot be said of England in this period, as it has been written of *ancien régime* France, that government made no impact upon the problem of the poor.[25] Admittedly England was a fraction of the size of France, both in area and population, and after 1650 Whitehall was fortunate to have a decisive improvement in demographic and economic conditions following a century of upheaval and hardship. Many vagrancy policies, moreover, were inhumane and repressive, while some such as the bridewell failed in their purposes. Yet by other criteria those policies were successful. To those in power vagabonds were a threat to the established order, and ultimately that danger was averted. Compared with the continent there were few rebellions of the poor, notwithstanding the rapid pace of economic change and civil wars among the 'better sort', and that was partly, at least, due to their determination and ingenuity in wielding political power. They adapted fourteenth-century legislation to the needs of their time, greatly expanding its compass and the means to enforce it. The country gentlemen who dominated the House of Commons were equally pre-eminent in local government, and they found useful allies at parish level among the prosperous freeholders and tenant-farmers. In addition to controlling vagrancy, they enforced poor relief and settlement laws which, whatever their faults, significantly eased the lot of the needy. Obviously, by comparison with today, the lives of the poor remained desperately harsh in seventeenth-century England. But like should be compared with like; it is unnecessary to endorse the Whig interpretation of history to conclude that, compared with other states of the period, England's ruling élites did manage to take effective action on the social front. High-mindedness and charity may well have motivated them in part – but so, no doubt, did the resolve to perpetuate their own hegemony.

Notes

The place of publication is London unless otherwise stated.

INTRODUCTION

1 Sources listed in Appendix, Table I. For 1630s, see PRO SP 16 *passim*; and Slack, 'Vagrants and vagrancy'. It should be stressed that this study makes little use of indictment records, and none at all where vagrants' occupations are concerned. Cf. J. S. Cockburn, 'Early modern assize records as historical evidence', *Journal of the Society of Archivists*, V (1975), 222–4; J. S. Cockburn, 'Trial by the book? Fact and theory in the criminal process, 1558–1625', in J. H. Baker (ed.), *Legal Records and the Historian* (1978), 66; and *infra*, Chapter 6, introductory remarks, 86.

2 J. H. Langbein, *Prosecuting Crime in the Renaissance* (Cambridge, Mass., 1974), is an authoritative discussion of examination procedure; see also J. G. Bellamy, *Criminal Law and Society in Late Medieval and Tudor England* (New York, 1984), Chapter 2 and below, 12–13, 157–8.

3 Leonard; Webbs, *Old Poor Law*.

4 R. Fuller, *The Beggars' Brotherhood* (1936); G. Salgādo, *The Elizabethan Underworld* (1977). Better use of the literature was made by F. Aydelotte, *Elizabethan Rogues and Vagabonds* (Oxford, 1913).

5 P. Clark, 'The migrant in Kentish towns, 1580–1640', in *Crisis and Order*; Slack, 'Vagrants and vagrancy'; A. L. Beier, 'Vagrants and the social order in Elizabethan England', *P&P*, 64 (1974).

6 M. Walzer, *The Revolution of the Saints* (1966), 199.

7 Mainly relying upon *Statutes*; W. Lambarde, *Eirenarcha: Or Of the Office of the Justices of Peace* . . . (1581); M. Dalton, *The Countrey Justice* . . . (1618); E. Coke, *Institutes of the Laws of England* (1642–4).

8 G. Dubin and R. H. Robinson, 'The vagrancy concept reconsidered: problems and abuses of status criminality', *New York University Law Review*, XXXVII (1962), 105, 114–15.

9 Howard S. Becker, *Outsiders: Studies in the Sociology of Deviance* (1963), cited by S. Cohen, *Folk Devils and Moral Panics* (1972), 12–13.

CHAPTER 1. THE NEW POVERTY

1 H. Butterfield, *The Whig Interpretation of History* (1931), 10–17.

2 P. O'Connor, *Britain in the 'Sixties: Vagrancy* (Harmondsworth, 1963).

3 J.-P. Gutton, *La société et les pauvres en Europe (XVIᵉ-XVIIIᵉ siècles)* (Paris, 1974), 93–7; R. W. Southern, *Western Society and the Church in the Middle Ages* (Harmondsworth, 1970), 279–89; and R. H. Hilton's review of M. Mollat, *Les pauvres au moyen-âge:étude sociale* (Paris, 1978) in *English Historical Review*, XCIV (1979), 116–18.

4 B. Tierney, *Medieval Poor Law* (Berkeley, Calif., 1959), 11, 58–60.

5 S. Wenzel, *The Sin of Sloth* (Chapel Hill, 1960), 143–4, 177–9.

6 H. Baron, 'Franciscan poverty and civic wealth as factors in the rise of humanistic thought', *Speculum*, XIII (1938), 11, 21; J. Jusserand, *English Wayfaring Life in the Middle Ages* (1920, 2nd edn), 297–311, 358–64; J. Sumption, *Pilgrimage. An Image of Medieval Religion* (1975), 257–9, 289–90; 2 Thessalonians 3: *The New English Bible. New Testament* (Oxford, 1961), 355.

7 F. Graus, 'The late medieval poor in town and countryside', in S. Thrupp (ed.), *Change in Medieval Society. Europe North of the Alps, 1050–1500* (1964), 316–17; J. Le Goff, 'The town as an agent of civilization, 1200–1500', in C. M. Cipolla (ed.), *Fontana Economic History of Europe* (1972), I.90.

8 C. Misraki, 'Criminalité et pauvreté en France à l'époque de la guerre de cent ans', in M. Mollat (ed.), *Etudes sur l'histoire de la pauvreté* (Paris, 1974), II.545; R. Manselli, 'De Dante à Coluccio Salutati: discussion sur la pauvreté à Florence au XIVᵉ siècle', ibid., II.645; Charles de la Roncière, 'Pauvres et pauvreté à Florence au XIVᵉ siècle', ibid., 742–3; R. Favreau, 'Pauvreté en Poitou et en Anjou à la fin du moyen-âge', ibid., 608; B. Geremek, *Truands et misérables dans l'Europe moderne (1350–1600)* (Paris, 1980), chs 1–5; R. M. Clay, *The Medieval Hospitals of England* (1909; repr. 1966), 6–7, 28.

9 E. Le Roy Ladurie, *Les Paysans de Languedoc* (Paris, 1966) I.320–2; Geremek, op. cit., ch. 5; B. Pullan, 'Catholics and the poor in early modern Europe', *TRHS*, XXVI (1976); R. Jütte, 'Poor relief and social discipline in sixteenth-century Europe', *European Studies Review*, XI (1981); Webbs, *Old Poor Law*, 29–41.

10 E. Dudley, *The Tree of Commonwealth* (1509; Cambridge, 1948), ed. D. M. Brodie, 40; Sir Thomas Smith, *De Republica Anglorum* (1583; Cambridge, 1982), ed. M. Dewar, 141.

11 J. J. Scarisbrick, *Henry VIII* (1968), 405.

12 F. J. Furnivall (ed.), *Philip Stubbes's Anatomy of Abuses*, New Shakespeare Soc., Series VI, no. 12 (1882), ii.42; S[amuel] H[artlib], *The Parliament's Reformation* (1646), 1–2; P. Chamberlen, *The Poor Man's Advocate* (1649), 37.

13 J.-L. Vives, *Concerning the Relief of the Poor* (Bruges, 1526), transl. M. M. Sherwood, Studies in Social Work, no. 11 (New York, 1917), 8; J. Gore, *The Poor Man's Hope* (1635), 22.

14 Vives, op. cit., 7–8; A. Gerardus, *The Regiment of the Poverty* (1572), transl. H. Tripp, sig. A.5.a.

15 Vives, op. cit., 44; R. Morison, *A Remedy for Sedition* (1536; 1933 edn), E. M. Cox (ed.), 30.

16 Morison, op. cit., 31, 35; *The Sermons of Mr. Henry Smith* (1593), 1114; T. Hobbes, *Leviathan* (1651; new edn, Harmondsworth, 1968), ed. C. B. Macpherson, 238.

17 F. W. Chandler, *The Literature of Roguery* (New York, 1907; repr. 1974), 2 vols; also, E. von Kraemer, *Le type du faux mendiant dans les littératures romanes depuis*

le moyen âge jusq'au XVIIe siècle, Commentationes humanarum litterarum, XIII (Helsingfors, 1944). F. Aydelotte, *Elizabethan Rogues and Vagabonds* (Oxford, 1913) remains the best study of the English variant.

18 S. Brandt, *The Ship of Fools*, transl. A. Barclay (1509; Edinburgh, 1874; repr. New York, 1966), I.302; collections of the English tracts in Judges, and in G. Salgãdo (ed.), *Cony-Catchers and Bawdy Baskets* (Harmondsworth, 1972). I am indebted in this section to J. Shuter, 'Sympathy or sensationalism? Attitudes to the vagrant in the cony-catching literature, 1536–1626', University of Lancaster B.A. dissertation, 1976.

19 Judges, 3–4, 51–62, 110–13.

20 ibid., 495.

21 Cf. G. Salgãdo, *The Elizabethan Underworld* (1977) and G. Salgãdo (ed.), *Cony-Catchers and Bawdy Baskets*, 15, for a different approach to the literary sources.

22 Judges, 71, 99, 121, 131.

23 ibid., 150–1.

24 ibid., 36, 51, 65, 67–9, 107–8, 308–9, 368–9, 378, 387, 420–1.

25 ibid., 24, 79, 84–5, 113–17, 121–3, 135.

26 ibid., 73, 318ff.; Chandler, op. cit., I.58–9; Shuter, op. cit., 11–12, 32.

27 *Dictionary of National Biography*, 'Thomas Harman'; Harrison, *Description*, 184–5.

28 R. H. MacDonald (ed.), *The Library of Drummond of Hawthornden* (Edinburgh, 1971), 222; N. A. Smith (comp.), *Catalogue of the Pepys Library at Magdalene College, Cambridge* (Cambridge, 1978), I.85; F. S. Boas (ed.), *The Diary of Thomas Crosfield* (1935), 33.

29 R. Holinshed, *Chronicles* (1577; 1808 edn), ed. H. Ellis, III.1061.

30 *Statutes*, III.329, IV.i.5, 115, 411, 591, ii.899.

31 *TED*, I.339–42.

32 Caernf. RO QSR 1577 (B); NLW Wales 4/592/1/25; WCL Court of Burgesses, 1610–13/52, 235, 272; Wilts. CRO QSR East.1621/191; Cunnington, *Wilts.*, 33; NRQS, I.202; WYRO, WRQS, 1653–60/253a–b.

33 *Calendar of Close Rolls, Edward IV* (1953), II.298–9; *TRP*, I.32; *SRP*, I.360.

34 *Statutes*, III.559, IV.i.6, 116–17, 593, 611, ii.902.

35 ibid., II.58, III.328–30, 560, IV.i.590–1, ii.899.

36 C. Phythian-Adams, 'Urban decay in late medieval England', in P. Abrams and E. A. Wrigley (eds), *Towns in Societies* (Cambridge, 1978), 181–2.

37 *Statutes* IV.i.155; and for later Acts, ibid., IV.i.591–2, ii.899.

38 Somers. RO Q/SR 6/20; Chesh. RO QJF 4/2/29; WCL Court of Burgesses, 1610–13/156. Cf. K. Thomas, *Religion and the Decline of Magic* (1971), 552–6; A. Macfarlane, *Witchcraft in Tudor and Stuart England* (New York, 1970), 174.

39 Devon RO Exeter Act Bk. IV.308 and *passim*; *BJF*, 63; *NCM 1630–1*, 77, 84, 100; *NCM 1632–5*, 20; *SE 1570–94*, 10–11; Dorset RO DBC/49a–b; *LBR*, III.398–9; Leics. RO HP II/18/2/15/621–2.

40 Essex RO Q/SR 216/159; also PRO SP16/349/70.

41 P. Clark, 'The migrant in Kentish towns', in *Crisis and Order*, 122–3.

42 L. Stone, *The Causes of the English Revolution, 1529–1642* (1972), 62, 116.

43 J. H. Langbein, *Prosecuting Crime in the Renaissance* (Cambridge, Mass., 1974), 67, 75.

44 For developments on the Continent, E. Peters, *The Magician, the Witch and the Law* (Hassocks, 1978), 151–4.

45 Langbein, op. cit., 84–7.

CHAPTER 2. THE GROWTH OF VAGRANCY

1 Harrison, *Description*, 184; J. Kent, 'Social attitudes of Members of Parliament, 1590–1624', University of London Ph.D. thesis, 1971, 97–8.
2 *Stanleyes Remedy; Or, The Way How to Reform Wandering Beggars, Thieves, Highway Robbers and Pick-pockets* (1646), 2; [?Richard Haines], *Provision for the Poor* (1678), 5; Gregory King, repr. in D. C. Coleman, *The Economy of England, 1450–1750* (1977), 6.
3 *TED*, III.418; J. Bruce (ed.), *Diary of John Manningham, Barrister-at-Law, 1602–3*, Camden Society (1868), XCIX, 73.
4 *TED*, II.345; cf. D. M. Palliser, *The Age of Elizabeth* (1983), 121.
5 Arrest records in PRO SP 16, 1631–9 *passim* (the total given here corrects that in A. L. Beier, *The Problem of the Poor in Tudor and Early Stuart England* (1983), 32); constables' records in J. R. Kent, 'Population mobility and alms: poor migrants in the Midlands during the early seventeenth century', *Local Population Studies*, 27 (1981).
6 Search campaign documents in PRO SP 12 and SP 16 *passim*; population growth-rates calculated from E. A. Wrigley and R. S. Schofield, *The Population History of England, 1541–1871* (1981), 208–9.
7 P. Bowden, 'Agricultural prices, farm profits, and rents', *AHEW*, 621.
8 J. Patten, 'Village and town: an occupational study', *AgHR*, XX (1972), 4–5 (10 per cent has been added to the total poor on the grounds that military records excluded over-60s, for whom see N. P. Webb, 35, cited in n.9); C. Phythian-Adams, *Desolation of a City: Coventry and the Urban Crisis of the Late Middle Ages* (1979), 134.
9 N. P. Webb, 'The structure of poverty in some Elizabethan communities, based on censuses of the poor', University of Lancaster B.A. thesis, 1980, 31; A. L. Beier, 'The social problems of an Elizabethan country town: Warwick, 1580–90', in P. Clark (ed.), *Country Towns in Pre-Industrial England* (Leicester, 1981), 58–9; Palliser, *The Age of Elizabeth*, 122; P. Slack, 'Poverty and politics in Salisbury, 1597–1666', in *Crisis and Order*, 176; J. F. Pound (ed.), *The Norwich Census of the Poor, 1570*, Norfolk Record Society, XL (1971), 7, 10: of the English population of 10,625, a total of 2311 were listed as poor, or 21.75 per cent.
10 P. A. J. Pettit, *The Royal Forests of Northamptonshire. A Study in their Economy, 1558–1714*, Northamptonshire Record Society, XXIII (1968), 145, 200–3; A. L. Beier, 'Studies in poverty and poor relief in Warwickshire, 1540–1680', Princeton University Ph.D. thesis, 1969, 113. The figure of 16 per cent for pastoral Kent cited by A. M. Everitt, 'Farm labourers', *AHEW*, 397–8, is untypically low in that county. King's table repr. in Coleman, *The Economy of England*, 6; cf. G. S. Holmes, 'Gregory King and the social structure of pre-industrial England', *TRHS*, XXVII (1977), 62, 64, who is critical of many of King's estimates, but not those relating to the poor.
11 D. C. Coleman, 'Labour in the English economy of the seventeenth century', repr. Carus-Wilson, II.291 ff.; for contemporaries' views, *EHD*, 297–8; Morison, *A Remedy for Sedition* (1536; 1933 edn), 35, 47; *TED*, III.322.
12 Z. Razi, *Life, Marriage and Death in a Medieval Parish* (Cambridge, 1980), 30, 58–60, 66–8; F. M. Page, 'The customary poor law of three Cambridgeshire manors', *Cambridge Historical Journal*, III (1930), 127–9.
13 R. H. Hilton, *The Decline of Serfdom in Medieval England* (1969), 58–9; J. Hatcher, 'English serfdom and villeinage: towards a reassessment', *P&P*, 90 (1981), 38–9.
14 P. Goubert, *Beauvais et le Beauvaisis de 1600 à 1730* (Paris, 1960), I.604–12.

15 R. H. Tawney, *The Agrarian Problem in the Sixteenth Century* (1912), 46.
16 Webb, 'Structure of poverty', 33–41; Beier, 'Elizabethan country town', 59, 62.
17 Pettit, *The Royal Forests of Northamptonshire*, 141–8; Beier, 'Studies in poverty and poor relief in Warwickshire, 1540–1680', Princeton University Ph.D. thesis, 113–15.
18 Beier, 'Elizabethan country town', 59.
19 Wrigley and Schofield, op. cit., 208–9.
20 E. Kerridge, *The Agricultural Revolution* (1967), 39–40, 181; W. G. Hoskins, 'Harvest fluctuations and English economic history, 1620–1759', *AgHR*, XVI (1968), 25–8; Bowden, 'Agricultural prices', 606–7.
21 D. C. Coleman, 'Industrial growth and industrial revolutions', *Economica*, n.s., XXIII (1956), 14–16; Bowden, op. cit., 608 (quotation); J. Thirsk, 'Industries in the countryside', in F. J. Fisher (ed.), *Essays in the Economic and Social History of Tudor and Stuart England* (Cambridge, 1961).
22 Bowden, op. cit., 598–601; for the land question, W. G. Hoskins, *The Age of Plunder* (1976), 29–36.
23 M. Spufford, *Contrasting Communities* (Cambridge, 1974), totals calculated from 72–3, 90–1; E. Kerridge, *Agrarian Problems in the Sixteenth Century and After* (1969), 128–33; Everitt, 'Farm labourers', *AHEW*, 402.
24 Bowden, op. cit., 652–9; Everitt, op. cit., 399–412; Spufford, op. cit., 75–6; W. G. Hoskins, *The Midland Peasant* (1957), 214.
25 A. H. Johnson, *The Disappearance of the Small Landowner* (1909; new edn, 1963), 57–8.
26 Tawney, op. cit., 297, 300–1, 403–4; E. Kerridge, 'The movement of rent, 1540–1640', repr. Carus-Wilson, II.211, 220; Bowden, op. cit., 684–5.
27 Tawney, op. cit., 213–30; J. E. Martin, *Feudalism to Capitalism. Peasant and Landlord in English Agrarian Development* (1983), 132–40.
28 M. W. Beresford and J. Hurst, *Deserted Medieval Villages* (Lutterworth, 1971), 12–15, 35; J. Thirsk, 'Enclosing and engrossing', *AHEW*, 200–1; Martin, op. cit., 161–4.
29 Bowden, op. cit., 679–83.
30 P. Laslett, *The World We Have Lost – Further Explored* (3rd edn, 1983), 5.
31 C. Phythian-Adams, *Desolation of a City* (Cambridge, 1979), 204; P. Laslett, *Household and Family in Past Time* (Cambridge, 1972), 151–8; A. Kussmaul, *Servants in Husbandry in Early Modern England* (Cambridge, 1981), ch. 2. My understanding of the institution of dependent labour has been greatly increased through the work of Nicholas Webb, a Lancaster Ph.D. student.
32 Laslett, *World We Have Lost*, 1–5; S. R. Smith, 'The London apprentices as seventeenth-century adolescents', *P&P*, 61 (1973), 157–8.
33 Information from Nicholas Webb.
34 D. Knowles, *The Religious Orders in England* (Cambridge, 1959), III.260–4; G. W. O. Woodward, *The Dissolution of the Monasteries* (1966), 168–9; L. Stone, *The Crisis of the Aristocracy, 1558–1641* (Oxford, 1965), 187, 211–14, 584–5; F. Heal, 'The idea of hospitality in early modern England', *P&P*, 102 (1984), 90–1, for a more cautious assessment.
35 R. Finlay, *Population and Metropolis. The Demography of London, 1580–1650* (Cambridge, 1981), 66–7; and my paper on 'Engine of manufacture: the trades of London', in A. L. Beier and R. Finlay (eds), *London 1500–1700. The Making of the Metropolis* (forthcoming).
36 Essex RO Q/SR 1564–96; BCB 1597–1608; Norf. RO Norwich NCM 1564–1610, 1626–30; *NCM 1631–5*.
37 P. Spufford, 'Population mobility in pre-industrial England', *Genealogists'*

Magazine, XVII (1973), 422; J. Patten, 'Patterns of migration and movement of labour to three pre-industrial East Anglian towns', *Journal of Historical Geography*, II (1976), 122; L. Stone, 'Social mobility in England, 1500–1700', *P&P*, 33 (1966), 32; A. Kussmaul, 'The ambiguous mobility of farm servants', *EcHR*, 2nd s., XXXIV (1981), 223–5; D. Souden, *Local Population Studies*, 20 (1978), 57–8.

38 W. Gouge, *Of Domestical Duties* (1622), 599–605, 611, 647.
39 *TED*, I.340–1, 376–8; D. Marshall, *The English Domestic Servant in History* (1949), 10–11; indenture examples in *TED*, I.113, Cunnington, *Devizes*, pt. ii., 39–40.
40 e.g. *BJF*, 20–7, 57; Notts. RO QSM V.101; Wilts. CRO QSR Hil.1612/152.
41 C. Williams (ed.), *Thomas Platter's Travels in England, 1599* (1937), 182; instances of conflicts in S. R. Smith, 'London apprentices', 152–3; Cunnington, *Wilts.*, 53–4, 107–8, 125, 193; *Middlesex Co. Recds*, n.s. (1937), III.155, 250; F. S. Boas (ed.), *The Diary of Thomas Crosfield*, 68; Caernf. RO QS (no foliation), 30 Apr. 1571; Leics. RO HP II/18/16/20; F. Bamford (ed.), *A Royalist's Notebook* (1936), 55–6.
42 *TED*, I.361, III.430; Notts. RO QSM IV.175, IX.427; Wilts. CRO QSR East. 1618/161; *BJF*, 179; Essex RO Q/SBa 2/2; BCB 1620/203a.
43 Cunnington, *Devizes*, pt.1 43; Chester RO QSE 5/85, 6/13, 7/10, QSF 31/86; Scarborough Borough Records E.56, Box 23; Somers. RO Q/SR 42/111, 62/36.
44 Chesh. RO QJF 11/2/1.
45 BCB 1606/101a; also Wilts. CRO QSR Trin. 1612/179; Somers. RO Q/SR 76/39.
46 Notts. RO QSM III.177, V.8; Staffs. RO QSR (Charles I) 10/71.
47 K. J. Allison, 'An Elizabethan village "census"', *BIHR*, XXXVI (1963), 96–103; Kussmaul, *Servants in Husbandry*, 79.
48 Everitt, 'Farm labourers', *AHEW*, 397–8; King table repr. in Coleman, *Economy of England*, 6.
49 C. Hill, 'Pottage for freeborn Englishmen: attitudes to wage-labour', repr. in C. Hill, *Change and Continuity in Seventeenth-Century England* (1974), 220.
50 D. Woodward, 'Wage rates and living standards in pre-industrial England', *P&P*, 91 (1981), 43–5.
51 Bowden, 'Agricultural prices', 598–601, 864–5; Everitt, 'Farm labourers', 402; I. Blanchard, 'Labour productivity and work psychology in the English mining industry, 1400–1600', *EcHR*, 2nd s., XXXI (1978), 14.
52 Coleman, 'Labour in the English economy', Carus-Wilson, II.300–1; J. Thirsk, 'The farming regions of England', *AHEW*, 88.
53 B. E. Supple, *Commercial Crisis and Change in England, 1600–1642* (Cambridge, 1959), 14–19; W. G. Hoskins, 'Harvest fluctuations and English economic history, 1480–1619', *AgHR*, XII (1964), 29; F. J. Fisher, 'Commercial trends and policy in sixteenth-century England', Carus-Wilson, I.153; J. D. Gould, 'The crisis in the export trade, 1586–7', *English Historical Review*, LXXI (1956), 212–22.
54 S. R. Smith, 'The social and geographical origins of the London apprentices, 1630–1660', *The Guildhall Miscellany*, IV (1973), 199.
55 M. MacDonald, *Mystical Bedlam* (Cambridge, 1981), 40–1, 67.
56 A. Salerno, 'The social background of seventeenth-century emigration to America', *Journal of British Studies*, XIX (1979), 33, 44.
57 Doles based on Marston Trussell constables' accounts, 1616–74, Northants. RO MaT 102; Barcheston churchwardens' accounts, 1626–1725, War. CRO DR/17/1/6; DAD, DCA 1621–78; Upton parish accounts, 1600–51, and constables' accounts, 1640–66, Notts. RO PR 1709–10; St Mary le Strand, churchwardens' accounts, XXII, 1621–49, WCL. Cf. parish relief in S. C. Ratcliff and

H. C. Johnson (eds), *Warwick County Records, Sessions Order Book* (Warwick, 1935), I.6, 10, 17; W. Minchinton, *Wage Regulation in Pre-Industrial England* (Newton Abbot, 1972), 203 and Bowden, 'Agricultural prices', 657.

58 Webb, 'Structure of poverty', 8; Beier, 'Elizabethan country town', 77; P. Slack, 'Poverty and politics in Salisbury, 1597–1666', in *Crisis and Order*, 175–6.

CHAPTER 3. MIGRANTS AND VAGRANTS

1 E. S. Lee, 'A theory of migration', *Demography*, III (1966), 49; also L. A. Kosiński and R. M. Prothero (eds), *People on the Move* (1975), 2–3.

2 P. Clark, 'The migrant in Kentish towns', in *Crisis and Order*, 129–39.

3 P. Spufford, 'Population mobility in pre-industrial England', *Genealogists' Magazine*, XVII (1973), 422.

4 J. Patten, *Rural-Urban Migration in Pre-Industrial England* (School of Geography, University of Oxford, 1973), 11–22, provides a fair survey.

5 e.g. Z. Razi, *Life, Marriage & Death in a Medieval Parish*, 30.

6 ibid. 30–1; P. McClure, 'Patterns of migration in the late Middle Ages', *EcHR*, 2nd s., XXXII (1979), 175–7; S. Thrupp, *The Merchant Class of Medieval London* (Chicago, 1948), 209.

7 Razi, op. cit., 117–24.

8 Calculated from McClure, op. cit., 181; Thrupp, op. cit., 209–11.

9 A. F. Butcher, 'The origins of Romney freemen, 1433–1523', *EcHR*, 2nd s., XXVII (1974), 24–7; J. Hatcher, *Plague, Population and the English Economy, 1348–1530* (1977), 63.

10 Thrupp, op. cit., 208–11; C. I. Hammer, 'The mobility of skilled labour in late medieval England', *Vierteljahrschrift für Sozial- und Wirtschaftsgeschichte*, LXIII (1976), 203; G. D. Ramsay, 'The recruitment and fortunes of some London freemen in the mid-sixteenth century', *EcHR*, 2nd s., XXXI (1978), 528–9.

11 P. Clark, 'Migrant in Kentish towns', 129; P. Clark, 'Migration in England during the late seventeenth and early eighteenth centuries', *P&P*, 83 (1979), 68–70; D. Souden, 'Migrants and the population structure of later seventeenth-century provincial cities and market towns', in P. Clark (ed.), *The Transformation of English Provincial Towns, 1600–1800* (1984), 144. I am grateful to the editor for allowing me to see this paper in advance of publication.

12 Calculated from J. R. Kent, 'Population mobility and alms: poor migrants in the Midlands during the early seventeenth century', *Local Population Studies*, 27 (1981), 38, 42–3.

13 *Statutes*, III.329, 558, IV.i.7, 115, 593, 611, ii.899, V.401; and the sources cited in Chapter 1, n. 39.

14 *Statutes*, III.329, IV.ii.899.

15 *TED*, II.336; C. Read (ed.), *William Lambarde and Local Government* (Ithaca, 1962), 169.

16 Colchester data from Slack, 'Vagrants and vagrancy', 379.

17 For east-west roads, see H. C. Darby (ed.), *An Historical Geography of England before 1800* (Cambridge, 1936), 260, 342.

18 Note that the figure for the Irish in Somerset in Appendix, Table I is on the low side, because only those actually arrested were included; another seventy-six reportedly landed at Portishead point in May 1630: Somers. RO Q/SR 62/38–42.

19 Slack, op. cit., 379 (Cornwall and Devon).

20 If East Anglia were included in the reckoning, the South's fall would be still greater.
21 PRO SP 16/193/5.
22 ibid., 12/51/11, 67/45, 80/22, 60, 81/14, 44–6; A. D. Dyer, *The City of Worcester in the Sixteenth Century* (Leicester, 1973), 170–1.
23 Salop. RO SBR QS examinations, Elizabeth I – Charles I (uncalendered); Survey of Inmates (?1641), Box 15/734.
24 PRO SP 16/270/18, 271/92, 293/82 & I, 310/107, 329/26.
25 Slack, op. cit., 379 (Lancashire and Westmorland).
26 A. M. Everitt, 'The marketing of agricultural produce', *AHEW*, 497–8 (markets); D. Defoe, *A Tour Through England and Wales* (1724–6; 1928 edn), ed. G. D. H. Cole, II.269–70.
27 Only a handful – six to be precise – of the 156 Yorkshire vagrants were from Lincolnshire in the total of 88.
28 Cf. Slack, op. cit., 371, and the authorities cited there.
29 R. S. Schofield, 'The geographical distribution of wealth in England, 1334–1649', *EcHR*, 2nd s., XVIII (1965), 506–7.
30 W. G. Howson, 'Plague, poverty and population in parts of northwest England, 1580–1720', *Trans. Historic Soc. Lancs. & Chesh.*, CXII (1960), 54–5; Staffs. RO QSR, 1606–33, D1287/10/2, *passim*.
31 W. G. Hoskins, *Provincial England* (1963), 20n; counties examined in relation to Yorkshire include Cheshire, Lancashire, Nottinghamshire, Staffordshire and Westmorland.
32 Slack, op. cit., 375; Wilts. CRO QSR, *passim*, e.g. Trin. 1612/168, Trin. 1616/148, Mich. 1631/229. In Frome's case proximity to Wiltshire obviously played a part, but the town still led others with 15 vagrants as against 10 from Glastonbury and 8 from Bath.
33 e.g. Chester RO QSE 5/138; *NCM 1630–2*, 226.
34 G. Puttenham, *The Arte of English Poesie* (1589; Cambridge, 1936 edn, repr. 1970), 6; J. Cooke, *Unum necessarium: Or, The Poor Man's Case* (1648), 25; final quotation in Pettit, *The Royal Forests of Northamptonshire*, 133.
35 Quoted Pettit, op. cit. 163; A. M. Everitt, 'Farm labourers', *AHEW*, 411–12.
36 A. L. Beier, 'Studies in poverty and poor relief in Warwickshire', Princeton University Ph.D. thesis, 1969, 113–15; Pettit, op. cit., 141–5.
37 E. Lipson, *The History of the Woollen and Worsted Industries* (1921), 108; R. H. Tawney, *The Agrarian Problem in the Sixteenth Century* (1912; repr. New York, 1967), 22n.
38 Beier, op. cit., 98–103, 123–6; Pettit, op. cit., 152; J. Thirsk, 'The farming regions of England', *AHEW*, 37, 80; J. Thirsk, 'Industries in the countryside', in F. J. Fisher (ed.), *Essays in the Economic & Social History of Tudor & Stuart England, passim*.
39 Quoted Lipson, op. cit., 108 and W. K. Jordan, *Philanthropy in England, 1480–1660* (1959), 70; cf. Tawney, op. cit., 22n.
40 Cheshire, Somerset and Yorkshire evidence as in Table I (Appendix); Lancashire in PRO SP 16/364/122–3; Norfolk in PRO SP16/347/68, Norf. RO NCM 1603–14/103b, 1624–34/102b, 105b.
41 An urban centre is defined as a place holding a regular market: see A. M. Everitt, 'The marketing of agricultural produce', *AHEW*, 468–75.
42 P. Clark and P. Slack, *English Towns in Transition, 1500–1700* (Oxford, 1976), 11, 83; P. Corfield, 'Urban development in England and Wales in the sixteenth and seventeenth centuries', in D. C. Coleman and A. H. John (eds), *Trade, Government and Economy in Pre-Industrial England* (1976), 231.

43 Of course, vagabonds might have named larger, better-known places the farther from 'home' they were (cf. Slack, 'Vagrants and vagrancy', 376, Table 5), but that still seems insufficient to explain the preponderance of towns.

44 London figures in A. L. Beier and R. Finlay, 'Introduction', sect. II, *London 1500–1700*, forthcoming; cf. J. Graunt, *Natural and Political Observations . . . Made Upon the Bills of Mortality* (1662; repr. 1973), ed P. Laslett, 65; for Norwich: Clark and Slack, *Towns in Transition*, 86.

45 Beier, 'Studies in poverty and poor relief', 118–20, 126–9.

46 J. F. Pound, 'An Elizabethan census of the poor: the treatment of vagrancy in Norwich, 1570–80', *University of Birmingham Historical Journal*, VIII (1962), 139; A. L. Beier, 'The social problems of an Elizabethan country town: Warwick, 1580–90', in P. Clark, (ed.), *Country Towns in Pre-Industrial England* (Leicester, 1981), 53, 77; Cooke, *Unum necessarium*, 25.

47 Figures from R. Finlay and B. Shearer, 'Population growth and suburban expansion', in Beier and Finlay (eds), *London 1500–1700*, Table 5.

48 *TED*, III.418; CLRO Repert., 23/479b–480a, Journ., 24/322b–323a; A. L. Beier, 'Social problems in Elizabethan London', *Journal of Interdisciplinary History*, IX (1978), 204.

49 *TED*, III.438; J. Stow, *A Survey of London* (1598; new edn, 1956), 497.

50 Beier, 'Elizabethan London', 206–7.

51 ibid., 207–8 and sources cited there.

52 P. Clark, 'The reception of migrants in English towns in the early modern period', paper presented to International Urban History Conference, Göttingen, 4–5, 12–13.

53 V. Pearl, 'Change and stability in seventeenth-century London', *London Journal*, V (1979), 4 ff.; S. R. Smith, 'The London apprentices as seventeenth-century adolescents', *P&P*, 61 (1973), 155–6; D. M. Bergeron, *English Civic Pageantry, 1558–1642* (1971), 2 ff.

54 BCB 1620–1 (25 March 1620 – 24 March 1621), 1528 persons judged and punished; 1624–5, 1639. Not all were referred to as 'vagrants', but the majority probably were vagabonds: 815 were so described in 1624–5, but in addition another 581 were listed simply as 'sent in'.

55 Finlay and Shearer, op. cit., Table 3; Beier, 'Elizabethan London', 208.

56 CLRO Repert., 17/425a (ff.), 446a, 32/157a–b, 41/151a–b; WCL St Margaret's parish overseers' accounts, E.146/15a, 26a, 28a.

57 N. Brett-James, *The Growth of Stuart London* (1935), 67; CLRO Remembrancia II, nos. 74, 102; *APC 1597–8*, 427–8; Stow, op. cit., 116, 150, 365, 375.

58 E. D. Pendry (ed.), *Thomas Dekker* (1967), 233–4; Graunt, *Natural and Political Observations*, 58; M. D. George, *London Life in the Eighteenth Century* (1925), 82–5. For evidence of improved housing see M. J. Power, 'East London housing in the seventeenth century', in *Crisis and Order*, 240–1, 258–9.

59 PRO SP 16/415/95, 96, 417/25III, VIII, XI, XIII, XIV, XVI. (In Southwark and neighbouring suburbs 24 of 35 vagrants were from outside the Southeast.)

60 GLRO P92/SAV/1422–3; PRO SP 16/359/I–XXV, esp. XVII.

61 BCB, *passim*; G. Salgādo, *The Elizabethan Underworld* (1977), 19; A. Harbage, *Shakespeare's Audience* (New York, 1941), 81–3; cf. S. Brigden, 'Youth and the English Reformation', *P&P*, 95 (1982), 47–51.

62 J. D. Gould, *The Great Debasement* (Oxford, 1970), 125; F. J. Fisher, 'The development of the London food market, 1540–1640', Carus-Wilson, I.142–50; F. J. Fisher, 'The development of London as a centre of conspicuous consumption in the sixteenth and seventeenth centuries', ibid., II.197–207. The prolifer-

ation of new trades is examined in A. L. Beier, 'Engine of manufacture: the trades of London', in Beier and Finlay (eds), *London 1500–1700*, forthcoming.

63 J. U. Nef, 'The progress of technology and the growth of large-scale industry in Great Britain, 1540–1640', in Carus-Wilson, I. 104; cf. R. Davis, *The Rise of the English Shipping Industry in the Seventeenth and Eighteenth Centuries* (1962), 55–6; C. Wilson, *England's Apprenticeship, 1603–1763* (1965), 273.

64 Beier, 'Engine of manufacture'.

65 BCB 1597–1610.

66 F. J. Fisher, 'The growth of London', in E. W. Ives (ed.), *The English Revolution, 1600–1660* (1968), 78; Beier, 'Elizabethan London', 213–17, and sources cited there.

67 Wilts. CRO QSR East. 1631/138; also Essex RO Q/SR 85/26.

68 Salisbury cases from P. Slack (ed.), *Poverty in Early Stuart Salisbury*, Wiltshire Record Society, XXXI (1975), 17–65.

69 J. A. Chartres, 'Food consumption and internal trade', Table 16, forthcoming in Beier and Finlay (eds), *London 1500–1700*.

70 YCR, VII.159, VIII.49–50; *Statutes*, IV.ii.896; Somers. RO Q/SR 20/63; PRO SP 16/382/10, 388/7 XL.1.

71 BCB 1575/104a; CLRO Journ., 20.ii.fol.500b; *TED*, III.430; BCB 1601/217a (also 1602/335a, 1605/58b, 61b, 77a).

72 Quoted T. R. Forbes, *Chronicle from Aldgate. Life & Death in Shakespeare's London* (New Haven, 1971), 79–80. Further examples: G. W. G. Leveson Gower (ed.), *The Registers of St. Peter's Cornhill* (1877), Harleian Society, Register Section, I.134, 138, 146, 160; W. Bruce Bannerman (ed.), *The Registers of St. Helen's, Bishopsgate, 1575–1837* (1904), ibid., XXXI.291, 294; W. Bruce Bannerman (ed.), *The Registers of St. Olave, Hart Street, London, 1563–1700* (1916), ibid., XLVI.110, 121, 140, 155.

73 Leicester and Somerset sources as in Table I (Appendix); cf. P. Spufford, 'Population mobility in pre-industrial England', *Genealogists' Magazine*, XVII (1973), 425–6.

74 *Henry IV, Part Two*, V:iii; KCAO QM/SB 213; Dorset RO DBC/87a; *TED*, III.421, 438.

75 Beier, 'Elizabethan country town', 53ff.

76 PRO SP 16/536/17.

77 Beier, op. cit., 62; P. Slack, 'The local incidence of epidemic disease: the case of Bristol, 1540–1650', in *The Plague Reconsidered* (Matlock, 1977), 59 (which also finds (p. 55) that the poor in the better-off central parishes of Bristol were also stricken); Devon RO Exeter Act Book IV.15, 207, 274–5; Dorset RO DBC/212a, 229b; P. Slack, 'Poverty and politics in Salisbury, 1597–1666', in *Crisis and Order*, 178; Salop. RO SBR Box 15/734.

CHAPTER 4. A PROMISCUOUS GENERATION

1 J. Downame, *The Plea of the Poor* (1616), 38; R, J. *Proposals on Behalf of the Poor* (1653), 2; R. Younge, *The Poor's Advocate* (1654), 9–10.

2 P. Laslett, *Family Life and Illicit Love in Earlier Generations* (Cambridge, 1977), 13.

3 e.g. Leics. RO HP II/18/15/238, Somers. RO Q/SR 51/13.

4 J. F. Pound (ed.), *The Norwich Census of the Poor, 1570*, Norfolk Record Society, XL (1971), 95; A. L. Beier, 'The social problems of an Elizabethan country town: Warwick, 1580–90', in P. Clark (ed.), *Country Towns in Pre-Industrial England* (Leicester, 1981), 60–1.

5 *Statutes*, IV.ii.1161.

6 Beier, op. cit., 60–1.
7 Somers. RO Q/SR 46/1; *Herts. Co. Recds*, V.172–3.
8 *SE 1570–94*, 23; *BJF*, 106.
9 BCB 1560/72a; L. Stone, *The Family, Sex and Marriage in England, 1500–1800* (1977), 616–17; BCB 1578/297b, 1629/147a.
10 Stone, op. cit., 612–14; P. Laslett, 'Introduction', in *Bastardy and Its Comparative History* (1980), ed. P. Laslett, K. Oosterveen and R. M. Smith, 22–6; K. Wrightson, 'The nadir of English illegitimacy in the seventeenth century', ibid., 180–4.
11 Wrightson, op. cit., 186–8; J. A. Sharpe, 'Crime and delinquency in an Essex parish, 1600–1640', in J. S. Cockburn (ed.), *Crime in England, 1550–1800* (1977), 99; R. W. Malcolmson, 'Infanticide in the eighteenth century', ibid., 202; G. R. Quaife, *Wanton Wenches and Wayward Wives* (1979), 65, 67, 71–2, 74–6.
12 Quaife, op. cit., 98–9; Somers. RO Q/SR 33/133, 34/18.
13 BCB 1579/434b, 1604/4a, 5b; WCL E.146, fol. 15a (but London illegitimacy was undoubtedly high: see WCL Court of Burgesses, 1610–13, 1614, *passim*).
14 Single females made up 45 of 83 vagrants in St Margaret's Westminster overseers' accounts in the 1580s (WCL E.146), and 31 of 45 in Southwark (GLRO P92/SAV/1422C, 1423F); CLRO Journ., 29/177a.
15 WCL E.146/14a, 30a, 31a; Somers. RO Q/SR 33/133; Dorset RO DBC/229a–30a.
16 PRO SP 16/314/77; BCB 1603/397b, 434b; also Chester RO QSE 9/21.
17 At Ealing in 1599, 49 per cent were under 21: Allison, 'An Elizabethan village "census"', *BIHR*, (1963), 96–103, which is similar to Lichfield in 1695: D. V. Glass, 'Gregory King's estimate of the population of England and Wales, 1695', repr. in D. V. Glass and D. E. C. Eversley (eds) *Population in History* (1965), 207, 212. Wrigley and Schofield, *Population History*, 217–19, only show 39.6 per cent under 20 in 1695, but do not cite the Ealing case and themselves state that their sixteenth-century evidence is weak.
18 Slack, 'Vagrants and vagrancy', 366 (Colchester); BCB 25 March 1630 – 24 March 1631.
19 R. Morison, *A Remedy for Sedition* (1536; 1933 edn), 30; BL Lansdowne MS 95/51–5.
20 R. Newton, 'The decay of the Borders', in C. Chalklin and M. Havinden (eds), *Rural Change and Urban Growth, 1500–1800* (1974), 10; Historical Manuscripts Commission, *Report on the Records of the City of Exeter* (1916), Series 73, vi.
21 PRO SP 16/385/27; *LBR*, III.222; Staffs. RO D1287/10/2, 5 Oct. 1614 (no foliation).
22 *TED*, III.433; J.-L. Vives, *Concerning the Relief of the Poor* (Bruges, 1526), transl. M. M. Sherwood, Studies in Social Work, no. 11 (New York, 1917), 8, 21–2; Hartlib, *Parliament's Reformation* (1646), 6; *Statutes*, IV.i.611; I. Pinchbeck and M. Hewitt, *Children in English Society* (1969), I.100 (quotation), 127–32.
23 WCL E.146/32a–33a; Norf. RO NCM 1595–1603/501 (also 1603–14/153a).
24 Somers. RO Q/SR 67/241; Notts. RO QSM XI.26; Essex RO D/B/3/3/125/1, 211; BCB 1602/323a, 1640/313a, 318b, 319a, 1641/348a–b.
25 BCB 1575/120b, 1603/368a (also 1600/190a).
26 *TED*, II.345; Judges, 345; cf. J. F. Pound, *Poverty and Vagrancy in Tudor England* (1971), 29.
27 Essex RO Q/SR 19A/61; Wilts. CRO QSR Trin. 1629/112, East.1632/111, 170.
28 Essex RO Q/SR 113/40, 40a; Leics. RO HP II/18/17/269.
29 R. O. Jones, 'The mode of disposing of gipsies and vagrants in the reign of Elizabeth', *Archaeologia Cambrensis*, 4th s., XIII (1882), 226–9.

30 *Statutes*, III.327, IV.i.242, 448–9; E. O. Winstedt, 'Early British gypsies', *Journal of the Gypsy Lore Society*, n. s., VII (1913–14), 10–12.

31 Winstedt, op. cit., 8, 10, 16, 18; *TED*, II.345; Judges, 345, 420–1; Ribton-Turner, 489.

32 *Herts. Co. Recds*, V.471; Essex RO Q/SR 196/16–18; *NRQS*, I.11, 21; PRO Assi 45/3/2/141–3; J. S. Cockburn (ed.), *Calendar of Assize Records, Sussex Indictments, Elizabeth I* (1975), 128.

33 Calculated from T. W. Thompson, 'Gleanings from constables' accounts and other sources', *Journal of the Gypsy Lore Society*, VII, 3rd s., (1928), 31–4; Anon., 'Sowerby in olden times', *Halifax Antiquarian Society Papers* (1901–3), no pagination: 20 groups total.

34 Winstedt, op. cit., 8 (hearsay example); Ribton-Turner, 489.

35 Judges, 421–2; Ribton-Turner, 603–4.

36 Winstedt, op. cit. 11; Thompson, op. cit., 36, 43–4; Leics. RO HP II/18/4/117; H. T. Crofton, 'Early annals of the gypsies in England', *Journal of the Gypsy Lore Society*, I (1888), 24.

37 B. Vesey-FitzGerald, *Gypsies of Britain* (1944; repr. Newton Abbot, 1973), 121–2; T. San Roman, 'Kinship, marriage, law and leadership in two urban gypsy settlements in Spain', in F. Rehfisch (ed.), *Gypsies, Tinkers and Other Travellers* (1975), 174–5.

38 Although in Paris in 1427, 100 or so gypsies were reported to have a 'duke' and a 'count' representing them: J. Shirley (ed.), *A Parisian Journal, 1405–1449* (Oxford, 1968), 216–18.

39 Quoted from Vesey-FitzGerald, op. cit., 120; A. and F. Rehfisch, 'Scottish travellers or tinkers' in Rehfisch (ed.), op. cit., 278.

40 GLRO Middlesex QS Calendar, Sessions Book, 1639–44, IA, 45, 49; Devon RO QSOB 1592–1600/250; Hants. RO 4M53/140/104a; *Herts. Co. Recds*, V.471; Wilts. CRO QSR Mich. 1608/125; PRO Assi 45/3/2/141–3 (16 of 24 had the same surname; 14 of 24 were related to at least one other in the group).

41 A. Sutherland, 'The American Rom: a case of economic adaptation', in Rehfisch (ed.), op. cit., 3n.

42 PRO Assi 45/3/2/141–3; Judges, 421; J. Sampson, 'Cant words in the New English Dictionary', *The Times Literary Supplement* (21 June 1928), 468.

43 *Statutes*, III.327; Judges, 421.

44 PRO SP 16/281/83; Hocus-Pocus Junior, *The Anatomy of Legerdemain* (4th edn, 1634), sig. A.4.a.; Vesey-FitzGerald, op. cit., 179.

45 Shirley (ed.), op. cit., 218; Judges, 345.

46 *Statutes*, III.327, IV.i.242–3, 448; F. Aydelotte, *Elizabethan Rogues and Vagabonds* (Oxford, 1913), 152 (my italics); Derbyshire quotation from Thompson, op. cit., 35.

47 Thompson, op. cit., 36; Wilts. CRO QSR Mich. 1608/125; Essex RO Q/SR 196/16–18.

48 *Statutes*, IV.i.448; Essex RO Q/SR 258/95; GLRO Middlesex QS Calendar, Sessions Book 1639–44, IA, 45, 49; Devon RO QSOB 1592–1600/250.

49 *Statutes*, IV.i.449.

50 Cromwell, quoted Ribton-Turner, 487; Winstedt, op. cit., 17–18; Crofton, op. cit., 23.

51 PRO SP 16/265/34; Wilts. CRO QSR Trin.1629/112, Trin.1637/174. In the last instance 'Malagall', County Cork, is assumed to be Mallow, and 'Messelton', Mitchelstoun.

52 D. B. Quinn, *The Elizabethans and the Irish* (Ithaca, 1966), 80–1, 168; B. Barnes, 'Irish travelling people', Rehfisch (ed.), op. cit., 237–42.

53 R. Carew, *The Survey of Cornwall* (1602; 1953 edn), ed F. E. Halliday, 139.

54 Somers. RO Q/SR 62/38–42.

55 J. C. Beckett, *The Making of Modern Ireland, 1603–1923* (1966), 20–1, 61, 82–94, 101–2; quotation from L. Stone, *The Causes of the English Revolution, 1529–1642* (1972), 78.

56 Quinn, op. cit., ch. 7, for English attitudes.

57 *Statutes*, IV.i.596; J. R. Chanter and T. Wainright (eds), *Reprint of the Barnstable Records* (Barnstable, 1900), II.127, 129, 158; Judges, 496; Devon RO QSOB 1592–1600/314.

58 BCB 1628/92a; CLRO Remembrancia VI, nos. 172–3; PRO SP 16/234/57, 248/71, 265/34, 63, 266/4, 426/87, *CSPD 1633–4*, 462.

59 e.g. BCB 1628/*passim*; WCL St Mary le Strand, churchwardens' accounts, 1586–1650, vol. 22; also R. R. Tighe and J. E. Davis, *Annals of Windsor* (1858), II.116–17; H. J. Wilkins, (ed.), *Church Register, 1558–1718, of . . . Westbury-upon-Trym*, Westbury and Bristol Records, III (Bristol, 1912), *passim*.

60 Judges, 113; *TED*, II.345.

61 C. V. Wedgwood, *The King's Peace* (New York, 1955), 469–81; cf. R. Clifton, 'The popular fear of Catholics during the English Revolution', *P&P*, 52 (1971), 49–51.

62 K. Wrightson and D. Levine, *Poverty and Piety in an English Village: Terling, 1525–1700* (1979), 125–33; R. Houlbrooke, *Church Courts and the People during the English Reformation, 1520–1570* (Oxford, 1979), ch. 3; M. J. Ingram, 'Ecclesiastical justice in Wiltshire, 1600–1640, with special reference to cases concerning sex and marriage', University of Oxford, D.Phil. thesis, 1976, 374–7.

63 *Statutes*, IV.ii.1028; Devon RO Exeter Act Book IV.250; BCB 1604/447a (also Cunnington, *Devizes*, pt. ii, 21–2; Leics. RO HP II/18/8/555–6, 589).

64 Wiltshire and Leicester sources as in Appendix, Table I; examples in Dorset RO DBC/14b–15a, 229a–b.

65 Dorset RO DBC 106b–107a, 222b–223a.

66 e.g. Wilts. CRO QSR Trin.1612/168, East.1631/130, Mich.1631/178–9; Leics. RO HP II/18/8/335, 20/59; Chester RO QSF 61/130; G. R. Quaife, *Wanton Wenches and Wayward Wives* (1979), 59–62.

67 BCB 1606/111a; Stone, *The Family*, 31; Leics. RO HP II/18/10/286.

68 D. J. Steel, *National Index of Parish Registers* (1968), I.295, 313, 319–20 (I owe this reference to Dr R. A. P. Finlay); Somers. RO Q/SR 34/19; Leics. RO HP II/18/19/415.

69 Historical Manuscripts Commission, Series 6, *Seventh Report* (1879), 621; Stone, op. cit., 31.

70 e.g. Leics. RO HP II/18/4/106–7, 10/286; Essex RO Q/SR 103/13; Cunnington, *Devizes*, pt. ii, 21–2.

71 BCB 1641/354a, 358a.

72 Winstedt, 'Early British gypsies', 18; Essex RO Q/SR 54/39.

73 BCB 1621/222a, 1624/375b (also Somers. RO Q/SR 18/79–81, which is actually a document written by Dorset justices).

74 Notts. RO QSM VI.169; Staffs. RO QSR (James I), 50/13–14.

75 Essex RO Q/SR 54/39; Staffs. RO QSR (James I) 50/13–14; *RR*, II.348, 353–4.

76 Norf. RO NCM 1562–9/286; BCB 1624/371b.

77 Chester RO QSE 5/110, 123; Somers. RO Q/SR 42/89.

78 Cited by Slack, 'Vagrants and vagrancy', 363.

CHAPTER 5. ON THE ROAD

1 Harrison, *Description*, 180.
2 NLW Wales 4/126/pt.2/15; Leics. RO HP II/18/3/248–51; *BJF, passim*; Chesh. RO QJF 4/1/22; Chester RO QSF 74/8, no.2.
3 *TED*, II.343; Notts. RO QSM IX.6; Staffs. RO QSR (Charles I) 22/6; *BJF*, 97–8.
4 *BJF, passim*; these figures correct those in 'Vagrants and social order', *P&P*, 64, 18.
5 *RR, passim*; Reading vagabonds moved fewer total miles than those of Warwick, but that is partly caused by under-reporting; hence the lower numbers of days reported, too.
6 Essex RO Q/SR 19A/53; Wilts. CRO QSR Hil.1626/150; PRO SP 16/197/13.
7 Slack, 'Vagrants and vagrancy', 369; *BJF*, 58–9; Salop. RO SBR QS examinations (uncatalogued) 2 December 43 Elizabeth I.
8 Somers. RO Q/SR 40/89–90; BCB 1603/369a.
9 Leics. RO HP II/18/4/(?)376, 4/231; *SE 1570–1594*, 36.
10 *Statutes*, IV.i.7; estimates of urban population in P. Clark and P. Slack, *English Towns in Transition* (Oxford, 1976), 11, 83; markets listed in A. M. Everitt, 'The marketing of agricultural produce', *AHEW* 468–75, and are mapped on 497.
11 *Judges*, 7; Chester RO QSF 30/50; Wilts. CRO QSR Mich.1631/227; BCB 1620/200b, 204a, 1640/318b; CLRO Journ., 26/320b; *TED*, III.430.
12 M. T. Hodgen, 'Fairs of Elizabethan England', *Economic Geography*, XVIII (1942), 395; *BJF, passim*; Salop. RO SBR QS examinations, ?27 June 1616; Chester RO QSE 11/57, 13/25, QSF 36/103, 66/71–4; *RR*, III.77, 125.
13 F. Aydelotte, *Elizabethan Rogues and Vagabonds* (Oxford, 1913), 161; *Judges*, 368 (doubts persist whether Dekker was the author, however: *Judges*, 514; E. D. Pendry (ed.), *Thomas Dekker, Selected Prose Writings* (1967), 322–3); PRO SP 16/197/13, 329/12.
14 *BJF*, 116–17, 124–5; Wilts. CRO QSR Mich. 1631/227.
15 A. M. Everitt, 'Farm labourers', *AHEW* 435 (quotation); P. Clark, 'The migrant in Kentish towns', *Crisis and Order*, 138; PRO SP 16/197/40 (quotation).
16 Harman, repr. *TED*, III.409; B. Jonson, *Bartholomew Fair*, III:v; Cunnington, *Devizes*, pt.i., 54; CLRO Journ., 31/343a; Chester RO QSF 36/103, 61/16; Leics. RO HP II/18/3/105, 105a, 5/684, 700; Salop. RO SBR QS examination, ?27 June 1616.
17 Salop. RO SBR QS examinations, 3 August 1578, 24 June 1601; Chester RO QSE 9/66, QSF 30/71–2 (quotation); *BJF*, 108.
18 CLRO Journ., 28/63b, 95b; quotations from E. P. Thompson, 'Patrician society, plebeian culture', *Journal of Social History*, VII (1974), 392; *WRQS*, II.8–9; Staffs. RO QSOB III.19b; Wilts. CRO QSR Trin.1612/179; also ibid. Hil.1617/101–2; Somers. RO Q/SR 34/19, 42/9–11.
19 L. Stone, *The Crisis of the Aristocracy, 1558–1641* (Oxford, 1965), 575; Somers. RO Q/SR 21/50; BCB 1632/265a; CLRO Repert., 34/102b.
20 *Statutes*, IV.ii.900; e.g. WCL E.146, 36a; *RR*, II.414; Hants. RO QSOB 1627/79b; Somers. RO Q/SR 38/73, 42/16, 51/13; Essex RO Maldon D/B/3/3/211; Wilts. CRO QSR Mich.1613/167, Mich.1631/229.
21 Leics. RO HP II/18/7/117; *BJF*, 134; Somers. RO Q/SR 7/59; NLW Wales 4/128/pt.5/42–5; *NCM 1632–5*, 159.
22 Ribton-Turner, 72; *TRP*, I.211, 302–3; Remembrancia V, no.8, VII, no.103; BCB 1630/206a; GLRO Calendar of Middlesex Sessions Books, 1639–44 (I-A), 71.
23 *Judges*, 4; V., B., *The Run-away's Answer* (1625), sig. A.4.a.
24 Sir Thomas Smith, *De Republica Anglorum* (1583; Cambridge, 1982), ed M.

Dewar, 106; Aydelotte, op. cit., 152–4, 156–7; J. Strype, *Annals of the Reformation* (Oxford, 1824), I.ii.554–8; see also an apparent schedule for searches in Sir William Cecil's hand in PRO SP 12/41/76, fols. 2a–b.

25 Cf. Slack, 'Vagrants and vagrancy', 370.

26 *BJF*, 27–8; PRO Assi 45/4/3/55.

27 Langland quoted Ribton-Turner, 56; W. G. Hoskins, 'Harvest fluctuations and English economic history', *AgHR* XII (1964), 29–30, 44–6, ibid., XVI (1968), 28–31; Slack, op. cit., 369–70; CLRO Journ., 32/146b.

28 Chester RO QSF 61/2; Essex RO Maldon D/B/3/3/211 (9 April); Halliwell, 17; G. D. Owen, *Elizabethan Wales* (Cardiff, 1962), 188–9.

29 Hodgen, op. cit., 395–6 (the figure of 128 fairs for August in 'Vagrants and social order', *P&P*, 64, 26n, should be corrected to 148).

30 CLRO Journ., 26/274a. The only winter fair that did not attract high numbers was Chester, 1570–1600, but that might be explained by the smallness of the sample. Cf. Slack, 'Vagrants and vagrancy', 370 (Norwich and Salisbury).

31 CLRO Repert., 13.i/42a; J. Hill, 'Poor relief in seventeenth-century Shropshire', University of Liverpool M.A. thesis, 1973, 127.

32 H. J. Dyos and D. H. Aldcroft, *British Transport. An Economic Survey from the Seventeenth Century to the Twentieth* (Leicester 1969), emphasizes goods rather than persons; J. Parkes, *Travel in England in the Seventeenth Century* (1925) and J. Crofts, *Packhorse, Waggon and Post* (1967), are largely anecdotal.

33 Essex RO Q/SBa 2/2 (3 September 1621); also Chester RO QSE 8/21; *BJF*, 47.

34 Parkes, op. cit. 80; J. A. Chartres, 'Road carrying in England in the seventeenth century: myth and reality', *EcHR*, 2nd s., XXX (1977), 78–81 (and C. H. Wilson and J. A. Chartres in ibid., XXXIII (1980)).

35 CLRO Repert., 16/436b–437a, 17/378b, 401a; BCB 1606/87b.

36 CLRO Journ., 19/171b–172a; Lincs. AO PSJ/1/A/10/11; Wilts. CRO QSR East.1632/110; S. H[artlib], *London's Charity Inlarged* (1650), 2–4.

37 Stone, *Crisis of the Aristocracy*, 582–5; cf. F. Heal, 'The idea of hospitality in early modern England', *P&P*, 102 (1984), 90.

38 T. Becon, *The Early Works* (Cambridge, 1843), ed. J. Ayre, 20; E. Sandys, *Sermons* (Cambridge, 1842), ed. J. Ayre, 400; C. Dalechamp, *Christian Hospitalitie* (1632), 7 (italics mine).

39 A. Everitt, 'The English urban inn, 1560–1760', in A. Everitt (ed.), *Perspectives in English Urban History* (1973), 93–4; P. Clark, *The English Alehouse: A Social History, 1200–1800* (1983), 14–15.

40 Summarized from Wilts. CRO QSR Hil.1613/154.

41 Dorset RO DBC/163a; Somers. Q/SR 29/17–19.

42 F. J. Furnivall (ed.), *Philip Stubbes's Anatomy of Abuses*, New Shakespeare Soc., Series VI, no.4 (1877–9), i.107; J. Cooke, *Unum necessarium: Or, The Poor Man's Case* (1648), 18.

43 *TED*, I.330; Staffs. RO QSR (Mich.1622) 67/7.

44 *Herts. Co. Recds*, I.24–5; Cunnington, *Wilts.*, 143; *NRQS*, IV.33; Hants. RO 4M53/140/21a.

45 Essex RO Q/SR 122/26; Somers. RO Q/SR 32/244.

46 Staffs. RO QSR (James I) 64/12; Lancs. RO QSB 1/136/27.

47 *NRQS*, I.170–1; Staffs. RO QS Mich.1621 65/56.

48 Parkes, op. cit., 143; Chester RO QSE 8/21, QSF 70/20; Somers. RO Q/SR 16/3.

49 NLW Wales 4/128/pt.5/42–5.

50 Chester RO QSF 49/29, 74/93; Lancs. RO QSB 1/142/7; Clark and Slack, 'Introduction', *Crisis and Order*, 18 (also *BJF*, 168).

51 Salop. RO SBR QS examinations, 15 July 20 Elizabeth I; *NRQS*, I.143, III.290.

52 *Statutes*, IV.i.597; Hants. RO 'Notes by J. S. Furley on minutes of sessions of the peace and gaol delivery', 1–19 Elizabeth I, 15; *BJF*, 109; Leics. RO HP II/18/4/248, 8/335.
53 Chesh. RO QJF 12/2/17; Judges, 108–9.
54 Chester RO QSF 40/27, 73/67; Chesh. RO QSF 7/1/7.
55 *TED*, II.336; Somers. RO Q/SR 33/14, 50/66 (also Chester RO QSE 5/85).
56 Chester RO QSE 8/16; Staffs. RO QS (James I) 78/15.
57 M. Prestwich, *Cranfield* (Oxford, 1966), 529; *Herts. Co. Recds*, V.292–4; also PRO SP 16/241/61.
58 BCB 1577/164a; Wilts. CRO QSR Hil.1613/167; J. H. Parry, 'Transport and trade routes', in E. E. Rich and C. H. Wilson (eds), *Cambridge Economic History of Europe* (Cambridge, 1967), IV, 186; E. Le Roy Ladurie, *Histoire du climat depuis l'an mil* (Paris, 1967), ch. 4.
59 *TED*, III.66; NLW Wales 4/969/pt.3/16; Somers. RO Q/SR 23/33, 37d.
60 *BJF*, 133; PRO Assi 45/5/2/23; Wilts. CRO QSR Mich. 1614/122.
61 *TED*, III.430 (also *Stubbes's Anatomy of Abuses*, ii.43).
62 WCL E.145–6; CLRO Journ., 26/320b.

CHAPTER 6. DANGEROUS TRADES

1 *TED*, III.406; Harrison, *Description*, 183; T. Adams, *Mystical Bedlam, Or the World of Mad-Men* (1615), 62–3.
2 For indictments, J. S. Cockburn, 'Early modern assize records as historical evidence', *Journal of the Society of Archivists*, V (1975), 222–4; J. S. Cockburn, 'Trial by the book? Fact and theory in the criminal process, 1558–1624', in J. H. Baker (ed.), *Legal Records and the Historian* (1978), 66. It is worth mentioning in passing that in his references to my work Dr Cockburn is mistaken in implying that I have relied upon indictments in researching vagrants' occupations; and, that I am a sociologist.
3 W. G. Hoskins, *Provincial England* (1963), 94–5; E. Kerridge, 'Social and economic history [of Leicester], 1509–1660', *VCH Leicestershire*, IV (1958), 76 ff.
4 B. E. Supple, *Commercial Crisis and Change in England, 1600–1642* (Cambridge, 1959), *passim*; Norwich, it seems, expelled immigrant clothworkers; *NCM 1630–1*, 154–5, 158.
5 *BJF*, 75–6; quoted W. L. Woodfill, *Musicians in English Society from Elizabeth to Charles I* (Princeton, 1953), 128.
6 *TED*, I.344; *Statutes*, IV.i.592; F. Aydelotte, *Elizabethan Rogues and Vagabonds* (Oxford, 1913), 160.
7 *BJF*, 51; BCB 1601/244; Wilts. CRO QSR Mich. 1614/122, Mich. 1633/172; Staffs. RO QSR (Trin.1624) 76/25; Leics. RO HP II/18/16/125.
8 Wilts. CRO QSR Mich. 1614/122, 126.
9 Essex RO Q/SBa 2/14.
10 Leics. RO HP II/18/15/276; Caernf. RO QSR 1620 (June).
11 Sir F. Bridge, *The Old Cryes of London* (1921), plate between 24–5; R. Samuel, 'Comers and goers', in H. J. Dyos and M. Wolff (eds), *The Victorian City* (1973), I.123–60; T. W. Bagshaw, 'The itinerants', *Bedfordshire Magazine*, VIII (1961–2), nos. 59–60; J. R. Dolan, *The Yankee Peddlers of Early America* (New York, 1964).
12 J. J. Jusserand, *English Wayfaring Life in the Middle Ages* (1920 edn), 235; *Statutes*, IV.i.155, 591–2, ii.899.
13 *OED* 'chapman' etc.; *Statutes*, IV.ii.1024, 1052; Remembrancia IV, no. 83.
14 Act IV, Sc.iv.

15 Chester RO QSF 31/83; Wilts. CRO QSR Hil.1619/171. For another approach to the subject, M. Spufford, *The Great Reclothing of Rural England. Petty Chapmen and Their Wares in the Seventeenth Century* (1984), esp. ch. 6.

16 Leics. RO HP II/18/17/533; Somers. RO Q/SR 2/41–2.

17 *BJF*, 125; *RR*, III.83; Spufford, op. cit., ch. 5.

18 *TED*, III.109; CLRO Journ., 26/6a–7a; *NCM 1632–5*, 52; Spufford, op. cit., 54–8, 168, 172.

19 *OED* 'tinker' etc.

20 Wilts. CRO QSR Trin.1620/146; Somers. RO Q/SR 6/84.

21 CLRO Journ., 26/6a–7a.

22 Essex RO Maldon D/B/3/3/211 (also Leics. RO HP II/18/15/410, 20/212); Spufford, op. cit., 54–67.

23 Norf. RO NCM 1603–14/103b, 1626–30/102b, 105b, 109a; *RR*, III.83, 125–6.

24 Norf. RO NCM 1603–10/103b; Wilts. CRO QSR East.1616/187; Leics. RO HP II/18/15/347; Chester RO QSF 69/53 (1–4); Somers. RO QSR 40/105–6.

25 Somers. RO Q/SR 17/31 (tinker), 33/125 (chapman); Essex RO Maldon D/B/3/3/125.

26 *TED*, II.45; G. Roberts (ed.), *Diary of Walter Yonge*, Camden Society, XLI (1848), 52–3; Cunnington, *Devizes*, pt.ii, 81.

27 Derbys. RO QS bundles no. 236(?); *APC 1621–3*, 214–15; Supple, *Commercial Crisis and Change*, 56–7, 103–4, 111, 117–18, 244–5; A. L. Beier, 'Poor relief in Warwickshire, 1630–1660', *P&P*, 35 (1966), 86–7.

28 D. Thomas, *A Long Time Burning* (1969), 8–15; W. M. Clyde, *The Struggle for the Freedom of the Press from Caxton to Cromwell* (1934), 296; H. S. Bennett, *English Books and Readers, 1558–1603* (Cambridge, 1965), 267; M. Spufford, *Small Books and Pleasant Histories* (1981), ch. 5 (although mainly later Stuart).

29 Quoted Bennett, op. cit., 267.

30 Leics. RO HP II/18/8/704 (n. d. but probably 1600–6); Clyde, op. cit., 57–66, 193–4, 243, 276; CLRO Repert., 55/411a; BCB 1642/384b, 388a (2), 389a.

31 DAD DCA Oct.1621–Oct.1622, Oct.1627–Oct.1625, and Appendix, Table XI.

32 C. S. L. Davies, 'Slavery and Protector Somerset', *EcHR*, 2nd s., XIX (1966), 538; *TRP*, I.489, 498; Guildhall, Worcester, A.6, View of Frankpledge, I.71–3.

33 C. Barnett, *Britain and Her Army, 1509–1970* (1970), 43; *TED*, II.343, 345; *Statutes*, IV.ii.966–8.

34 Barnett, op. cit., 61–2, 73, 108; C. H. Firth, *Cromwell's Army* (3rd edn, 1921), 13; CLRO Journ., 34/52b; PRO Privy Council Registers P.C. 2/38, vol. 4, 605.

35 Rich, quoted C. G. Cruickshank, *Elizabeth's Army* (Oxford, 2nd edn, 1966), 26; Navy quotation from C. Lloyd, *The British Seaman, 1200–1860* (1968), 60–1; H. J. Webb, 'Elizabethan soldiers: a study in the ideal and the real', *Western Humanities Review*, IV (1950), 152–3.

36 Quoted Barnett, op. cit., 41; Hants. RO 4M53/140/155a–b.

37 *Henry IV, Part One*, IV:ii; *BJF*, 78.

38 Cruickshank, op. cit., 26–7.

39 Harrison, *Description*, 194; also More, *Complete Works*, IV.63.

40 T. Wright (ed.), *Queen Elizabeth and Her Times* (1838), II.29; Cruickshank, op. cit., 168–9; L. Boynton, 'The Tudor provost-marshal', *English Historical Review*, LXXVII (1962), 444–5; *TRP*, III.44–8, 96–7, 106, 134, 196–7; C. Bridenbaugh, *Vexed and Troubled Englishmen, 1590–1642* (New York, 1967), 268–9.

41 J. S. Cockburn (ed.), *Calendar of Assize Records, Hertfordshire Indictments, Elizabeth I* (1975), 173; Essex RO Q/SR 113/39, 39a; KCAO QM/SB 72, 459, 486, 635, 692; Chester RO QSF 49/138; J. S. Cockburn (ed.), *Calendar of Assize Records, Sussex Indictments, Elizabeth I*, 380, 389, 408, 412.

42 Judges, 7–8, 84.

43 Cruickshank, op. cit., 172–3; Barnett, op. cit., 16, 62–3.

44 Leonard, 73, 78, 135–6, 169–70; Devon RO QSOB 1592–1600/114–15, 118, 1625–33 and 1633–40, *passim*; Hants. RO QO/1, 1607–28/2–6; Firth, *Cromwell's Army*, 266–75; cf. Hants. RO QSOB 1650–3, 1662.

45 Essex RO Q/SBa 2/21; also Wilts. CRO QSR East.1609/102.

46 *Statutes*, IV.i.591, ii.899; V. Gildersleeve, *Government Regulation of the Elizabethan Drama* (1908; repr. New York, 1961), 226; M. E. James, *Social Problems and Policy During the Puritan Revolution* (1930; repr. 1966), 287.

47 F. S. Boas (ed.), *Diary of Thomas Crosfield* (1935), 54.

48 E. K. Chambers, *The Elizabethan Stage* (Oxford, 1923), I.320; J. T. Murray, *English Dramatic Companies, 1558–1642* (1910), II.354–9; *NCM 1632–5*, 100, 116, 161, 212–13.

49 Chambers, op. cit., IV.209; E. K. Chambers, *The Mediaeval Stage* (Oxford, 1903), I.44; *TRP*, I.341.

50 Chambers, *Mediaeval Stage*, I.45; M. C. Bradbrook, *The Rise of the Common Player* (Cambridge, Mass., 1962), 31, 34–5.

51 Wright (ed.), *Queen Elizabeth*, II.227; Staffs. RO QSR (James I) 31/107; Bradbrook, op. cit., 51; Chambers, *Elizabethan Stage*, IV.266–7, 269, 273, 276–7, 287.

52 Bradbrook, op. cit., 27–8, 37–8 (quotation at 37), 41–3; A. W. Ward and A. R. Waller (eds), *Cambridge History of English Literature* (Cambridge, 1910), VI.ii.272.

53 Woodfill, *Musicians in English Society*, 129; Wilts. CRO QSR Trin.1614/129, 139; Chester RO QSE 13/25.

54 Woodfill, op. cit., 129–30; *NRQS*, I.105; Notts. RO QSM IV.181.

55 Chesh. RO QJF 7/2/16; *RR*, II.160–1; Staffs. RO QSR (Charles I) 22/23; Essex RO Maldon D/B/3/3/211.

56 Chambers, *Mediaeval Stage*, I.54–5; Bradbrook, op. cit., 22–4; J. E. Stevens, *Music and Poetry in the Early Tudor Court* (1961), 299; Woodfill, op. cit., 102–8, 119, 122, 125–6.

57 Chambers, *Mediaeval Stage*, I.63–5, 68–9, II.185; G. E. Dawson (ed.), *Records of Plays and Players in Kent, 1450–1642* (1965), Malone Society Collections, VII.xi–xiii.

58 C. R. Baskervill, *The Elizabethan Jig* (Chicago, 1929), 31–2; *The Winter's Tale*, IV:iii–iv; *Bartholomew Fair*, III:v; Norf. RO NCM 1595–1603/489, 498, 545; BCB 1642/410; Wilts. CRO QSR Mich. 1620/186.

59 P. Burke, 'Popular culture in seventeenth-century London', *London Journal*, III (1977), 154; Gildersleeve, *Government Regulation*, 227; CLRO Repert., 55/411a; Bristol RO Sessions Minute Book 1653–71/6a; Cunnington, *Wilts.*, 230.

60 R. Scot, *The Discovery of Witchcraft* (1584; new edn, Carbondale, Ill., 1964), ed. H. R. Williamson, 268–9; L. B. Wright, 'Juggling tricks and conjury on the English stage before 1642', *Modern Philology*, XXIV (1927), 272, 280.

61 Scot, op. cit., 283–91.

62 Leics. RO HP II/18/5/694; P. Slack (ed.), *Poverty in Early Stuart Salisbury*, Wiltshire Record Society, XXXI (1975), 37, 39.

63 The best general guide is M. Pelling and C. Webster, 'Medical practitioners', in *Health, Medicine and Mortality in the Sixteenth Century* (Cambridge, 1979), ed. C. Webster; see also C. Hill, *Intellectual Origins of the English Revolution* (Oxford, 1965), 74–7, 80, 83; C. Hill, 'The medical profession and its radical critics', repr. in C. Hill, *Change and Continuity in Seventeenth-Century England* (1974), ch. 7; C. Webster, *The Great Instauration* (1975), ch. 4.

64 *Statutes*, III.330; Halle reprinted in T. J. Pettigrew (ed.), *Early English Poetry, Ballads, and Popular Literature of the Middle Ages*, Percy Society (1844), XI, 3, 8, 11–16, 18, 26 (a reference that I owe to Lucinda McCray Beier).
65 *Statutes*, III.31; Halle, op. cit., 27; *BJF*, 176–7 (also Dorset RO DBC/333a).
66 Halle, op. cit., 13, 16–19 (cf. Leics. RO HP II/18/15/255).
67 *Statutes*, III.32; Halle, op. cit., 19–23.
68 Quoted G. N. Clark, *The Royal College of Physicians* (Oxford, 1964), I.56; *BJF*, 49; and Halle, op. cit., 9, 27 (also *BJF*, 176–7).
69 Halle, op. cit., 6, 8–9, 12, 14; Somers. RO Q/SR 9/25 (also Dorset RO DBC/333a, 336b).
70 *Statutes*, III.906; *BJF*, 49, 176–7; C. H. Mayo (ed.), *Municipal Records of the Borough of Dorchester* (Exeter, 1908), 653 (also Somers. RO Q/SR 70/51A).
71 *Statutes*, III.906; Halle, op. cit., 17, 22–3; W. S. C. Copeman, *Doctors and Disease in Tudor Times* (1960), 143.
72 E. Duckett, *The Wandering Saints* (1959); R. W. Southern, *Western Society and the Church in the Middle Ages* (Harmondsworth, 1970), 286–7; H. Waddell, *The Wandering Scholars* (1927), 161–2, 174, 180–1, 184–5; *Statutes*, II.58.
73 *Statutes*, III.330, IV.i.592, ii.899.
74 *CSPD 1547–80*, 410; *LBR*, III.378–80, 396, 409; BCB 1606/149b (also *BJF*, 3).
75 L. Stone, 'The educational revolution in England, 1560–1640', *P&P*, 28 (1964), graph facing p. 49; ibid., 75 (citing M. Curtis, 'The alienated intellectuals of early Stuart England', *P&P*, 23 [1962]; idem, *P&P*, 24 [1962], 101–2).
76 Somers. RO Q/SR 45/47; Dorset RO DBC/12a, 80b, 218a–b.
77 *Statutes*, III.330, IV.i.591, ii.899; K. Thomas, *Religion and Magic* (1971), 245–7, 442–3.
78 Thomas, op. cit., 245–7, 442–3; A. Macfarlane, *Witchcraft in Tudor and Stuart England* (New York, 1970) 116–20 (residences). Cases involving accusations of witchcraft and vagrancy are Staffs. RO QSR (James I) 16/51–3; Somers. RO Q/SR 9/21; Caernf. RO QSR 1636–7 (H. Lloyd).
79 PRO Assi 45/3/2/141–3.
80 Somers. RO Q/SR 53/76–7; Caernf. RO QSR 1636–7 (H. Lloyd).
81 PRO Assi 45/4/2/70.

CHAPTER 7. THE SEMINARY OF VAGABONDAGE

1 T. F. Merrill (ed.), *William Perkins, 1558–1602, English Puritanist* (Nieuwkoop, 1966), 226; *The Sermons of Mr Henry Smith* (1593), 1108, 1124–5; *Three Sermons on Homilies* (1596), sig. B.2.b.
2 Tawney, *Agrarian Problem*, 268.
3 *Statutes*, III.328, IV.i.116, 413, 598, ii.897.
4 J. F. Pound, 'An Elizabethan census of the poor: the treatment of vagrancy in Norwich, 1570–80', *University of Birmingham Historical Journal*, VIII (1962), 136–7; A. L. Beier, 'The social problems of an Elizabethan country town: Warwick, 1580–90' in P. Clark (ed.), *Country Towns in Pre-Industrial England* (Leicester, 1981), 77; K. Thomas, *Religion and the Decline of Magic* (1971) 552–5; A. Macfarlane, *Witchcraft in Tudor and Stuart England* (New York, 1970), 174.
5 *Statutes*, III.331–2, 558; IV.i.116, 592, ii.898–900.
6 Leverton overseers' accounts, 1562–98, fol.12a (parish chest); DAD DCA, 1621–2, 1627–8 (£11 13s 4d as against £1 13s 7d); Warwicks. CRO DR17/1/6; Notts. RO PR 1709.

7 Essex RO Q/SR 58/56–7; Dorset RO DBC/212a; Essex RO Maldon D/B/3/3/125 (6 July 1635).

8 Devon RO Exeter Act Book IV/300; Somers. RO Q/SR 23/82, 33/14, 99; Chester RO QSE 5/109, QSF 63/11, no.2.

9 DAD DCA 1621–2, 1627–8; WCL St Mary le Strand churchwardens' accounts, vol. 22; Slack, 'Vagrants and vagrancy', 368.

10 *TRP*, II.161–2; *SE 1570–94*, 83–4; Judges, 54, 81.

11 Leics. RO HP II/18/7/319; Somers. RO Q/SR 42/87.

12 Somers. RO Q/SR 7/8–9, 26/53; Judges, 94.

13 PRO P.C. 2 42/240, 413; Cunnington, *Wilts.*, 317–19.

14 Essex RO Q/SR 85/37–8; Somers. RO Q/SR 21/133, 40/75–6.

15 Somers. RO Q/SR 21/133.

16 ibid., 45/32–4 (Bowden was incorrigible as well as inept: he was caught yet again in 1625 with a false passport: ibid., 53/79); Cunnington, *Wilts.*, 113.

17 DAD, DCA, Oct. 1621–Oct. 1622 (32 of 373 = 8.6 per cent); P. Rowland James, *The Baths of Bath in the Sixteenth and Early Seventeenth Centuries* (1938), 95, 109 (Abbey cemetery and St James's: 406 of 2209); R. Lennard, 'The watering places', in R. Lennard (ed.), *Englishmen at Rest and Play* (Oxford, 1931), 4–10; WCL St Margaret's overseers' accounts, E.145–9 *passim*.

18 Judges, 55, 80–1; Somers. RO Q/SR 18/81.

19 W. S. Weeks, *Clitheroe in the Seventeenth Century* (Clitheroe, n. d.), 58; GLRO P92/SAV/1423E/32; also, York City Archives, House Books 31/341a.

20 Leics. RO BR 11/18/1/34; Cunnington, *Wilts.* 223–5; *Herts. Co. Recds*, V.47–8; WYRO QSOB 1638–42/15a.

21 PRO SP 12/86/16/XIII, 16/388/7/XL.7; BCB 1640/286a (also Norf. RO NCM 1603–14/7, 82a, 97a, 127b, 173b, 175a, 214a, 234a).

22 Judges, 53, 372; *King Lear*, III: iv.

23 J. Aubrey, *The Natural History of Wiltshire* (1685; repr. Newton Abbot, 1969), ed. K. G. Ponting, 93; Ribton-Turner, 172; also R. Graves, J. Lindsay and P. Warlock, *Loving Mad Tom* (1927; repr. New York, 1970).

24 R. N. Hadcock and D. M. C. Knowles, *Medieval Religious Houses* (2nd edn, 1971), 372; M. MacDonald, *Mystical Bedlam* (Cambridge, 1981), 121–2; Judges, 494, 496–7; BCB 1624/368a–69a.

25 BCB 1624/368a–69a; MacDonald, op. cit., *passim*.

26 M. Foucault, *Folie et déraison. Histoire de la folie à l'âge classique* (Paris, 1961), 76.

27 Essex RO Q/SR 219/126; *NCM 1632–5*, 88.

28 BCB 11 Dec. 1578 (no foliation); Wilts. CRO QSR East.1618/168.

29 BCB 1576/233b; Wilts. CRO QSR Trin.1614/129 (also BCB 1621/224a, 1630/190a; Chester RO QSE 5/130).

30 R. Hunter and I. Macalpine, *Three Hundred Years of Psychiatry* (1963), 12–15, 55; MacDonald, op. cit., 173ff.

31 Essex RO Q/SR 205/119, 258/95 (also 208/123, 209/105).

32 Judges, 91; BCB 1560/89a.

33 Wilts. CRO QSR East.1613/218–19; Somers. RO Q/SR 18/80.

34 Judges, 85–90, 117–18 (and plates facing 90, 117).

35 CLRO Repert., 16/149a.

36 ibid., Repert., 3/197a, 11/364a, 394b; Thomas, *Religion and Magic*, 198–9.

37 BCB 1578/339a, 1620/198a; for the subject generally, see the absorbing study by M. Pelling, 'Appearance and reality: barber-surgeons, the body and disease', forthcoming in A. L. Beier and R. Finlay (eds), *London 1500–1700*; final example from BCB 1560/99b.

38 Halliwell, 17.
39 ibid., 19–20 (to glaver means to flatter: *OED*); G. D. Owen, *Elizabethan Wales* (Cardiff, 1962), 188–9; Caernf. RO QSR 1618; cf. Pound, 'Elizabethan census of the poor', 138; Beier, 'Elizabethan country town', 60–1.
40 CLRO Repert., 9/190b, Journ., 25/257a; BCB 1621/219b, and entry for 28 April (no foliation); *BJF*, 48.
41 *TED*, II.335; Judges, 70; Essex RO Q/SR 194/73; York City Archives, York QS F.7/259a.
42 More, *Complete Works*, IV.67, 71; J. M. Cowper (ed.), *Four Supplications*, Early English Text Society, extra s., XIII (1871), 79.
43 Wilts. CRO QSR East.1623/217; Lincs. AO Lindsey QS A.6/158 (also Somers. RO Q/SR 75/63).
44 Salop. RO SBR QS examinations (3 April, 20 James I); E. Sussex RO QS files January 1626/109/2.
45 Herts. RO HAT/SR2/128; Wilts. CRO QSR Mich.1617/154; Judges, 69; Somers. RO Q/SR 46/87.
46 *SE 1570–94*, 28; KCAO QM/SB 526; Somers. RO Q/SR 3/198 (also Essex RO Q/SR 73/54).
47 PRO SP 16/189/60; Dorset RO DBC/80b, 218a–b.
48 Essex RO Q/SR 47/17; Wilts. CRO QSR Trin.1614/129; BCB 1605/15a.
49 Somers. RO Q/SR 17/42; KCAO QM/SB 658.
50 *SE 1570–94*, 28; KCAO QM/SB 526.
51 F. Thompson, *Lark Rise to Candleford* (1954 edn), 126–8.

CHAPTER 8. THE UNDERWORLD UNCOVERED

1 Judges; G. Salgādo, *The Elizabethan Underworld* (1977).
2 Salgādo, op. cit., 44.
3 J. F. Pound, *Poverty and Vagrancy in Tudor England* (1971), 29.
4 Wilts. CRO QSR examinations and constables' presentments, 1603–38.
5 BCB: in Oct. 1602, 9 of 41 vagrants were stated to have been in Bridewell before; in Feb. 1631, 25 of 85.
6 Salgādo op. cit., 44–5; cf. *TED*, II.337–8.
7 Pound, op. cit., 29; cf. *TED*, II.345.
8 KCAO QM/SB 228.
9 Essex RO Q/SR 54/39; PRO Assi 45/5/7/27; M. Prestwich, *Cranfield* (Oxford, 1966), 529.
10 Judges, 113–15, 522–32; F. Grose, *A Classical Dictionary of the Vulgar Tongue* (1785; repr., Menston, 1968), ed. R. C. Alston.
11 Essex RO Q/SR 76/56, Somers. RO Q/SR 18/79, 81.
12 Judges, 24, 64; *Liber Vagatorum*, trans.J. C. Hotten, D. B. Thomas (ed.), *The Book of Vagabonds and Beggars* (c.1509; repr. 1932), 18, 136–83.
13 *OED*, 'cant'.
14 KCAO QM/SB 643–4; Essex RO Q/SR 113/40, 40a.
15 Judges, 35–6; Essex RO Q/SR 76/56, 113/40a.
16 P. Linebaugh, 'The Tyburn riot against the surgeons', in D. Hay *et al.*, *Albion's Fatal Tree* (New York, 1975), 66; G. Irwin, *American Tramp and Underworld Slang* (New York, 1931); E. Partridge, *A Dictionary of the Underworld, British and American* (1961).
17 *A New Canting Dictionary* (1725).
18 Calculated from J. S. Cockburn, 'The nature and incidence of crime in England, 1559–1625: a preliminary survey', in J. S. Cockburn (ed.), *Crime in*

England, 1550–1800 (1977), 55 (figures for thefts include burglary and highway robbery).

19 In 718 of 1604 examinations (44 per cent), it is unclear whether an offence had been committed. Examples of thorough examinations: Chester RO QSF 74/6, Leics. RO HP II/18/4/172, 5/742, 8/584. BCB 25 March 1624–24 March 1625.

20 J. Bellamy, *Crime and Public Order in England in the Later Middle Ages* (1973), 30; M. J. Ingram, 'Communities and courts: law and disorder in early seventeenth-century Wiltshire', in Cockburn, op. cit., 132–3.

21 *BJF*, 123; Derbys. RO QS bundles, no. 294; Norf. RO NCM 1595–1603/37; Chester RO QSF 51/60, 63, 69/53, 73/78; Leics. HP II/18/4/163, 12/32-P, 17/493, 500–1; Essex RO Q/SBa 2/2 (Davy Jones); *RR*, II.348; Dorset RO DBC/229a–b; PRO Assi 45/2/2/54–5, 4/3/52, 2/1/115.

22 Judges, 378–9; Wilts. CRO QSR Hil.1610/143, Mich.1627/218.

23 Essex RO Q/SR 79/92; KCAO QM/SB 643; DAD DCA 1621–2 (17 July 1622); Notts. RO QSM.VI.209, 222; *BJF*, 62; BCB 1603/369b.

24 Judges, 65, 70–4.

25 BL Royal MS.17.A.XIII/29b–30a; R. West, *The Court of Conscience, Or Dick Whippers Sessions* (1607), sig. D.1.b.

26 Somers. RO Q/SR 45/21; KCAO QM/SB 462; BL Royal MS.17.A.XIII/30a; BCB 1620/187a, 1621/214b, 1630/194a, 206a, 1641/323a.

27 Judges, 49; *TED*, II.338–9.

28 BCB 1576/3a, 1578/273a, 1579/380a (also 1577/67b, 1620/212a).

29 Judges, xlix–lii; Aydelotte, *Elizabethan Rogues and Vagabonds*, 82; BL Royal MS.17.A.XIII/47b.

30 Chester RO QSE 10/9 (also QSF 59/22), 66/50.

31 Judges, 69; Essex RO Q/SR 214/75 (also KCAO QM/SB 643–4).

32 Judges, 54, 79, 156.

33 Chester RO QSE 5/94/103–4; Essex RO Q/SBa 2/6, *passim*.

34 *TED*, II.337–8.

35 Judges, 73, 172–3; Somers. RO Q/SR 21/7, 42/169 (also 33/32, 45/39–40).

36 Chester RO QSE 9/67 (also *BJF*, 107); Wilts. CRO QSR Mich.1610/104.

37 *BJF*, 50; Leics. RO HP II/18/15/426; BCB 1621/214b.

38 e.g. NLW Wales 4/126/pt.1/8–10; KCAO QM/SB 1056; Leics. RO HP II/18/2/378.

39 NLW Wales 4/969/pt.1/32; *BJF*, 182; Wilts. CRO QSR Mich.1627/220, Hil.1637/234; Leics. RO HP II/18/12/32-P.

40 W. Holdsworth, *A History of English Law* (3rd edn, 1923), VIII.304–5; J. F. Stephen, *A History of the Criminal Law of England* (1883; repr. New York, n. d.), III.150; Sir Edward Coke, *Third Part of the Institutes* (1644; repr. 1979), 63–5.

41 BL Lansdowne MS.79/9; cf. Salop. RO SBR QS examinations (Joan Nede, 15 July 30 Elizabeth I).

42 Cunnington, *Wilts.*, 16–24.

43 Judges, 175; Chester RO QSE 51/20; Notts. RO QSM.IX.223 (cf. Somers. RO Q/SR 40/19).

44 Wilts. RO QSR Mich.1621/170; PRO Assi 45/3/1/205; Chester RO QSF 69/54.

45 BL Lansdowne MS.79/9; *RR*,II.149, 152, 155–6 (also Cunnington, *Wilts.*, 17).

46 *RR*,II.348 (also KCAO QM/SB 643–4).

47 *RR*,II.146–9, 150–2, 156–61; Cunnington, *Wilts.*, 21–2.

48 *RR*,II.147–52; Cunnington, *Wilts.*, 16–17.

49 Summ. from *RR*,II.151–2 (the maid reported seeing four or five men, making the task easier, but she was in bed and the widow answered the door).

50 Chester RO QSF 69/54; Salop. RO SBR QS examinations, 3 April 20 James I.
51 Holdsworth, op. cit., III.363.
52 Cunnington, *Wilts.*, 16–24; cf. K. Hart, 'Informal income opportunities and urban employment in Ghana', in R. Jolly (ed.), *Third World Employment* (Harmondsworth, 1973), 66–7.
53 Cunnington, *Wilts.*, 17; KCAO QM/SB 643–4; Wilts. CRO QSR Hil.1619/171, Hil.1620/184; Somers. RO Q/SR 42/197.
54 Somers. RO Q/SR 34/97 (also *NRQS*,I.170–1; Lincs. AO Lindsay QS A.6/154).
55 Somers. RO Q/SR 18/82; *Herts. Co. Recds*, I.59–60.
56 Holdsworth, op. cit., III.362; Stephen, op. cit. II.121, III.124, 126 (neither source is very helpful).
57 W. P. Baker, 'The observance of Sunday', in R. Lennard (ed.), *Englishmen at Rest and Play* (Oxford, 1931) 119; L. Stone, *The Crisis of the Aristocracy, 1558–1641* (Oxford, 1965), 568–9; K. Thomas, *Religion and the Decline of Magic*, 21.
58 Chester RO QSF 66/71–5; *RR*, II.139.
59 Wilts. CRO QSR Mich.1631/180; Leics. RO HP II/18/19/457; *RR*, II.294–7.
60 *RR*, II.263–4 (possible fourth group: Somers. RO Q/SR 8/51).
61 Wilts. CRO QSR Hil.1614/107, East.1614/171, Hil.1632/234; Norf. RO NCM 1626–30/140b, 272b.
62 Judges, 44, 493.
63 CLRO Journ.,19/353b; Wilts. CRO QSR Hil.1614/107, East.1614/171, Mich.1631/180, 234, Hil.1632/167; Chester RO QSF 66/71–5; *RR*, II.138–9, 264, 294–7.
64 ibid. (with exception of first three references); Leics. RO HP II/18/12/31.
65 Somers. RO Q/SR 40/32–3; *RR*, II.263–4; Leics. RO HP II/18/19/457; Wilts. CRO QSR Hil.1632/167.
66 Somers. RO Q/SR 8/51, 40/32–3; *RR*, II.138–40.
67 Fairs: Somers. RO Q/SR 8/5, Leics. RO II/18/12/30–1, Chester RO QSF 66/71–4, Wilts. CRO QSR Hil.1617/101–2, Hil.1632/167. Mobility: Chester RO QSF 66/71–5, Somers. RO Q/SR 40/32–3, Wilts. CRO QSR Mich.1631/180, Leics. RO HP II/18/19/457.
68 Norf. RO NCM 1562–69/507, 643, 650; ibid. 1569–76/47, 53; CLRO Repert.,13.ii.407b, 16/37b; P. Slack (ed.), *Poverty in Early Stuart Salisbury*, Wiltshire Record Society, XXXI (1975), 32; cf. Thomas, *Religion and Magic*, 198–9.
69 BCB 1578/287a, 1579/364a, 380a; *RR*, II.140; documents CLRO Repert.,11/364a–b; Somers. RO Q/SR 2/23–4; Notts. RO QSM.IV.181.
70 Holdsworth, op. cit., III.368; Stephen op. cit., III.149; J. Parkes, *Travel in England in the Seventeenth Century* (1925), 164, 175–6; Ribton-Turner, 39, 53, 173; Bellamy, *Crime and Public Order*, 42, 154.
71 Judges, 415–17.
72 Leics. RO HP II/18/1/110; *SE 1570–94*, 87–8; PRO Assi 45/4/2/43–4; *NRQS*, V.232.
73 BL Lansdowne MS.79/9/20a–22a.
74 J. Bernard, *Le guide des chemins d'Angleterre* (Paris, 1579), 73; Parkes, op. cit., 168; H. Smith, *Sermons* (1593), 1114; Bellamy, op. cit., 42.
75 BL Lansdowne MS.79/9/20b; KCAO QM/SB 275 (also Leics. RO HP II/18/1/110; PRO Assi 45/3/1/81, 4/2/43–4).
76 BL Lansdowne MS.79/9/20a–b: KCAO QM/SB 275; Parkes, op. cit., 175; also *SE 1639–44*, 8–9; PRO Assi 45/4/2/43–4.

77 KCAO QM/SB 107.

78 BCB 1641/337b.

79 Stone, *Crisis of the Aristocracy*, 223–34 (quotation at 226); J. Samaha, *Law and Order in Historical Perspective* (New York, 1974), 27.

80 Staffs. RO QSR (James I) 62/64; PRO Assi 45/1/4/10.

81 BCB 1606/84a, 1630/186a (also 1575/102b, 1607/193a, 1639/248a); cf. *RR*, III.360.

82 Staffs. RO D1287/10/2 (30 May 1614 – no foliation); BCB 1630/203a, 209a (also *BJF*, 183; *SE 1570–94*, 95–6; Wilts. CRO QSR Mich.1619/155, Trin.1620/147).

83 *NRQS*, II.101–2; BCB 1621/220a (also 1630/207b, 1631/220b).

84 *RR*, II.348, 353–4; Essex RO Q/SR 54/39; *BJF*, 182; Chester RO QSE 5/130.

85 Wilts. CRO QSR Hil.1610/121–6; Leics. RO HP II/18/20/20 (also *BJF*, 134–5).

86 G. R. Elton, *The Tudor Constitution* (Cambridge, 2nd edn, 1982), 59–61, 419–23, 442–8; Holdsworth, op. cit., VIII.339–40; although see J. Bellamy, *The Tudor Law of Treason* (1979), chs 1–2, who takes a cautious line.

87 Elton, *Policy and Police* (Cambridge, 1972), chs 2–3, esp. 63, 74; *CSPD 1547–80*, 353.

88 C. Z. Wiener, 'The beleaguered isle', *P&P*, 51, *passim*; R. Clifton, 'The popular fear of Catholics', ibid., 52 and *passim*; C. Haigh, 'The continuity of Catholicism in the English Reformation', ibid., 93 (1981), 58–60; quotation from Hants. RO 4M53/140/130b.

89 J. Bossy, 'The character of Elizabethan Catholicism', in T. H. Aston (ed.), *Crisis in Europe, 1560–1660* (1965), 223–33; *BJF*, 114–15.

90 J. Gerard, *The Autobiography of a Hunted Priest* (New York, 1952), 11, 17.

91 BCB 1606/158b; Chester RO QSE 8/12, 10/38, 11/3, QSF 49/100–2; KCAO NR/JQp 1/28; *SE 1622–7*, 54–8.

92 C. Hill, *The World Turned Upside Down* (1972), 22; Elton, *Tudor Constitution*, 458; BCB 1620/206a.

93 Hill, op. cit., 40 and *passim*; Cunnington, *Wilts.*, 231.

94 BCB 1575/125b; Leics. RO HP II/18/15/244.

95 BCB 1606/108a; Staffs. RO QSOB II.88 (also *RR*, III.9; Dorset RO DBC/61a, 69a–b, 307a).

96 J. Gardiner (ed.), *Letters and Papers, Foreign and Domestic, of the Reign of Henry VIII* (1888), XI.332–3; Elton, *Policy and Police*, 63, 74; J. Strype, *Annals of the Reformation* (Oxford, 1824), I.ii.346; Hill, op. cit. 37; BCB 1642/366b.

97 Quotation from Holdsworth, op. cit., VIII.340; Elton, *Tudor Constitution*, 59–64; Bellamy, *Tudor Law of Treason*, 32–4.

98 KCAO NR/JQf 1/2/15; Dorset RO DBC/78b.

99 Dorset RO, 'Calendar of local archives, borough and county of the town of Poole', 37; BCB 1606/87b.

100 BCB 1560/80b; PRO SP 16/258/45 I–II; BCB 1641/334a (also *SE 1639–44*, 39; Cunnington, *Wilts.*, 226).

101 Somers. RO Q/SR 42/87; Leics. RO HP II/18/16/82. For refusals to make statements: Somers. RO Q/SR 23/56, Dorset RO DBC/357a; and for an instance of the penalty being applied in 1641, Cunnington, *Wilts.*, 135–7.

102 Stephen, *History of the Criminal Law*, III.178; Leics. RO HP II/18/16/68–9, 19/547; PRO Assi 45/2/2/25.

103 Somers. RO Q/SR 29/18–19.

104 *Statutes*, IV.i.592; Essex RO Q/SR 76/56.

105 e.g. *BJF*, 62, 66; Essex RO Q/SR 47/17, 76/56, Q/SBa 2/18; Somers. RO Q/SR 23/20, 31/14; E. Sussex RO QS files 1614/7A/54; Dorset RO DBC/107a, 299a;

Wilts. CRO QSR East.1619/179, Trin.1623/152; cf. Slack, 'Vagrants and vagrancy', 364, who quotes prices which seem rather on the high side.
106 Wilts. CRO QSR Trin.1620/147 (also BCB 1578/16 July (no foliation), a vagrant with a sheaf of the documents, which he obtained from a 'scholar of Oxford' for two pots of beer); Somers. RO Q/SR 40/118 (also Chester RO QSF 49/27).
107 Essex RO Q/SR 79/92; Wilts. CRO QSR Trin.1615/114, East.1619/179; Somers. RO Q/SR 18/79–82.
108 Wilts. CRO QSR Trin.1626/139, 153.
109 Essex RO Q/SR 79/92; Wilts. CRO QSR Trin.1615/114.
110 Essex RO Q/SR 47/17; Somers. RO Q/SR 18/79–82; Dorset RO DBC/14b–15a; also Wilts. CRO QSR Trin.1615/114, Somers. RO Q/SR 19/126, Dorset RO DBC/12a, Norf. RO NCM 1569–76/75.
111 Somers. RO Q/SR 18/80; Aydelotte, *Elizabethan Rogues and Vagabonds*, 173–4 and plate between 40 and 41.
112 Wilts. CRO QSR Mich.1610/102–3, Trin.1614/148a–b.
113 Bellamy, *Crime and Public Order*, 6, 70–2, 75; G. Howson, *Thief-Taker General. The Rise and Fall of Jonathan Wild* (1970), 312–14.

CHAPTER 9. STATE POLICY: FROM *UTOPIA* TO THE PENAL COLONY

1 I owe this point to my friend and colleague Dr A. Grant.
2 A. G. R. Smith, *The Government of Elizabethan England* (1967), 83.
3 L. Stone, *The Causes of the English Revolution, 1529–1642* (1972), 62, 116; K. Pickthorn, *Early Tudor Government. Henry VII* (Cambridge, 1949), 73–4.
4 F. Aydelotte, *Elizabethan Rogues and Vagabonds* (Oxford, 1913), 66–7; L. D. Frasure, 'Shakespeare's constables', *Anglia*, LVIII (1934), 387–90; cf. J. Kent, 'The English village constable, 1580–1642', *Journal of British Studies*, XX (1981), 28–9.
5 D. Woodward, 'The background to the Statute of Artificers', *EcHR*, 2nd s., XXXIII (1980), 39–42; Leonard, 129.
6 A. Fletcher, *A County Community in Peace and War: Sussex, 1600–1660* (1975), 213; cf. P. Clark, *English Provincial Society from the Reformation to the Revolution* (Hassocks, 1977), 352, 360; T. G. Barnes, *Somerset, 1625–1640* (Cambridge, Mass., 1961), 162–3; A. H. Smith, 'Justices at work in Elizabethan Norfolk', *Norfolk Archaeology*, XXXIV (1967), 101.
7 K. Wrightson, 'Two concepts of order: justices, constables and jurymen in seventeenth-century England', in J. Brewer and J. Styles (eds), *An Ungovernable People* (1980), 40–3; Wrightson and Levine, *Poverty and Piety in an English Village*, 176–83.
8 Quoted J. S. Cockburn (ed.), *Calendar of Assize Records: Sussex Indictments, James I* (1975), 11; (also KCAO QM/SB 946).
9 BL Lansdowne MS.49/29; BL Royal MS.17.A.XIII/29b–30a.
10 NLW Wales 4/128/pt.4/25; Staffs. RO QSR (James I) 24/33.
11 Wilts. CRO QSR 1603–38, *passim* (130 of 333 parishes listed in the 1831 census reported, excluding urban ones); Wrightson, 'Two Concepts of Order', 37.
12 Sources as in Table I (Appendix); Slack, 'Vagrants and vagrancy' (Salisbury), 360ff.; Northants. RO MaT 102.
13 *Statutes* IV.ii.900; F. G. Emmison, *Catalogue of Essex Parish Records, 1240–1894* (Chelmsford, 2nd edn, 1966), 17–19, 76, 111, 137, 203; *Essex Review*, XLII (1933), 41–2; records for Bisley (parish register, 1547–1700), Canewdon (parish register, 1636–1772), and Crondall (churchwardens' accounts, tran-

script, fols. 182–98) are still in the parish chests, and I must thank the incumbents for permission to see them. I am especially grateful to John Bromley of Lockington in the East Riding, who provided me with a transcript of records of vagrants punished there from 1650 to 1654.

14 Original records in PRO SP 12 and SP 16; see discussion *supra*, 15–17.

15 'Recidivism' rate assumed to be 1 in 3.4, as in London in 1631: see above, 124.

16 For projects generally, J. Thirsk, *Economic Policy and Projects* (Oxford, 1978); J. O. Appleby, *Economic Thought and Ideology in Seventeenth-Century England* (Princeton, 1978), ch. 6; James, *Social Problems and Policy during the Puritan Revolution*, 271–83.

17 More, *Complete Works*, IV.61 (quotation)–73, 81, 241.

18 G. R. Elton, 'An early Tudor poor law', *EcHR*, 2nd s., VI (1953); G. R. Elton, *Reform and Renewal* (Cambridge, 1973), 73, 75–6, 122–4. Original drafts in PRO SP 6/7/71, 73, BL Royal MS.18.C.VI.

19 BL Royal MS.18.C.VI/1a–2a, 3b–6a, 32a–33a. Whether or not the draft's proposal of capital punishment for incorrigible vagrants constituted 'mild treatment', as it has been suggested (Elton, op. cit., *EcHR*, VI, 58), their proposed prosecution as felons in this bill was a new departure, and one that was taken up in the poor law passed that year: *Statutes*, III.560.

20 BL Royal MS.18.C.VI/29a–30b (italics mine).

21 Reprinted in E. Arber (ed.), *An English Garner* (Birmingham, 1879), II.141–3.

22 ibid., III–IV; G. K. Fortescue (ed.), *Catalogue of the Pamphlets . . . Collected by George Thomason, 1640–1661* (1908), I.33; T. W. Fulton, *The Sovereignty of the Sea* (1911), 95–8, 202, 239–45.

23 A. E. Bland, P. A. Brown and R. H. Tawney (eds), *English Economic History, Select Documents* (1914), 435–6.

24 BL Cotton Titus B.10/267–70.

25 BL Royal MS.17.A.XIII, *passim* and fol. 80.

26 Plagiarism from document reprinted in *TED*, II.307; cf. *Stanleyes Remedy . . .* (1646), 5.

27 CLRO Remembrancia IV, no.83.

28 James, op. cit., chs 6–7; W. Schenk, *The Concern for Social Justice in the Puritan Revolution* (1948), ch. 9; C. Webster, *The Great Instauration* (1975), chs 1–2.

29 Hartlib, *The Parliament's Reformation* (1646), 1–4; *London's Charity Inlarged* (1650), 10–14; Webster, op. cit., 361ff.; V. Pearl, 'Puritans and Poor Relief. The London Workhouse, 1649–1660', in D. H. Pennington and K. Thomas (eds), *Puritans and Revolutionaries* (Oxford, 1978), 218–22.

30 Chamberlen, *Poor Man's Advocate*, 37, 47; Hartlib, *The Parliament's Reformation*, 5. Cf. Webster, op. cit., 360–9.

31 The best available study is L. Boynton, 'The Tudor provost-marshal', *English Historical Review*, LXXVII (1962), 437–40, upon which these paragraphs rely greatly; *TRP*, I.106ff.; *Statutes*, III.560; CLRO Repert., 9/253a.

32 Boynton, op. cit., 444–5; Chesh. RO DDX 358/68b.

33 *SRP*, I.360–2.

34 Boynton, op. cit., 455n.; *APC 1621–3*, 224–5.

35 Boynton, op. cit., 446; CLRO Journ., 24/95a, 113b, 150b–151a, 225b, Repert., 40/70b–72a; BCB 1597 onwards, *passim*.

36 Boynton, op. cit., 448–9; PRO SP 16/189/79, 195/31, 233/90 (figures cited), 265/85; *Herts. Co. Recds*, V.398.

37 Boynton, op. cit., 447; *Herts. Co. Recds*, V.67–8, 398.

38 C. Read (ed.), *William Lambarde and Local Government*, 107; also A. H. Smith, *County and Court: Government and Politics in Norfolk, 1558–1603* (Oxford, 1974), 130–3.
39 Quoted Boynton, op. cit., 446.
40 *Statutes*, II.58, 569, III.328–9, IV.i.413, 591–2.
41 *Statutes*, III.562, IV.i.416; *TRP*, II.47; *NCM 1630–1*, 147ff.; Dorset RO DBC/49a–b, 186a; Chester RO QSF 30/70; Wilts. CRO QSR Trin.1612/176; Essex RO Q/SR 205/37–8.
42 *Statutes* IV.i.592, ii.899–900.
43 W. J. Ashley, *An Introduction to English Economic History and Theory* (1893), pt.ii.361–2; B. Geremek, 'Criminalité, vagabondage, paupérisme: la marginalité à l'aube des temps modernes', *Revue d'histoire moderne et contemporaine*, XXI (1974), 369–70.
44 CLRO Repert., 3/98b (also Journ., 11/305a); *YCR*, III.46.
45 *Statutes*, IV.i.413–14 (enforced in Leicester: *LBR*, III.xlv); CLRO Repert., 25/49a.
46 Ribton-Turner, 36–7; CLRO Journ., 5/97b, Repert., 2/200a, 204b, 3/11b; Phythian-Adams, 'Urban decay', in Abrams and Wrigley (eds), *Towns in Societies*, 181–2.
47 *Statutes*, II.569, III.559, IV.ii.1160; *TRP*, I.89, 193; Wilts. CRO QSR 1603–38, *passim*.
48 Summarized from document reprinted in F. Aydelotte, *Elizabethan Rogues and Vagabonds* (Oxford, 1913), 155–6.
49 ibid., 156–7.
50 *TRP*, II.136–8, 187–94, 202–3; *TED*, I.325–30; *YCR*, VI.20–1; Cunnington, *Devizes* pt.i, 43; Essex RO Q/SR 11A. Cf. Leonard, 80.
51 C. Russell, *The Crisis of Parliaments* (1971), Chapter 6, especially pp. 304 ff.; and locally, Barnes, *Somerset*, 172–5.
52 P. Slack, 'Books of Orders: the making of English social policy, 1577–1631', *TRHS*, 5th s., XXX (1980), 16–18; B. Quintrell, 'The making of Charles I's Book of Orders', *English Historical Review*, XCV (1980), 553, 571.
53 *Statutes*, II.33, 569, III.329, 559–60, IV.i.5, 591, 610, ii.899–900, 1025, 1160; M. Dalton, *The Countrey Justice* (1618), 96, 103.
54 BL Add. MS.11405/44a–48b (c.1597); J. Kent, 'Attitudes of members of the House of Commons to the regulation of "personal conduct"', *BIHR*, XLVI (1973), 51–3; J. H. Baker, 'Criminal courts and procedure at common law, 1550–1800', in J. S. Cockburn (ed.), *Crime in England, 1500–1800* (1977), 21–4.
55 Quoted Judges, xlv, 503–4; Kent, op. cit. 51; J. H. Langbein, *Prosecuting Crime in the Renaissance* (Cambridge, Mass., 1974), 25–6, 33–4.
56 *Statutes*, II.569; CLRO Journ.,20.ii/502b (art.47).
57 K. Wrightson, 'Aspects of social differentiation in rural England, c.1580 –1660', *Journal of Peasant Studies*, V (1977–8), 43–5.
58 E. Peters, *The Magician, the Witch and the Law* (Hassocks, 1978), 151–4.
59 Langbein, op. cit., 206n, 209; *Statutes*, III.330; Dalton, op. cit., 267.
60 R. Pugh, *Imprisonment in Medieval England* (Cambridge, 1968), 208.
61 N. Walker, *Crime and Punishment in Britain* (Edinburgh, 1965), 127–8, for the distinction between redress and retribution.
62 *Statutes*, I.312, II.56, 569; J. Bellamy, *Crime and Public Order in England in the Later Middle Ages* (1973), 182, states that all villages were to have stocks.
63 *YCR*, VIII.160; W. Andrews, *Bygone Punishments* (1899), 209–26.
64 *Statutes*, III.329, IV.i.591, ii.899.

65 L. Stone, *The Crisis of the Aristocracy, 1558–1641* (Oxford, 1965), 34–5; L. Stone, *The Family, Sex and Marriage in England, 1500–1800* (1977), 163–7 (quotation at 164); W. M. Cooper, *A History of the Rod in All Countries* (n.d.), 385–97, 423–50.

66 *Statutes*, I.367, IV.i.5; Bellamy, op. cit. 182.

67 *Statutes*, IV.i.591,ii.1025; Essex RO Q/SR 51, 205/30; NRQS, I.195 90, II.98,101,191; BCB 1620/180b; Somers. RO Q/SR 29/12–13, 31/14, 33/38.

68 Bellamy, op. cit., 184–5; J. S. Davies, *A History of Southampton* (1883), 294; CLRO Repert., 13.i./194a; BCB 1609/362a, 1610/439b, 1620/179b.

69 CLRO Repert., 4 (no foliation), 11 June 1520, 5/198a, 9/165b, 252b.

70 *Statutes*, III.560, IV.i.6, 591, 610–11, ii.900, 1025; *Middlesex Co. Recds* (1886), I.94, 101–3, 221, 266–7; *BJF*, 103; Ribton-Turner, 490.

71 Wilts. CRO QSR 1603–38, *passim*.

72 Stone, *Crisis of the Aristocracy*, 34–5.

73 Baker, 'Criminal courts and procedure', 21; Judges, xlv, 91–2.

74 *Statutes*, II.32–3, 58, 569, IV.i.610, ii.900; *BJF*, 78–9.

75 *Statutes*, III.558, IV.i.5, ii.900.

76 ibid., IV.i.591; W. J. Hardy (ed.), *Calendar to the Records of the Borough of Doncaster*, 1899–1903), III.185; *BJF*, 99–100, 123; *Middlesex Co. Recds* (1886), I.101–3.

77 *Statutes*, IV.i.611, ii.901, but cf. ibid., 1159.

78 H. J. Hewitt, *The Organization of War Under Edward III* (Manchester, 1966), 29–30 (a reference kindly supplied by Dr A. Grant).

79 CLRO Repert., 13.i/148a, Journ.25/22a–b, 277b(ff.), 32/330a, 33/23b; BCB 1597–1642, *passim*, e.g. 1598/36b, 1605/37a, 42b, 43a, 44b.

80 Norf. RO NCM 1624–34/128a; *Herts. Co. Recds*, V.267; BCB 1598/36b, 1599/80a.

81 D. L. Keir, *The Constitutional History of Modern Britain since 1485* (8th edn, 1966), 305–6; F. W. Maitland, *The Constitutional History of England* (Cambridge, 1911), 275–80; D. J. Medley, *A Student's Manual of English Constitutional History* (3rd edn, 1902), 478.

82 S. R. Gardiner, *The Constitutional Documents of the Puritan Revolution* (Oxford, 1899), 243; J. R. Tanner, *English Constitutional Conflicts of the Seventeenth Century* (Cambridge, 1928), 120.

83 CLRO Journ., 20.ii/502b.

84 *Statutes*, IV.ii.900; *SRP*, I.52–3.

85 A. E. Smith, *Colonists in Bondage* (1947; new edn, Gloucester, Mass., 1965).

86 ibid., chs 4–9; BCB 1607/220a; CLRO Journ.,31/129a. For a view of indentured servants as a 'subset' of migrants, see D. Souden, '"Rogues, whores and vagabonds"? Indentured servant emigrants to North America', *Social History*, III (1980), 28ff. No doubt some of the indentured went voluntarily, but how many is uncertain.

87 R. C. Johnson, 'The transportation of vagrant children from London to Virginia, 1618–1622', in H. S. Reinmuth (ed.), *Early Stuart Studies* (Minneapolis, 1970), 138–46; BCB 1597–1660, *passim*.

88 W. H. Blumenthal, *Brides from Bridewell* (Rutland, Vermont, 1962), 65 (quotation), 105; P. Clark, *English Provincial Society*, 372; Smith, *Colonists in Bondage*, 143.

89 Blumenthal, op. cit., 64, 66; *CSPD 1611–18*, 594; CLRO Journ., 31/128b; quotation from Johnson, op. cit., 143–4.

90 BCB 1620/185b; Cunnington, *Wilts.*, 241.

91 CLRO Journ., 31/125a, 128b.

92 E. S. Morgan, 'The first American boom: Virginia, 1618 to 1630', *William and Mary Quarterly*, 3rd s., XXVIII (1971), 170; Johnson, op. cit., 147.

93 Johnson, op. cit., 147–9; Morgan, op. cit., 184–6, 195–7.

94 T. H. Breen and S. Foster, 'Moving to the New World', *William and Mary Quarterly*, 3rd s., XXX (1973), 217–19; R. B. Morris, *Government and Labor in Early America* (1946; repr., New York, 1965), 502–3; and latterly, D. W. Galenson, *White Servitude in Colonial America* (Cambridge, 1982).

95 Quoted J. H. Langbein, 'The historical origins of the sanction of imprisonment for serious crime', *Journal of Legal Studies*, V (1976), 48–9; cf. M. Foucault, *Discipline and Punish. The Birth of the Prison* (New York, 1979), 7–8, 128.

96 J. Stow, *Survey of London* (1598; new edn 1956), 64, 351–2, 369, 438–41; J. Webb, *Poor Relief in Elizabethan Ipswich*, Suffolk Records Society, IX (1966), 12–14; Leonard, 101, 112–14; Cunnington, *Devizes*, pt.i.88.

97 Smith, *County and Court*, 104; Leonard, 227–9; J. S. Cockburn (ed.), *Calendar of Assize Records: Hertfordshire Indictments, James I* (1975), 275; Fletcher, *A County Community*, 167; S. C. Ratcliff and H. C. Johnson (eds), *Warwick County Records* (Warwick, 1935–53), I.11, 223, IV.58, VII.cviii–cviix, 229.

98 *TED*, II.307–8, 311; *Statutes*, IV.i.611; Coke quoted Leonard, 241.

99 BL Lansdowne MS.5/30/102a; *Statutes*, IV.i.611, ii.899–900, 1161; *TED*, II.340.

100 F. M. Eden, *The State of the Poor* (1797), III, Appendix, cxlii–cxliii.

101 BL Lansdowne MS.5/30/102a; *TED*, II.320 (also Eden, op. cit., cxlii–cxliii).

102 PRO SP 16/190/948–50, 967–70; Eden, op. cit., cxl; BL Lansdowne MS.5/30/103b–4b; *TED*, II.320–2. Governors of Bridewell attending Court Meetings are listed in BCB, *passim*.

103 Eden, op. cit., cxli, cxliv; Essex RO Q/SR 197ff.; Hants. RO 4M53/140/102a–b, 103b–104a; Wilts. CRO QSR Trin. 1624/183, Hil. 1634/156; Stamford Borough Records, QS Roll 1629–30 (photocopy supplied by Lincs. AO).

104 PRO SP 16/190/941–70; Suffolk RO, Bury St Edmunds, D6/4/1/14; also *TED*, II.321–2; Hants. RO 4M53/140/82b.

105 PRO SP 16/190/948; *TED*, II.319; also Essex RO Q/SR 207/99; Hants. RO 4M53/140/82b; Cunnington, *Wilts.*, 58.

106 CLRO Remembrancia II, no. 85; A. L. Beier, 'An Elizabethan country town: Warwick, 1580–90', in P. Clark (ed.), *Country Towns in Pre-Industrial England* (Leicester, 1981), 75; Chesh. RO QJF 13/1/2; Halliwell, 21–2.

107 BCB 1600/164a; CLRO Journ., 26/336b–338a; quotation from *Stanleyes Remedy . . .*, discussed in the second section of this chapter. Cf. Wilts. CRO QSR East. 1623/222; Leics. RO HP II/18/20/312.

108 BCB 1600–1 (25 March–24 March), and the pattern was broadly similar in 1560–1, 1578–9, 1620–1, 1630–1, and 1640–1; Essex RO QSR 197ff.; Wilts. CRO QSR Trin. 1624/183, Trin. 1630/142, Hil. 1634/156; *NCM 1630–1, passim*. Cf. debate with J. F. Pound in *P&P*, 71 (1976), 127–8, 132–3.

109 Leonard, 227; Barnes, *Somerset*, 183n. (quotation). See also CLRO Journ. 21/205a; *LBR*, III.xlviii; J. A. Sharpe, *Crime in Seventeenth-Century England* (Cambridge, 1983), 150–2.

110 BL Cottonian MS. Titus B.10/268b; CLRO Repert., 45/90b–91a.

111 CLRO Remembrancia II, no. 85.

112 ibid.; *TED*, III.439.

113 *Middlesex Co. Recds* (1887), II.130; Dorset RO DBC/218a; Chamberlen, *Poor Man's Advocate*, 47.

114 Chester RO QSF 61/119; Wilts. CRO QSR Hil. 1637/223; Cooper, *A History of*

the Rod, 197–8; J. S. Cockburn (ed.), *Hertfordshire Indictments, James I*, 261; BCB 1630/208b.
115 Dorset RO DBC/218a; BCB 1620/190b.
116 BCB 1606/118a, 1639/245a, 1641/354a (matrons' searches); for references to hair-cropping see n. 68 in this chapter.
117 BCB 1560/79b, 91b (also Wilts. CRO QSR 1631/138).
118 Cunnington, *Wilts.*, 66–7, 108; also Staffs. RO QSR (James I) 77/4, 5.
119 BL Addit. MS.11405/44a–48b.
120 Webbs, *Old Poor Law*, 107–9, 215ff.; V. Pearl, 'The London workhouse', in Pennington and Thomas (eds), *Puritans and Revolutionaries*, 230–2; Appleby, *Economic Thought and Ideology*, ch. 6; J. R. Poynter, *Society and Pauperism* (1969), 69–70, 311–16.

CONCLUSIONS

1 Quoted M. James, *Social Problems and Policy during the Puritan Revolution* (1930; repr. 1966), 287.
2 Webbs, *Old Poor Law*, 361–6; Wilts. CRO QSR for the 1660s and 1690s.
3 Webbs, op. cit., 374, 379–83, 387–91; and for an indication of the scale of the pass system: S. R. Broadbridge, 'The Old Poor Law in the parish of Stone', *North Staffordshire Journal of Field Studies*, XIII (1973), 15.
4 Keir, *Constitutional History*, 234.
5 E. Lipson, *Economic History of England* (2nd edn, 1934), III.264–5.
6 C. Hill, *Reformation to Industrial Revolution* (New York, 1967), 106, 113–14.
7 E. A. Wrigley and R. S. Schofield, *The Population History of England, 1541–1871* (1981), 208–9; D. C. Coleman, *The Economy of England, 1450–1750* (1977), 102–3 (quotation at 103); E. H. Phelps-Brown and S. V. Hopkins, 'Seven centuries of the prices of consumables, compared with builders' wage-rates', *Economica*, n.s., XXIII (1956), 305.
8 E. L. Jones, 'Agriculture and economic growth in England, 1660–1750', *Journal of Economic History*, XXV (1965), 2–5; A. H. John, 'Agricultural productivity and economic growth in England, 1700–1760', ibid., 19–21, 31.
9 Coleman, op. cit., 134, 145–6, 159 (quotation).
10 P. Clark, 'Migration in England during the late seventeenth and early eighteenth centuries', *P&P*, 83 (1979), 70, 72–3, 81, 85–6 (quotation at 85).
11 *Statutes*, III.329, 558, IV.i.7, 115, 593, 611, ii.899, V.401.
12 These regulations are well summarized in P. Styles, 'The evolution of the law of settlement', repr. in his *Studies in Seventeenth-Century West Midlands History* (Kineton, 1978), 177–84; also *supra*, ch. 1, 11 and sources cited there.
13 *Herts. Co. Recds*, V.36; Essex RO Q/SR XIXB.482; Hants. RO QSOB 1607–28/344 –5, 467–8, 474; Staffs. RO QSR (James I) 76/25; Notts. RO QSM III.20, IX.392, X, *passim*; Wilts. CRO QSR Trin. 1627/117, Hil. 1636/176; Leics. RO HP II/18/14/ 204.
14 Styles, op. cit. 189–90.
15 ibid., 190–2; R. A. Pelham, 'The immigrant population of Birmingham, 1686–1725', *Transactions of the Birmingham Archaeological Society*, LXI (1937), 50; J. S. Taylor, 'The impact of pauper settlement, 1691–1834', *P&P*, 73 (1976), Appendix, 70–4.
16 N. P. Webb, 'The structure of poverty in some Elizabethan communities', University of Lancaster BA thesis, 1980, 49; A. L. Beier, 'Studies in poverty and poor relief in Warwickshire, 1540–1680', Princeton University PhD thesis,

1969, 168–9 (based on petitions to Warwickshire quarter sessions, S. C. Johnson and H. C. Ratcliff (eds), *Warwick County Records, Sessions Order Books*, I–V, VII.); *Statutes* IV.ii.897; cf. Clark, 'Migration', 87–8.

17 A. Willet, *Synopsis Papismi* (1614), 1220; T. Ruggles, *The History of the Poor* (1793–4), I.167–70; Webbs, *Old Poor Law*, 152–3; for higher figures, C. Wilson, *England's Apprenticeship, 1603–1763* (1965), 235.

18 PRO CO 388/5/2, 3 (returns from 4460 parishes, although it is unclear whether these were the only ones levying rates, or the rest simply did not report); Webbs, op. cit., 152–3.

19 Warwicks. CRO DR 266/44, DR 404; Crondall (Hants.) overseers' accounts, parish chest; Hants. RO 25M60/6 (Fawley); I. F. Jones, 'Aspects of poor law administration, seventeenth to nineteenth centuries, from Trull overseers' accounts', *Somerset Archaeological and Natural History Society, Proceedings*, XCV (1951), 79–80; C. Brears, *Lincolnshire in the Seventeenth and Eighteenth Centuries* (1940), 82, 170; J. Hill, 'Poor relief in seventeenth-century Shropshire', University of Liverpool MA thesis, 1973, 113; Clark, 'Migration', 86.

20 A. L. Beier, 'Studies in poverty and poor relief in Warwickshire', Princeton University PhD thesis, 1969, 184–95, 266–7; Cobbett quoted by M. D. George, *England in Transition* (1931), 198.

21 P. G. M. Dickson, *The Financial Revolution in England* (1967), 7, 10; quotation from L. Radzinowicz, *A History of English Criminal Law* (1968), IV.80. For the disruptive effects of demobilization see D. Hay, 'War, dearth and theft in the eighteenth century', *P&P*, 95 (1982), 135–46.

22 Clark, 'Migration', 89.

23 New studies of gaols are required, but in the meantime see S. and B. Webb, *English Prisons Under Local Government* (1922; repr. 1963), 3ff.; Clark, op. cit., 83 (Corporations).

24 D. Hay, 'Property, authority and the criminal law', in D. Hay *et al.*, *Albion's Fatal Tree* (New York, 1975), 18, 22–3.

25 O. H. Hufton, *The Poor of Eighteenth-Century France, 1750–1789* (Oxford, 1974), 367.

Appendix: Tables

Table 1 *Regional origins of vagrants, 1516–1660*

PLACES OF ORIGIN

PLACES OF ARREST
(1) *The Southeast*

	Colchester 1630–64		Essex examinations 1564–96		1621–44		Essex house of correction 1597–1620		1621–44	
	No.	%	No.	%	No.	%	No.	%	No.	%
The Southeast*	98	41.5	15	45.4	25	43.8	48	51.6	35	37.2
South and West	5	2.1	5	15.2	7	12.3	4	4.3	7	7.4
E. Midlands	9	3.8	3	9.1	0	0	5	5.4	4	4.2
W. Midlands	11	4.7	0	0	5	8.8	3	3.2	3	3.2
The Northwest	6	2.5	1	3.0	2	3.5	0	0	5	5.3
The Southwest	0	0	0	0	0	0	1	1.1	3	3.2
E. Anglia	62	26.3	5	15.2	10	17.5	24	25.8	23	24.5
Lincolnshire/Yorkshire	13	5.5	3	9.1	5	8.8	3	3.2	9	9.6
The Northeast	5	2.1	0	0	0	0	0	0	1	1.1
Ireland	20	8.5	1	3.0	0	0	3	3.2	3	3.2
Scotland	3	1.3	0	0	0	0	0	0	1	1.1
Wales	4	1.7	0	0	3	5.3	2	2.2	0	0
'The North'	0	0	0	0	0	0	0	0	0	0
The Continent	0	0	0	0	0	0	0	0	0	0
Totals	236	100.0	33	100.0	57	100.0	93	100.0	94	100.0

Table I (*continued*)

PLACES OF ARREST
(1) The Southeast (continued)

PLACES OF ORIGIN	Hertfordshire 1588–96		1636–9		Kent, Surrey, Sussex 1632–9	
	No.	%	No.	%	No.	%
The Southeast	24	40.0	37	43.5	328	53.8
South and West	4	6.7	16	18.8	126	20.7
E. Midlands	2	3.3	9	10.6	22	3.6
W. Midlands	6	10.0	13	15.3	30	4.9
The Northwest	2	3.3	0	0	10	1.6
The Southwest	1	1.7	1	1.2	11	1.8
E. Anglia	9	15.0	7	8.2	39	6.4
Lincolnshire/Yorkshire	7	11.7	0	0	20	3.3
The Northeast	0	0	0	0	0	0
Ireland	2	3.3	0	0	17	2.8
Scotland	0	0	0	0	1	0.2
Wales	0	0	2	2.4	6	0.9
'The North'	0	0	0	0	0	0
The Continent	3	5.0	0	0	0	0
Totals	60	100.0	85	100.0	610	100.0

Table I (*continued*)

PLACES OF ORIGIN

PLACES OF ARREST
(1) The Southeast (*continued*)

| | London | | | | | | | | | | | | Westminster | |
| | 1516–66 | | 1574–9 | | 1597–1604 | | 1604–10 | | 1620–1 | | 1634–42 | | 1581–4 | |
	No.	%	No.	%	No.	%	No.	%	No.	%	No.	%	No.	%
The Southeast	13	37.1	45	45.0	171	63.8	192	58.4	98	62.4	73	55.7	27	22.1
South and West	3	8.6	17	17.0	21	7.8	32	9.7	14	8.9	17	13.0	25	20.5
E. Midlands	4	11.4	4	4.0	8	3.0	11	3.3	3	1.9	5	3.8	5	4.1
W. Midlands	2	5.7	4	4.0	13	4.9	8	2.4	6	3.8	8	6.1	8	6.6
The Northwest	2	5.7	4	4.0	2	0.7	7	2.1	5	3.2	0	0	5	4.1
The Southwest	0	0	4	4.0	9	3.4	3	0.9	4	2.6	2	1.5	19	15.6
E. Anglia	2	5.7	10	10.0	13	4.9	15	4.6	9	5.7	9	6.9	19	15.6
Lincolnshire/Yorkshire	4	11.4	6	6.0	13	4.9	9	2.8	3	1.9	6	4.5	3	2.5
The Northeast	2	5.7	0	0	0	0	1	0.3	5	3.2	1	0.8	2	1.6
Ireland	1	2.9	3	3.0	6	2.2	29	8.8	8	5.1	3	2.3	2	1.6
Scotland	1	2.9	1	1.0	5	1.9	5	1.5	0	0	0	0	0	0
Wales	1	2.9	1	1.0	3	1.1	10	3.1	2	1.3	1	0.8	7	5.7
'The North'	0	0	0	0	2	0.7	2	0.6	0	0	1	0.8	0	0
The Continent	0	0	1	1.0	2	0.7	5	1.5	0	0	5	3.8	0	0
Totals	35	100.0	100	100.0	268	100.0	329	100.0	157	100.0	131	100.0	122	100.0

Table 1 (*continued*)

	Reading 1623–41		(2) South and West 1603–20		Wiltshire 1621–9		1630–8		(3) The Southwest Somerset 1607–36	
PLACES OF ORIGIN	No.	%	No.	%	No.	%	No.	%	No.	%
The Southeast	55	39.9	46	14.5	37	15.2	57	13.9	36	8.1
South and West	42	30.4	153	48.3	103	42.2	162	39.5	94	21.3
E. Midlands	7	5.1	3	0.9	4	1.6	7	1.7	14	3.2
W. Midlands	6	4.4	14	4.4	5	2.1	23	5.6	9	2.0
The Northwest	5	3.6	5	1.6	0	0	7	1.7	1	0.2
The Southwest	14	10.2	83	26.2	46	18.9	84	20.5	232	52.5
E. Anglia	0	0	5	1.6	4	1.6	7	1.7	1	0.2
Lincolnshire/Yorkshire	2	1.4	3	0.9	3	1.2	4	1.0	4	0.9
The Northeast	2	1.4	0	0	0	0	2	0.5	0	0
Ireland	2	1.4	1	0.3	29	11.9	35	8.5	25	5.7
Scotland	0	0	0	0	2	0.8	0	0	2	0.5
Wales	2	1.4	4	1.3	9	3.7	22	5.4	22	4.9
'The North'	0	0	0	0	0	0	0	0	0	0
The Continent	1	0.8	0	0	2	0.8	0	0	2	0.5
Totals	138	100.0	317	100.0	244	100.0	410	100.0	442	100.0

PLACES OF ARREST

Table I (continued)

PLACES OF ORIGIN

PLACES OF ARREST
(4) The Midlands

	Elizabethan (various)		Leicester 1584–1612		Leicester 1613–40		Nottinghamshire 1604–39		Staffordshire 1606–33	
	No.	%	No.	%	No.	%	No.	%	No.	%
The Southeast	20	8.2	21	17.7	14	9.4	8	8.9	0	0
South and West	28	11.4	7	5.9	7	4.7	0	0	0	0
E. Midlands	72	29.4	36	30.3	49	32.9	31	34.8	6	9.2
W. Midlands	41	16.7	23	19.3	23	15.4	11	12.4	37	56.9
The Northwest	26	10.6	3	2.5	8	5.4	3	3.4	14	21.6
The Southwest	10	4.1	2	1.7	1	0.7	0	0	0	0
E. Anglia	7	2.9	8	6.7	4	2.7	1	1.1	2	3.1
Lincolnshire/Yorkshire	24	9.8	18	15.1	31	20.8	32	36.0	5	7.7
The Northeast	5	2.0	0	0	5	3.3	3	3.4	0	0
Ireland	2	0.8	0	0	6	4.0	0	0	0	0
Scotland	0	0	0	0	1	0.7	0	0	0	0
Wales	10	4.1	1	0.8	0	0	0	0	1	1.5
'The North'	0	0	0	0	0	0	0	0	0	0
The Continent	0	0	0	0	0	0	0	0	0	0
Totals	245	100.0	119	100.0	149	100.0	89	100.0	65	100.0

Table I (continued)

PLACES OF ARREST
(5) The North

PLACES OF ORIGIN	1570–1600		Cheshire 1601–20		1621–30		Yorkshire 1638–60	
	No.	%	No.	%	No.	%	No.	%
The Southeast	3	2.25	5	3.4	2	2.6	7	4.5
South and West	3	2.25	7	4.7	1	1.3	0	0
E. Midlands	0	0	4	2.7	0	0	14	9.0
W. Midlands	27	20.3	30	20.1	11	14.5	5	3.2
The Northwest	54	40.6	38	25.5	33	43.5	17	10.9
The Southwest	4	3.0	3	2.0	0	0	1	0.6
E. Anglia	4	3.0	0	0	0	0	0	0
Lincolnshire/Yorkshire	11	8.3	12	8.0	9	11.8	88	56.4
The Northeast	2	1.5	3	2.0	1	1.3	19	12.2
Ireland	2	1.5	1	0.7	5	6.6	0	0
Scotland	0	0	0	0	0	0	5	3.2
Wales	17	12.8	45	30.2	14	18.4	0	0
'The North'	2	1.5	0	0	0	0	0	0
The Continent	0	0	0	0	0	0	0	0
Isle of Man	4	3.0	1	0.7	0	0	0	0
Totals	133	100.0	149	100.0	76	100.0	156	100.0

Table I (continued)

PLACES OF ARREST
(6) East Anglia

PLACES OF ORIGIN	Norwich 1564–72		Norwich 1595–1609		Norwich 1626–30		Norwich 1631–5		Suffolk 1642–60	
	No.	%	No.	%	No.	%	No.	%	No.	%
The Southeast	42	23.2	41	12.5	23	10.4	16	10.2	19	26.8
South and West	16	8.8	11	3.4	7	3.2	1	0.6	2	2.8
E. Midlands	3	1.7	12	3.7	12	5.4	3	1.9	4	5.6
W. Midlands	3	1.7	7	2.1	7	3.2	1	0.6	2	2.8
The Northwest	4	2.2	11	3.4	8	3.6	1	0.6	2	2.8
The Southwest	3	1.7	7	2.1	2	0.9	0	0	2	2.8
E. Anglia	88	48.6	177	54.0	122	55.0	121	77.1	35	49.3
Lincolnshire/Yorkshire	15	8.3	40	12.2	29	13.1	10	6.4	4	5.6
The Northeast	6	3.3	8	2.4	3	1.3	0	0	1	1.5
Ireland	0	0	0	0	4	1.8	2	1.3	0	0
Scotland	0	0	4	1.2	1	0.4	2	1.3	0	0
Wales	1	0.5	7	2.1	3	1.3	0	0	0	0
'The North'	0	0	0	0	0	0	0	0	0	0
The Continent	0	0	3	0.9	1	0.4	0	0	0	0
Totals	181	100.0	328	100.0	222	100.0	157	100.0	71	100.0

Sources: Colchester, Hertfordshire 1636–9, Kent, Surrey and Sussex 1632–9: Slack, 'Vagrants and vagrancy', 379; Essex Examinations and House of Correction Calendars, Essex RO Q/SR 1564–1644; Hertfordshire 1588–96, Herts. RO HAT/SR 1–8; London 1516–66, Repert. and Journ. CLRO; London 1574–1642, BCB; Westminster 1581–4, WCL E.146; Reading 1623–41, RR, I–IV; Wiltshire 1603–38, Wilts. CRO QSR; Somerset 1607–36, Somerset RO Q/SR; Midlands, Elizabethan (various), *BJF*, PRO SP 12/51/11, 67/45, 80/22, 27–9, 55, 81/14, 21, 24–5, 44–6; Leicester 1584–1640, Leics. RO HP; Nottinghamshire 1604–39, Notts RO QSM vols I–XI; Staffordshire 1606–33, Staffs. RO QSR 1606–33, D1287/10/2; Cheshire 1570–1630, Chester RO QSE & QSF, Ches. RO QJF; Yorkshire 1638–60, PRO Assi, WYRO, QSOB 1638–60, East Yorks. RO, QSOB 1647–51, Lockington overseers' accounts, 1650–4 (parish chest); Norwich 1564–1635, Norfolk RO NCM 1564–30, NCM 1630–1, 1632–5; Suffolk 1642–60, Suffolk RO, Ipswich Branch, QSOB 1639–62, 105/2/1–4.

*Counties are ranged under regional rubrics as follows: the *Southeast*: Beds., Essex, Herts., Kent, London and Middx., Surrey, Sussex; *South and West*: Berks., Bucks., Dorset, Hants, Glos., Oxon., Wilts.; *E. Midlands*: Leics., Northants, Notts, Rutland, War.; *W. Midlands*: Derby., Heref., Salop, Staffs., Worcs.; *Northwest*: Ches., Lancs., Cumb., Westml.; *Southwest*: Corn., Devon, Somerset; *E. Anglia*: Camb., Hunts., Norfolk, Suffolk; *Northeast*: Durham, Northumb. Derived with some modifications from J. Thirsk, 'The farming regions of England', *AHEW*, IV, ch. 1. Southwark has been included in Surrey, Greenwich in Kent and Bristol in Gloucestershire.

Table II *Vagrants of urban origin, 1516–1642*

Places of arrest		Total places†	% with markets*
Cheshire	1571–1600	140	37.1
	1601–30	191	46.1
Leicester	1584–1612	118	59.3
	1613–40	141	49.6
London	1516–66	27	77.8
	1574–9	92	90.2
	1597–1604	205	90.2
	1604–10	240	90.0
	1634–42	99	85.6
Norwich	1596–1603	139	61.0
Reading	1623–41	135	67.4
Somerset vagrants in Wiltshire	1598–1638	171	51.5
Various	1564–87	442	62.2
Westminster	1581–4	113	92.9
Yorkshire vagrants in in various counties	c.1590–1630	100	46.0

Sources: As in Table I, apart from Somerset vagrants in Wilts. 1598–1638, Wilts. CRO QSR 1603–38, P. Slack (ed.), *Poverty in Early Stuart Salisbury*, Wiltshire Record Society, XXXI (1975), 17–64; Various 1564–87, as in A. L. Beier, 'Vagrants and the social order in Elizabethan England', *P&P*, 64 (1974), 21–2 and sources cited there; Yorkshire vagrants in various counties, Ches. RO QJF, Chester RO QSE & QSF, Notts RO, QSM; Staffs. RO QSR; Leics. RO HP; PRO SP16/ (1630s), Lancashire and Westmorland.

†Towns and villages only; counties and 'countries' excluded.

*As in A. M. Everitt, 'The marketing of agricultural produce', *AHEW*, IV.468–75.

Table III *Family structures among vagrants, 1516–1644*

Place, records	Date	Single males*		Single females*		Couples†		Children		Uncertain		Totals	
		No.	%	No.	%	No.	%	No.	%	No.	%	No.	%
Cheshire	1570–1600	129	51.4	48	19.1	62	24.7	6	2.4	6	2.4	251	100.0
	1601–34	139	53.0	51	19.5	56	21.4	16	6.1	0	0	262	100.0
Essex constables	1564–72	94	58.8	42	26.2	14	8.8	9	5.6	1	0.6	160	100.0
	1613–14	31	38.3	17	21.0	26	32.1	7	8.6	0	0	81	100.0
Essex house of correction	1597–1620	69	67.0	18	17.5	12	11.6	4	3.9	0	0	103	100.0
	1621–44	55	53.4	23	22.3	20	19.4	4	3.9	1	1.0	103	100.0
Hertfordshire Q.S.	1588–96	91	67.4	30	22.2	14	10.4	0	0	0	0	135	100.0
	1636–9	68	51.5	41	31.1	12	9.1	11	8.3	0	0	132	100.0
Hertfordshire constables	1584–1612	72	50.0	21	14.6	48	33.3	3	2.1	0	0	144	100.0
	1613–40	70	40.5	31	17.9	64	37.0	8	4.6	0	0	173	100.0
London	1516–59	147	78.6	38	20.3	0	0	2	1.1	0	0	187	100.0
	1560–1	55	79.7	12	17.4	2	2.9	0	0	0	0	69	100.0
	1578–9	127	65.8	50	25.9	0	0	16	8.3	0	0	193	100.0
	1600–1	403	72.5	151	27.2	0	0	2	0.3	0	0	556	100.0
	1624–5	453	55.5	320	39.2	18	2.2	25	3.1	0	0	816	100.0
Norwich	1564–72	155	60.1	45	17.4	38	14.7	18	7.0	2	0.8	258	100.0
	1597–1609	186	49.6	106	28.3	36	9.6	43	11.5	4	1.0	375	100.0
	1626–35	245	57.4	114	26.7	48	11.2	18	4.2	2	0.5	427	100.0
Wiltshire exams	1603–20	98	70.5	9	6.5	28	20.1	4	2.9	0	0	139	100.0
	1621–38	83	50.3	18	10.9	42	25.5	22	13.3	0	0	165	100.0
Wiltshire constables	1603–20	112	48.1	55	23.6	34	14.6	22	9.4	10	4.3	233	100.0
	1621–38	319	41.5	144	18.8	154	20.1	122	15.9	28	3.7	767	100.0

Sources: As in Table I, adding Essex RO, Constables 1564–72 (Q/SR); 1613–14 (Q/SBa3); Wilts. CRO Constables (QSR).
* 'Single' at the time of arrest only; some were without spouses.
† Male/female couples only, whether legally married or not.

Table IV *The ages of vagrants, c.1570–c.1640*

		Below age 16*		Below age 21*		Total
		No.	%	No.	%	cases
1570–1622						
Crompton, Lancs.	1597	10	50.0	15	75.0	20
Crondall, Hants.	1598–1622	9	30.0	13	43.3	30
London	1602	20	54.1	36	97.3	37
Norwich	1595–1609	24	52.2	33	71.7	46
Various Quarter	1570–1622					
Sessions exams		7	22.6	13	41.9	31
Totals		70	42.7	110	67.1	164
1623–1639						
Essex and Kent	1630s	33	44.0	45	60.0	75
Various Quarter	1623–39					
Sessions exams		9	47.4	12	63.2	19
Westmorland	1630s	12	12.8	31	33.0	94
Totals		54	28.7	88	46.8	188

Sources: Crompton: Lancs. RO UDCr; Crondall, churchwardens' accounts, 1598–1622, fols. 182–98 (parish chest); London 1603: BCB; Norwich 1595–1609, Norf. RO NCM; Various QS examinations 1570–1639: Chester RO QSE & QSF, Somers. RO Q/SR, Wilts. CRO QSR; Essex and Kent 1630s: PRO SP16/241/60, 314/77, 328/7, 363/100, 415/96, 424/112, Essex RO D/B/3/3/125, 211, *Essex Review*, XLII (1933) 41–2; Westmorland 1630s: PRO SP16/388/7.
*Includes 'children' and 'boys'.

Table v Sizes of vagrant groups, 1570–1644

Table v Sizes of vagrant groups, 1570–1644

		One No.*	One %	Two No.	Two %	Three No.	Three %	Four No.	Four %	Five No.	Five %	Six No.	Six %	Seven No.	Seven %	Eight† No.	Eight† %
Chester	1570–1600	33	37.9	42	48.3	12	13.8	0	0	0	0	0	0	0	0	0	0
	1601–30	113	42.2	102	38.0	33	12.3	20	7.5	0	0	0	0	0	0	0	0
Essex, house of correction vagrants	1597–1620	51	53.1	34	35.4	6	6.3	0	0	5	5.2	0	0	0	0	0	0
	1621–44	33	33.0	28	28.0	15	15.0	8	8.0	0	0	6	6.0	0	0	10	10.0
Essex, house of correction non-vagrants	1597–1620	82	84.5	12	12.4	3	3.1	0	0	0	0	0	0	0	0	0	0
	1621–44	46	64.8	22	31.0	3	4.2	0	0	0	0	0	0	0	0	0	0
Leicester	1584–1612†	64	41.8	60	39.2	9	5.9	16	10.5	0	0	0	0	0	0	0	0
	1613–40‡	43	24.4	72	40.9	33	18.8	12	6.8	5	2.8	0	0	0	0	9	5.1
Wiltshire exams	1603–20	50	36.2	56	40.6	9	6.5	12	8.7	5	3.6	6	4.4	0	0	0	0
	1621–38	43	26.7	40	24.8	18	11.2	20	12.4	20	12.4	0	0	7	4.4	13	8.1
Wiltshire constables	1603–20	100	45.9	46	21.1	33	15.1	16	7.3	10	4.6	6	2.8	7	3.2	0	0
	1621–38	213	30.3	150	21.3	108	15.4	72	10.2	85	12.1	42	6.0	7	1.0	26	3.7

Sources: As in Table I.
*Includes total number of persons falling into each category, i.e. 42 equals 21 groups of two members each.
†Four cases were unclear (2.6 per cent).
‡Two cases were unclear (1.2 per cent); two groups of two members were possibly a group of four; three groups of two were possibly together, making a group of six members; and three groups of four persons each may have been linked.

Table **VI** *Distances from 'home' of vagrants at times of arrest, 1516–1660 (percentages)*

		0–50	51–100	101–50	Miles 151–200	200+	Totals
Cheshire	1570–1600	59.4	27.4	7.0	5.5	0.7	100.0
	1601–20	51.6	35.3	7.8	5.3	0	100.0
	1621–30	61.3	22.7	12.0	4.0	0	100.0
Essex	1564–96	55.5	13.9	14.6	8.3	7.7	100.0
	1597–1620	49.2	26.2	13.3	6.7	4.6	100.0
	1621–44	45.4	27.3	13.0	6.7	7.6	100.0
Leicester	1584–1612	44.9	48.3	5.9	0.9	0	100.0
	1613–40	48.3	36.1	5.4	5.4	4.8	100.0
London	1516–66	48.6	11.4	8.6	14.3	17.1	100.0
	1574–9	51.5	24.8	10.9	8.9	3.9	100.0
	1597–1604	66.7	10.7	9.6	6.9	6.1	100.0
	1604–10	62.0	13.4	9.4	4.6	10.6	100.0
	1620–1	62.7	12.0	8.9	7.6	8.8	100.0
	1634–42	59.3	19.5	13.0	4.9	3.3	100.0
Norwich	1564–71	48.6	25.4	15.5	7.2	3.3	100.0
	1595–1609	51.3	17.8	15.3	10.6	5.0	100.0
	1626–35	60.2	20.0	9.6	6.2	4.0	100.0
Reading	1623–41	58.6	27.1	5.7	4.3	4.3	100.0
Somerset	1607–36	49.4	28.8	12.6	5.3	3.9	100.0
Suffolk	1642–60	59.4	20.3	8.7	5.8	5.8	100.0
Westminster	1581–4	23.8	41.8	22.1	6.6	5.7	100.0
Wiltshire constables	1603–20	66.5	16.1	9.3	8.1	0	100.0
	1621–38	48.3	20.3	13.2	4.1	14.1	100.0
Wiltshire exams	1603–20	50.4	25.6	16.0	6.4	1.6	100.0
	1621–38	45.3	36.7	13.7	2.9	1.4	100.0
Yorkshire	1638–60	57.1	33.8	2.6	2.6	3.9	100.0

Sources: As in Table I. For evidence relating to Colchester, Devon and Cornwall, Hertfordshire, Lancashire and Westmorland, Kent, Sussex and Surrey, and Salisbury, see Slack, 'Vagrants and vagrancy', 369.

Table VII *Vagrants' stated reasons for being en route, 1555–1644*

		I* Kin, personal		II Specific destinations		III Seeking work		IV Business		V Miscellaneous business		VI Crime		VII Miscellaneous		Totals	
		No.	%	No.	%	No.	%	No.	%	No.	%	No.	%	No.	%	No.	%
Cheshire	1573–1600	14	15.7	12	13.5	8	9.0	25	28.1	9	10.1	21	23.6	0	0	89	100.0
	1601–30	39	26.5	25	17.0	25	17.0	38	25.9	4	2.7	16	10.9	0	0	147	100.0
Essex	1573–1620	6	17.7	2	5.9	1	2.9	1	2.9	1	2.9	19	55.9	4	11.8	34	100.0
	1621–44	9	17.3	10	19.2	1	1.9	15	28.9	0	0	9	17.3	8	15.4	52	100.0
Leicester	1584–1612	23	32.4	6	8.5	5	7.0	27	38.0	10	14.1	0	0	0	0	71	100.0
	1613–40	35	33.7	19	18.3	4	3.8	30	28.8	4	3.8	10	9.6	2	2.0	104	100.0
Reading	1623–41	25	19.2	25	19.2	16	12.3	49	37.7	10	7.7	0	0	5	3.9	130	100.0
Somerset	1607–36	49	17.4	66	23.4	28	9.9	49	17.4	27	9.6	58	20.6	5	1.7	282	100.0
Warwick	1580–7	15	14.7	3	2.9	18	17.7	31	30.4	3	2.9	32	31.4	0	0	102	100.0
Wiltshire	1555–1620	16	16.8	30	31.6	7	7.4	17	17.9	4	4.2	19	20.0	2	2.1	95	100.0
	1621–38	8	10.0	27	33.7	7	8.7	15	18.8	0	0	22	27.5	1	1.3	80	100.0

Sources: As in Table I, adding *BJF* for Warwick 1580–7; Cunnington, *Devizes* (Wiltshire pre-1603).

*I Business involving family, 'friends' and acquaintances.

II Travelling to a specific place; returning home (including soldiers and mariners).

III Seeking work or service.

IV Working, buying and selling, and other legal subsistence activities.

V Business that was sometimes personal, sometimes for gain.

VI Confessed crimes such as begging, wandering, theft.

VII e.g., entertainment, 'making merry'.

Table VIII *The market town and the vagrant, 1570–1644*

Places of arrest	Dates	No. places visited*	No. with markets†	% with markets
Cheshire	1570–1600	186	77	41.4
	1601–30	304	137	45.1
Essex	1573–96	98	40	40.8
	1597–1644	91	52	57.1
Leicester	1584–1612	351	215	61.3
	1613–40	335	219	65.4
Reading	1623–41	265	186	70.2
Somerset	1607–36	1248	768	61.5
Warwick	1580–7	442	262	59.3

Sources: As in Table I, adding *BJF* for Warwick 1580–7.
* As reported to magistrates in examinations; not including places in which vagrants were arrested.
† As listed in Everitt, 'The marketing of agricultural produce', *AHEW*, IV.468–75.

Table ix Arrests of masterless men, month by month, 1516–1644

Places and dates		Months & six-month totals													
---	---	Apr.	May	June	July	Aug.	Sept.	Total	Oct.	Nov.	Dec.	Jan.	Feb.	Mar.	Total
Cheshire	1570–1600	35	14	19	15	3	3	89	12	0	0	4	2	7	25
Chester	1570–1600	2	4	31	0	2	9	48	6	9	5	2	2	9	33
	1601–30	18	8	61	7	14	6	114	39	23	13	25	14	12	126
Essex	1564–96	9	15	15	19	16	20	94	14	3	6	2	0	3	28
	1597–1620	34	10	20	7	6	8	85	10	9	15	10	1	29	74
	1621–44	32	12	26	25	8	12	115	13	2	12	5	1	12	45
Leicester	1584–1612	13	27	10	3	5	2	60	11	24	28	6	7	8	84
	1613–40	11	22	24	9	7	6	79	14	14	21	24	6	12	91
London	1516–66	27	26	19	19	23	31	145	7	48	25	39	13	17	149
	1578–9	16	15	4	8	23	12	78	2	35	5	28	6	32	108
	1600–1	66	11	183	35	45	16	356	14	19	15	38	36	73	195
	1624–5	32	43	50	38	38	31	232	63	46	30	58	228	153	578
Norwich	1564–1609	95	70	64	68	41	37	375	45	58	36	47	24	49	259
	1626–35	44	38	39	83	27	13	244	43	37	32	21	41	41	215
Reading	1623–41	8	23	2	27	6	8	74	24	22	7	15	24	10	102
Somerset	1607–36	52	80	49	36	39	45	301	19	24	19	15	11	52	140
Warwick	1580–7	15	4	1	3	27	9	59	21	13	14	5	7	9	69
Wiltshire	1603–38	95	69	89	99	93	77	522	74	77	64	47	7	80	349

Sources: As in Table I, adding BJF for Warwick 1580–7; cf. Slack, 'Vagrants and vagrancy', 370.

Table x Hospitality to vagrants, 1570–1641

Places and dates

		Type of provision*															
		Alehouses, inns		Barns, etc.		Churches, hospitals		Gent 'masters'		Kin, friends		In nature		Non-gent		Officials†		Total	
		No.	%	No.	%	No.	%	No.	%	No.	%	No.	%	No.	%	No.	%	No.	%
Cheshire	1570–1600	13	17.1	14	18.4	0	0	4	5.3	6	7.9	2	2.6	36	47.4	1	1.3	76	100.0
	1601–30	37	29.1	15	11.8	0	0	4	3.2	5	3.9	0	0	64	50.4	2	1.6	127	100.0
Leicester	1584–1612	74	51.0	0	0	2	1.4	9	6.2	11	7.6	0	0	43	29.7	6	4.1	145	100.0
	1613–40	48	49.5	0	0	0	0	5	5.2	12	12.4	1	1.0	31	31.9	0	0	97	100.0
Reading	1623–41	77	53.9	6	4.2	0	0	3	2.1	3	2.1	1	0.7	49	34.3	4	2.8	143	100.0
Somerset	1607–36	78	32.4	24	10.0	2	0.8	19	7.9	20	8.3	8	3.3	82	34.0	8	3.3	241	100.0
Warwick	1580–7	24	24.5	0	0	0	0	22	22.5	11	11.2	2	2.0	36	36.7	3	3.1	98	100.0
Wiltshire	1603–20	80	58.4	8	5.8	2	1.5	10	7.3	8	5.8	3	2.2	25	18.3	1	0.7	137	100.0
	1621–38	32	53.3	8	13.3	0	0	4	6.7	5	8.3	1	1.7	9	15.0	1	1.7	60	100.0
Totals		463	41.2	75	6.7	6	0.5	80	7.1	81	7.2	18	1.6	375	33.4	26	2.3	1124	100.0

Sources: As in Table I, adding BJF for Warwick 1580–7.
*Including food, drink, and lodging; figures relate to instances cited in examinations, not numbers of persons receiving hospitality.
†Including constables, houses of correction and gaols.

Table XI *Occupations and status of masterless men, c.1520–c.1640*

	c.1520–c.1600		c.1600–c.1620		c.1620–c.1640	
	No.	%	No.	%	No.	%
Agriculture	12	3.3	23	6.5	19	3.7
Apprentices/servants	59	16.3	77	21.9	120	23.2
Building	22	6.1	10	2.8	18	3.5
Cloth-making and sale	68	18.8	53	15.1	72	13.9
Distributive	5	1.3	0	0	7	1.3
Entertainment	4	1.1	14	4.0	12	2.3
Gentlemen	0	0	5	1.4	8	1.5
Labourers/journeymen	32	8.8	17	4.8	20	3.8
Leather	18	5.0	12	3.4	28	5.4
Metal/mining	8	2.2	13	3.7	22	4.3
Miscellaneous	18	5.0	6	1.7	6	1.2
manufacture	3	0.8	1	0.3	14	2.7
retailing	2	0.6	10	2.8	20	3.9
services	2	0.6	1	0.3	0	0
Petty chapmen	28	7.7	25	7.1	51	9.8
Professions	10	2.8	7	2.0	6	1.1
Sailors/soldiers	25	6.9	40	11.4	58	11.2
Tinkers	15	4.1	11	3.1	16	3.1
Transport	0	0	2	0.6	3	0.6
Victualling	31	8.6	25	7.1	18	3.5
Totals	362	100.0	352	100.0	518	100.0

Sources: Ches. RO QJF, Chester RO QSE & QSF (1570–1630); Leics. RO HP (1584–1640); Norfolk RO, NCM 1564–1630, *NCM 1631–5*; London 1516–66, Repert. and Journ. CLRO; London 1597–1608, BCB; Essex RO Q/SR 1564–1644; Wilts. CRO QSR 1603–38; Somerset RO Q/SR 1607–36; *RR*, vols I–IV; Cunnington, *Devizes*.

Table XII Suspected offences of masterless men examined by magistrates, 1571–1641*

Offences	Places																			
	Chester				Leicester				Reading		Somerset		Warwick		Wiltshire				Totals	
	1571–1600		1601–30		1584–1612		1613–40		1623–41		1607–36		1580–7		1603–20		1621–38			
	No.	%	No.	%	No.	%	No.	%	No.	%	No.	%	No.	%	No.	%	No.	%	No.	%
Desertion	0	0	6	2.7	0	0	0	0	0	0	0	0	0	0	0	0	10	6.1	16	1.0
Drunkenness, disorder	0	0	1	0.5	0	0	2	1.4	8	4.9	12	2.7	5	4.0	3	2.2	0	0	31	1.9
'Felony'	0	0	0	0	5	3.7	0	0	0	0	0	0	0	0	0	0	0	0	5	0.3
Fraud	0	0	0	0	1	0.7	6	4.2	8	4.9	7	1.6	0	0	2	1.5	5	3.0	29	1.8
Immorality	0	0	3	1.3	6	4.4	13	9.1	6	3.6	21	4.7	0	0	3	2.2	1	0.6	53	3.3
Miscellaneous†	0	0	3	1.3	2	1.5	1	0.7	4	2.4	0	0	5	4.0	0	0	0	0	15	0.9
Murder, wounding	0	0	0	0	1	0.7	0	0	5	3.0	0	0	0	0	0	0	0	0	6	0.4
Passport violations	0	0	7	3.1	5	3.7	2	1.4	1	0.6	30	6.7	6	4.8	20	14.7	5	3.0	76	4.8
'Suspicious'	6	9.4	2	0.9	1	0.7	2	1.4	7	4.2	0	0	0	0	3	2.2	0	0	21	1.3
Theft, burglary	30	46.9	152	67.9	41	30.2	47	32.9	74	44.9	186	41.8	45	35.7	60	44.1	82	49.7	717	44.7
Unclear	8	12.5	48	21.4	60	44.1	60	41.9	24	14.5	71	16.0	40	31.7	22	16.2	43	26.1	376	23.4
Vagrancy	20	31.2	2	0.9	14	10.3	10	7.0	28	17.0	118	26.5	25	19.8	23	16.9	19	11.5	259	16.2
Totals	64	100.0	224	100.0	136	100.0	143	100.0	165	100.0	445	100.0	126	100.0	136	100.0	165	100.0	1604	100.0

Sources: As in Table I, but adding B/F for Warwick 1580–7.

* Offences defined as in Introduction, n. 7.

† Mainly persons deviating from the official religion.

Index